Pathways to Progress

Recent Titles in
Libraries Unlimited Latinos and Libraries Series
John L. Ayala and Salvador Güereña, Series Editors

¡Hola amigos!: A Plan for Latino Outreach
Susana G. Baumann

Pathways to Progress

Issues and Advances in Latino Librarianship

John L. Ayala and Salvador Güereña, Editors

Latinos and Libraries Series

 LIBRARIES UNLIMITED

AN IMPRINT OF ABC-CLIO, LLC
Santa Barbara, California • Denver, Colorado • Oxford, England

Library of Congress Cataloging-in-Publication Data

Pathways to progress : issues and advances in Latino librarianship / John L. Ayala and Salvador Güereña, editors.
    p. cm. — (Latinos and libraries series)
  Includes bibliographical references and index.
  ISBN 978-1-59158-644-9 (pbk.) — ISBN 978-1-61069-117-8 (ebook) 1. Hispanic Americans and libraries. I. Ayala, John L. II. Güereña, Salvador.
  Z711.92.H56P38 2012
  027.6′3—dc23   2011027695

ISBN: 978-1-59158-644-9
EISBN: 978-1-61069-117-8

16 15 14 13 12   1 2 3 4 5

This book is also available on the World Wide Web as an eBook.
Visit www.abc-clio.com for details.

Libraries Unlimited
An Imprint of ABC-CLIO, LLC

ABC-CLIO, LLC
130 Cremona Drive, P.O. Box 1911
Santa Barbara, California 93116-1911

This book is printed on acid-free paper (∞)

Manufactured in the United States of America

Contents

Series Foreword

We are pleased to present to the library community a new series on Latino library services. Latinos and Libraries contributes to the relatively new field of serving Latinos in libraries in the United States. Because the literature in this field is somewhat thin, this series answers the call to add scholarship to this field of library endeavor. Our expectations are that, through the Latinos and Libraries series, we will bring new information to the area of serving Latinos, and that readers of this series will become more educated and informed about topics relevant to the Latino community.

This series covers public, academic, and special library issues; services; questions; problems; and solutions. In our attempt to be comprehensive, we have enlisted various library practitioners in the field of library service to Latinos. These librarians, library directors, and library and information science professors represent a wide spectrum of library endeavors.

The authors also represent a range of nationalities, including Chicano/Chicana, Colombian, Peruvian, Puerto Rican, Mexican, and Anglo. These practitioners have written and will continue to write articles and monographs on Latino library service, and we are honored to include their contributions in this series.

The publishers and editors of Latinos and Libraries have been working diligently and thoroughly in presenting this wide-ranging and in-depth coverage of library service. Our hope is that you will be pleased with the coverage and with the continuing addition of literature to the field that we believe will be forthcoming from this series.

Thank you to the publisher of the series and for their dedication to expanding the literature in the field of Latinos and libraries. There is more to come.

John L. Ayala and Salvador Güereña
Series Editors

Introduction

The present anthology brings to the fore some of the practitioners in the field of librarianship who, in their desire to share their expertise, their knowledge, and practices, have cast light on some of the continuing issues in the profession and have presented solutions to some of the unmet needs in Latino librarianship. The articles range from the historical to practical problems in public library service, academic issues and perspectives, leadership development, and the role of the various library associations in enhancing library service to Latinos. Several model programs are highlighted, and through these case studies they inform and give insights into specialized collection development. During the past decade, there has been much growth and development of the Internet, and how well this meets the needs of the Latino community also warranted some attention. We delve into one of the biggest challenges for public libraries today: how well they are able to meet the literacy needs of children and youth in our communities, to ensure that the next generations are equipped and ready.

Almost all the authors are current practitioners in the field of library service. They also represent a diverse range of Latino population subgroups such as Chicano, Colombian, Peruvian, Boricua, and Cuban. They range from graduate library students to librarians, library science professors, to retirees with decades of experience in librarianship. The editors are proud to include one of the last presentations of the late Yolanda Retter, a friend and colleague to many, who was a strong advocate for equity and the inclusivity that recognizes and provides space for the GLBTQ community.

The Latino community is large and diverse. The editors desire that this book will serve to educate, to inform, and enlighten on the issues and the challenges and will provide some guidance in addressing the unmet needs. The present book points to the progress that has been made in solving issues of Latino library service and to the advances in the solutions addressing these problems. However, it was not the intent that this book be comprehensive, nor can any book be that. Such books can only constitute the tips of the icebergs. This one, as part of a series, is only one of more books to follow. Our hope is that you will find it beneficial and useful.

Chapter 1

Common Denominators in the Development of Latino Library Leadership

Sergio Chaparro, PhD

The explosive growth of the Latino/Hispanic population in the United States has brought an enormous set of challenges for library and information science (LIS) service. Some of these challenges have been addressed by the increased provision of information services in Spanish at libraries and information centers. There is, however, the need to look at the challenges from a different perspective: LIS education in America needs to address the current and future information needs of Latinos/Hispanics. In order to address these challenges, one of the major targets of LIS education will be to recruit, instruct, and mentor a new group of information managers and library directors who will be able to develop a more solid structure of Latino/Hispanic librarianship and information services across the nation. This article explores, discusses, and proposes some ideas and methods to create and empower a new group of managers and library directors who can advocate for Latino/Hispanic librarianship at the highest levels of education in LIS. These implementation ideas will, in turn, increase the voice of Latino/Hispanic populations in the information arena.

The path toward increasing the role of Latinos in American librarianship is full of challenges. One of the major challenges is the problem of the lack of representation of Latinos/as within the leadership and management of libraries (Adkins & Hussey, 2006, p. 457). This chapter proposes that underrepresentation can be solved by appropriate actions taken in, among others, the area of LIS education. During the past 15 years, several authors and studies have addressed the major challenges for Latino librarianship (Bala & Adkins; Güereña & Erazo) and the degree to which multiculturalism represents an inevitable "now" in the history of LIS. Pawley (2006) points out the fact that the LIS curriculum is inevitably inherited from a "distant past," but there is an urgent need to reshape it in order to make it more viable regarding constant challenges such as "white privilege" and "race." We are of the opinion here that the reshaping task can be accomplished by competent individuals. Therefore, there is need for the Latino library field to rethink its positioning with LIS in America.

Güereña (1990) writes that: "The America of the next century will, in all likelihood, be a service economy. But the question is who will serve and who will be the servers?"

Güereña was basically sounding a warning about the leadership role that Latino librarians are facing and its importance for the future of Latino librarianship in America. Two major variables give even more importance to that role: the Internet and the new demographics of Latinos in the sphere of library services in America.

By the year 2000, Güereña and Erazo argue, the new demographics and the Internet had affected and reshaped the opportunities for Latino librarians, but they had also provided major new challenges. One of these challenges is the ability and power of Latinos/as to play a role in the design, use, and implementation of Internet information services (Güereña & Erazo, 2000, p. 177).

This chapter looks at one group of LIS professionals, managers, and directors of libraries who possess enormous power to increase the visibility of Latino librarians within the profession. I strongly believe that recruitment for the LIS profession has its base in the visibility factor. The more we see Latinos in a profession, the more compelled we feel to emulate their efforts. In addition, the LIS is a profession of a strong networking component where interpersonal links and communication play a seminal role in modifying and affecting its professional demographics. The Latino presence in American LIS will not be secure unless we develop channels and networks that are robust and secure for the Latino professional future. Young et al. have already made clear the seminal role of recruitment, presence, and leadership in librarianship: "To insure a vital and viable professional future, librarianship must embrace a commitment to the identification, recruitment, and nurturing of the next generation of leaders" (Young et al., 2004, p. 35).

We argue that this viable professional future for Latino librarians requires an exceptional component of mentoring that involves several different factors. Being the moderator at the recent Joint Conference of Librarians of Color (JCLC) Latino directors panel, I could not help being surprised by one factor that most speakers emphasized when reflecting on their successful careers: mentoring for leadership. I use the phrase "mentoring for leadership" because it makes the mentoring more specific than usual. It clearly suggests that developing leadership traits and abilities is the final goal. These characteristics will enable the Latino librarian to succeed and increase his visibility and in turn arouse in others the wish to emulate him. Let's make it clear: without a strong and sustainable presence of Latino managers and library directors in libraries all around America, our chances for success will be slim. Those who succeed to higher positions of management and leadership within LIS will still in be the minority. Current and future Latino managers and directors should pay attention to the following suggestions as a way to empower the presence of Latino librarianship:

Suggestions

1. Make the library less ambiguous to the Latino populations. State a clear path of learning, action, and knowledge for Latino library users. Explain and place emphasis on the fact that the library is a "made" object by people who may share their own problems and beliefs, and that the library as a public agency is shaped by its users and their needs. (This requires library managers and administrators to constantly evaluate the needs of their users.) In the context of Latino users, managers and administrators must make an effort to inform the patrons explicitly of what the library can do for them and what they can do for the library.

2. Strengthen the participation of LIS schools in the shaping of Latino librarianship. Make available to these schools a systematic reporting on the condition of Latino librarianship and its current problems. Invite deans and faculty to voice their opinions about what to do to improve the situation of Latino librarianship. This is a task that Latino library and information services organizations such as the National Association to Promote Library Services to Latinos and the Spanish Speaking (REFORMA) could promote by building up target-oriented resources on the status of Latino librarianship in the United States. Every library school in the country, particularly those that exist close to a large concentration of Latinos, should be adequately informed of the information needs.

3. Strengthen the leadership potential of Latino librarians by promoting the idea that Latinos as library directors and managers can reshape and solve the general problems of underrepresentation of Latino librarians and librarianship. This is the point in where leadership techniques and tools need to be integrated in the teaching and learning process. Every Latino library director and manager needs to be kept informed of the most innovative teaching and advocacy tools to use in leading and mentoring their peers.

4. Report on the current conditions of underrepresentation of Latino librarians. Use advocacy tools in order to bring attention to the problem of underrepresentation to library directors, managers of libraries, and LIS educators. Keep the library community informed of the progress and advances but also of the realities of underrepresentation. Ask for advice on new strategies to address the problem. Explore the conditions of underrepresentation through periodic reports that reach LIS higher authorities.

5. Establish islands and pockets of leadership. Implement spaces and groups where existing leaders can provide extensive mentoring and advice to future Latino library leaders. These pockets of leadership may become attached to major conferences (i.e., American Library Association, Association of College and Research Libraries) and take advantage of the presence of other library leaders. Exposure to them and personal contacts are absolutely necessary for new librarians to expand their knowledge of leadership practices.

6. Connect to LIS education. Enable management schools and LIS programs with a strong management and leadership component to systematically connect with Latino library directors and managers to develop cooperation programs and advocacy tools. Propose, discuss, and analyze the problems that the Latino population in the United States will face in the future. McCook (2006) suggests that the relation between libraries and human rights is an issue for the future. It seems certain that immigration is another one. How can libraries help in the process of building knowledge and resources for the Latino population? Courtright (2005) also proposes health information as an area for future research about the Latino population's informational needs. There needs to be a strong connection between the problems that the Latino community faces and what the library as a social agency can do to address these problems. LIS education must pay close attention to both.

7. Make funding for research on Latino library services a priority. Establish a long-term plan to secure funding for research evaluating Latino library services. Make use of that research and evaluation to advocate action to the proper bodies, government, nongovernment, library, and library education bodies. Persuade lenders that without funding and research of Latino library services, our perceptions can become blurred by useless discussions that will not promote change. It is absolutely necessary to enhance the quality of research regarding Latino library services in order to develop a better understanding of its needs and problems. Proper solutions will depend on the quality of that research.

References

ALSC International Relations Committee. (2004). Growing up Latino in the U.S.A.: A bibliography. *Children and Libraries: The Journal of the Association for Library Service to Children, 2*(3), 19–21.

Bala, B., & Adkins, D. (2004). Library and information needs of Latinos in Dunklin County, Missouri. *Public Libraries, 43*(2), 119–122.

Courtright, C. (2005). Health information-seeking among Latino newcomers: An exploratory study. *Information Research, 10*(2), paper 224. Retrieved from, http://InformationR.net/ir/10-2/paper224.html

Güereña, S. (1990). *Latino Librarianship: A handbook for professionals*. Jefferson, NC: McFarland & Co.

Güereña, S., & Erazo, E. (1996). Hispanic librarians celebrate 25 years with renewed commitment to diversity. *American Libraries, 27*(6), 77–78.

Güereña, S., & Erazo, E. (2000). Latinos and librarianship. *Library Trends, 49*(1), 138–181.

McCook, K. d. l. P., et. al. (2006). Public libraries and human rights. *Public Library Quarterly, 25*(1/2), 57–73.

Milo, A. (1995). Ten reasons why we buy Spanish books. *Public Libraries, 34*, 340–341.

Olney, C. A., Warner, D. G., Reyna, G., Wood, F. B., & Siegel, E. R. (2007). Medline Plus and the challenge of low health literacy. *Journal of the Medical Library Association (JMLA), 95*(1), 31–39.

Pawley, C. (2006). Unequal legacies: race and multiculturalism in the LIS curriculum. *The Library Quarterly, 76*(2), 149–168.

Young, A, et al. (2004). What will Gen next need to lead? *American Libraries, 35*(5), 32–35.

Chapter 2

Collection Development: An Overview for the Spanish Speaking

Sara Martínez

Public librarians seeking to develop a collection for their Spanish-speaking customers have more tools and resources than ever before at their disposal. This chapter will look at these tools and some of the issues to consider when developing a collection for this population. It will also consider the role that the thoughtful selection of Spanish language periodicals can play in a collection of this type. As access to Spanish language materials grows and publishers struggle to find the best ways to reach this booming demographic, collection development for Latinos and the Spanish speaking is consistently challenging, never dull, and definitely not for the faint of heart.

In Tulsa, Oklahoma—where explorer Cabeza De Vaca is thought to have trod so long ago—the Tulsa City-County Library System (TCCL) responded enthusiastically to the Latino community's request for library service in Spanish by creating the Hispanic Resource Center (HRC) in 1999. Hopefully, the lessons learned over the last 10 years will be helpful to others in similar situations. Any success is due in large part to the support of the National Association to Promote Library and Information Services to Latinos and the Spanish Speaking (REFORMA) and to the solidarity and generosity of librarian leaders such as Camila Alire and Yolanda Cuesta.

It is impossible to overstate the importance of becoming familiar with the Spanish-speaking community in any area served by the public library. Who currently uses the library, and who SHOULD be using the library? Who exactly lives in the service area? It is imperative to get out of the library and into the community where the user population is found. Based on the fact that approximately 64 percent of Hispanic people living in the United States emigrated from Mexico (Pew, 2008), it is safe to say that in most communities a majority of Spanish-speaking residents are from Mexico.

Furthermore, these individuals often emigrate from small towns in Mexico as trailblazers for family and friends. For example, a significant percentage of Spanish-speaking immigrants in Tulsa are natives of Casa Blanca, Zacatecas. In 2006, the *Tulsa World* newspaper sent a team to report on this symbiotic relationship. Tom Droege (2006) wrote that

> Casa Blanca, a gritty, dust-driven town in north central Mexico, has been on the move for decades. On the move to Tulsa. Some 3,000 people from the humble farming community have traveled to Tulsa over the years—mostly illegally. They paint Tulsa houses, landscape Tulsa yards and attend Tulsa schools. More Casa Blanca natives live in Oklahoma today than in Casa Blanca. It is, of course, part of a greater migration.

This type of demographic information is invaluable because it humanizes the community.

Besides staying abreast of community happenings, it is important to develop relationships with community gatekeepers, implement a population survey, and/or organize community focus groups. The Spanish-speaking community in Tulsa was found to be quite diverse, perhaps more so than other Midwestern communities. This is due to the unique history that Tulsa has with the aviation and oil industries, as well as to the support given to refugees from around the world by religious and nongovernmental organizations in Tulsa. In any given day, it is possible to encounter immigrants representing the spectrum of Latin American countries—including Mexico, Venezuela, Cuba, Puerto Rico, Guatemala, Honduras, Ecuador, and Peru. This community is further augmented by American Latinos, including Nuyoricans, California Chicanos, Texicans, and New Mexicans. Providing library services to such a diverse group of Latinos and Spanish speakers has been a formidable challenge that has ultimately enriched the TCCL system.

The importance of cultivating personal relationships within the community cannot be overstated. The following anecdote may illustrate how seemingly insurmountable barriers to good relationships can sometimes be overcome with a personal touch. When I first began working at the library, the organization had difficulty communicating with the publisher of Tulsa's only Spanish language magazine. The publisher wanted the library to purchase a magazine subscription, but the library's administration could not understand this request because the free periodical was delivered to several library locations each week. I convinced the administration that it would be most prudent to purchase a subscription as a goodwill gesture. This small gesture has indeed yielded huge results, as we now distribute his bilingual newspaper (the magazine is defunct) to our branches and display it on our newspaper rack as a subscription. And now the publisher will sometimes accede to promote our events.

The Hispanic Resource Center's campaign to serve the Spanish-speaking community initially focused on marketing the library as a welcoming and secure place for all. Many Spanish-speaking customers were not familiar with the North American concept of the public library. A *librería*—literally translated as bookstore—is what many Spanish-speaking customers popularly and affectionately called the library as well. Hiring bilingual, bicultural staff was made a priority in this campaign.

Once a level of comfort was achieved, the staff concentrated on collection development. This process focused on acquiring materials that balanced the needs and interests of families from Zacatecas, with those of the broader Latino community. In today's global culture, the worldwide Latino community shares many interests and concerns. Todd Douglas Quesada wisely points out that tastes vary widely among Spanish speakers, adding:

> It is more important for the public librarian to develop a balanced core collection of Spanish-language materials optimally designed for a high rate of circulation for the community *before* delving too profoundly into collecting the classics.
>
> . . . A purely life-skills based collection would be useful, but it would turn off patrons seeking pop-culture or current materials. Possessing a balanced collection of popular materials is a potent means for developing patron use. (Quesada, 2008)

Watching Spanish language television channels such as Univisión and perusing websites such as univision.com or esmas.com, are excellent ways to stay abreast of who and what are popular and timely. Local Spanish language newspapers may have a web page as well. *Hispano de Tulsa* (hispanodetulsa.com) and *La Semana del Sur* (lasemanadelsur.com) are both bilingual newspapers published in Tulsa.

Recommendations

Join REFORMA (reforma.org). REFORMA's website, listserv, and wiki contain a wealth of resources, including experts who are always ready to be of service with friendly advice.

Develop a relationship with a distributor who can assist in navigating the often bewildering Spanish language publishing world. Traditionally, East Coast distributors tend to be more familiar with communities rooted in the Caribbean—Puerto Rico and Cuba, while those on the West Coast and in Texas tend to be more familiar with Mexican and South American immigrant communities. Today, this is less true as publishers all over the world, from Spain to Mexico to the United States and beyond, compete for the literate Spanish-speaker's dollar.

According to Monica Hatcher at the *Miami Herald*:

> Publishers from Spain were for many years the only players serving the Hispanic market. But now they are competing with U.S. houses for new authors and translation rights. . . . While foreign-based publishers now must go head-to-head with their heavyweight U.S. counterparts, Norman said their participation has led to bigger market growth overall and is welcome. (Hatcher, 2007)

A distributor should help determine how best to meet Spanish language collection needs, as these professionals attend book fairs and are familiar with Spanish language publishers.

The Tulsa City-County Library System has been working with Rainbow Books as its primary distributor for Spanish language children's materials. Their sales representative brings samples and catalogs to the library. The children's manager, bilingual children's librarians, and Hispanic Resource Center Coordinator spend the afternoon perusing the selections and making thoughtful choices. Rainbow Books orders the chosen titles and sends the paperbacks to be bound—well worth the extra expense. Being able to examine the materials, in person, is a definite advantage in the collection development process.

The Collection

When the Hispanic Resource Center began, Bilingual Publications had put together two lists of 100 titles each for a core collection of Spanish language materials. The recommendations below are subjects, titles, and authors that are popular and have attracted Spanish-speaking neighbors into the library and even motivated many to become card-carrying library users.

Spanish language titles are generally more expensive than their English counterparts as they are either imported or translated. *Harry Potter and the Sorcerer's Stone* is a good example. Titles like this one can be up to double the price of their English language counterparts.

Publication dates are another factor to consider. Because many of the available nonfiction titles are translated editions, these materials may be dated. The difference in time between the original and translated publication dates may be significant, as the original publication may have already been a few years old before being translated.

Binding is yet another point of consideration. While it may be preferable to purchase nicely bound hardcover books, Spanish language books are generally more readily available and affordable in paperback.

English as a Second Language (ESL) Materials

The language course *Inglés Sin Barreras* (ISB) has been a great patron draw and good financial investment. This resource has been added to the collection of each branch with a significant Spanish-speaking demographic. ISB is well known to the Spanish-speaking community, as it is heavily marketed across Spanish language television and media outlets.

Fiction

Coelho, Paolo. *El Alquimista*.

Sánchez, Carlos Cuauhtémoc titles, especially *Juventud en Extasis; Volar sobre el Pantano*.

Tellado, Corín, romance—Barbara Cartland style classics—especially *Don Quijote*, Cervantes; *Cien años de soledad*, García Márquez.

Horror stories—Edgar Allen Poe, H. P. Lovecraft, and Carlos Trejo.

Nonfiction

Anything by Univisión personalities, especially Jorge Ramos, but also María Antonieta Collins, Enrique Grata, Giselle Blondet among others. Other high demand topics include these:

100s—Dream interpretation is always popular, as are horoscopes and Nostradamus.

200s—Bibles, catechism, and other books on spiritual issues.

300s—Success in the United States; citizenship (especially 100 questions from the official citizenship test).

600s—Pregnancy and general health issues, alternative medicine.

800s—*Poesía*—any! (Especially love poems); jokes and humor.

929s—Baby names.

Movies

Golden Age Mexican classics featuring actors like Pedro Infante, Pedro Armendariz, Cantinflas, María Félix, Dolores Del Río, and TinTan; humorous movies with la India María and El Chavo del Ocho are winners, too.

Music

Mexican *banda* music is hot—*duranguense*, *norteño*, and *grupera*; *reggaeton* for the young people; anything by Vicente Fernández, Lola Beltrán, and Los Tigres del Norte is always popular.

Children's Materials

It is important to purchase and provide access to children's picture books and easy readers in the original Spanish. This can be difficult because of limited availability.

New immigrant families may enjoy the bilingual format because it allows for acquiring new English language skills and sharing books in the native language.

Bilingual children's librarians may have their own preferences for the types of books utilized in story times and other presentations. Some may not want to purchase books published in Spain because some of the vocabulary may differ from that common to Latin America. This is a relatively minor consideration and is usually not a stumbling block to comprehension, utilization, or enjoyment.

The Barahona Center for the Study of Books in Spanish for Children and Adolescents at California State University—San Marcos, provides a phenomenal searchable resource for reviews, as well as continuing education opportunities focused on working with Spanish language children's materials.

Tim Wadham's book is a good starting place:

Wadham, Tim. *Libros Esenciales/Essential Books: Building, Marketing, and Programming a Core Collection of Spanish Language Children's Materials*. New York: Neal-Schuman Publishers, 2006. ISBN-10: 1555705758. ISBN-13: 978-1555705756.

José Luis Orozco's book/cd sets contain a wealth of traditional children's songs and rhymes that can enhance story times and enliven any collection.

Resources on the Web

Univisión's website has a books page (univision.com, by typing "libros" into the "buscar"—or search—field) that is a list of recommended reads and links to articles about books by and about stars from the Spanish-speaking world of beautiful people.

America Reads Spanish (americareadsspanish.org) is a web-based resource managed by the Spanish Institute for Foreign Trade and the Spanish Association of Publishers Guilds (from Spain).

The American Association of Publishers maintains a useful list of resources on its web page through its Publishing Latino Voices for America effort at publishers.org/main/Latino/latino_03.htm.

Spanish language bulletins on newly published titles are available from casadellibro.com—a Spanish (from Spain) Amazon.com style enterprise.

Another web source worth getting to know is gandhi.com.mx; Gandhi is a wonderful bookstore in Mexico City.

One strategy might be to work with these two web pages and put together title lists to share with distributors. It is also possible to order, for example, lovely copies of books like García Márquez's *El Amor en los Tiempos de Cólera* directly from casadellibro.com. This is not a good idea for large orders but will work for special cases.

Book Fairs and Conferences

Book fairs are true cultural events in Spain and Latin America. The general public is invited to film screenings, author presentations, and a multitude of children's activities. Professional workshops are held for information professionals, teachers, and writers; and book displays are also prevalent. The Feria Internacional del Libro (FIL) in Guadalajara, Mexico, is an experience well worth the expense. Attendees are exposed to the breadth and depth of Spanish language publishing with 1,600+ houses present, provided countless networking opportunities with 500,000+ other individuals, and countless continuing education opportunities. The American Library Association's (ALA) Free Pass program can help defray the expense. This program, a partnership between ALA and FIL provides three nights at a hotel, registration at the fair, and $100 toward the air fare for ALA personal members. The program also includes orientation and support at the FIL.

Book Expo America has had a pavilion dedicated to Spanish language publishing. The event includes activities specifically designed for librarians. Information and registration are available at bookexpoamerica.com.

Texas Library Association conferences boast the largest exhibit hall (of library conferences, after the ALA conference) and can be a resource for Spanish language materials.

Magazines

Spanish language periodicals can be an enticing component of any collection. TCCL continues to experiment with different titles and methods of delivery. Daily newspapers are limited to those delivered consistently to the branch locations—*Hispano de Tulsa* and *La Semana del Sur*.

Local neighborhood Mexican grocery stores are good places to find magazine titles. Browsing Amazon.com and the Mexican media conglomerate Televisa's website, esmas.com, can also be helpful.

The most popular magazine titles in the collection are:

15 a 20—Spanish language equivalent to *People* magazine for teens.
Muy Interesante—similar to *Popular Science* although some material and illustrations may be considered graphic for North American tastes.
People en español—Spanish language counterpart to *People*.
Selecciones—Spanish language counterpart to *Reader's Digest*.
TVyNovelas—similar to *Soap Opera Digest*.
Vanidades—general fashion interests.

Also popular is the ephemeral *novelita*—small graphic comics for adults—which could be considered *telenovelas* on paper. It is not necessary to invest in extensive processing for these works. Depending on the collection development policy, it may be necessary to review them for graphic sexual content, as some can be considered offensive. These *novelitas* can be quite an intelligent investment—as they are heavily used and modestly priced.

Other titles that TCCL subscribes to are

Buenhogar—Spanish language counterpart to *Good Housekeeping*.
Caracola—general interest for preschool and younger.
ESPN Deportes—Spanish language counterpart to *ESPN* Sports.
Iguana—general children's interests.
Men's Health en español—Spanish language equivalent to *Men's Health*.
Mexico Desconocido—geography and travel articles reacquainting readers with Mexico.
National Geographic en español—Spanish language counterpart to *National Geographic*.
Okapi es más—general children's interests.
Proceso—newsweekly similar to *Time* published in Mexico City.
Reporter Doc—science for children.
Ser Padres—Spanish language equivalent to *Parents*.

New titles TCCL recently added are

Casa y Estilo—similar to Architectural Digest.
Fútbol Total—universal soccer reporting and analysis.
LaTeen—Latina young women interests.
Lowrider—automobiles and lowrider culture.
Maxim en español—Spanish language counterpart to *Maxim*.

Getting Spanish language materials into the library is a challenge and can also be an adventure. It is essential for excellent service to the Spanish speakers in your barrio.

References

Droege, Tom. (2006). Bordering on a Problem. Tulsa as a Second Language. *Tulsa World*, April 16. http://www.tulsaworld.com/news/article.aspx?articleID=060416_Ne_A1_Tulsa44371 (accessed February 26, 2008).

Hatcher, Monica. (2007). Expanding the World of Books. *Miami Herald*, Nov. 5, 2007: 22G. http://infoweb.newsbank.com/iw-search/we/InfoWeb?p_product=NewsBank&p_theme=aggregated5&p_action=doc&p_docid=11CEEB9FF9C02630&p_docnum=2&p_queryname=3 (accessed February 28, 2008).

Quesada, Todd Douglas. (2008). "Give 'Em What They Want—How Melrose Park Got its Spanish-language Collection Right." *Criticas*, 2/4/2008. http://www.criticasmagazine.com/article/CA6528515.html?q=quesada (accessed 2/29/2008).

Bibliography of Resources

Here are some titles with suggestions on ways to get to know the Spanish-speaking people in any community:

Alire, Camila & Jacqueline Ayala. *Serving Latino Communities*. New York: Neal Schuman Publishers, 2007. ISBN-13: 978-1555706067.

Immroth, Barbara & Kathleen de la Peña McCook, eds. *Library Services to Youth of Hispanic Heritage*. Jefferson, NC: McFarland & Co, 2000. ISBN: 0786407905.

Moller, Sharon Chickering. *Library Service to Spanish Speaking Patrons. A Practical Guide*. Englewood, CO: Libraries Unlimited, 2001. ISBN: 1563087197.

Wadham, Tim. *Libros Esenciales/Essential Books: Building, Marketing, and Programming a Core Collection of Spanish Language Children's Materials*. New York: Neal-Schuman, 2006. ISBN-10: 1555705758. ISBN-13: 978-1555705756.

Distributors

Baker & Taylor
http://www.btol.com/p_library.cfm
(800) 775-1800

Bilingual Publications
Linda Goodman; lindagoodman@juno.com
270 Lafayette St. #705
New York City, NY 10012-3327
(212) 431-3500

BWI Books
www.bwibooks.com
1340 Ridgeview Drive
McHenry, IL 60050
(800) 888-4478 (815) 578-4592
Fax: (800) 888-6319 (815) 578-4680

Lists of Spanish and Spanish/English Titles

Ingram "Essential Español" electronic newsletter
http://www.ingrambook.com/MRKNG/Espanol/november07/espa
nol.html

Lectorum/Scholastic—sign up for electronic updates
http://www.lectorum.com/
(800) 853-3291
Carmen Rivera, Manager; crivera@scholastic.com

Rainbow Book Company
sales@rainbowbookcompany.com
500 East Main Street
Lake Zurich, IL 60047
(800) 255-0965 (847) 726-9930
Fax: (847) 726-9935

Brodart Español
http://www.espanol.brodart.com/
(800) 474-9802

Magazine Distributors

Ebsco Information Services
5724 Highway 280 E
Birmingham, AL 35242-6816
(205) 991-6600
Contact page—
http://www2.ebsco.com/en-US/app/ContactUs/Pages/ContactUs.aspx

Information page for public librarians
http://www2.ebsco.com/en-us/InfoProfs/public/Pages/index.aspx

Latin American Periodicals
1842 W. Grant Road
Suite 104
Tucson, AZ 85745
(520) 690-0643
Fax: (520) 690-6574

E-mail lapmagazines@worldnet.att.net
Owner: Bernardo Serrano
Manager: Sergio Andrade

Useful Websites

America Reads Spanish
www.americareadsspanish.org

American Association of Publishers
www.publishers.org/main/Latino/latino_03.htm

Barahona Center for the Study of Books in Spanish for Children and
    Adolescents
http://www.csusm.edu/csb/

Book Expo America
www.bookexpoamerica.com

Casa del Libro
www.casadellibro.com

Criticas
www.criticasmagazine.com

Feria Internacional del Libro
www.fil.com.mx

Librería Gandhi
www.gandhi.com.mx

List of Latin American & Iberian Booksellers
http://library.lib.binghamton.edu/salalm/booksellers/libreros.html

REFORMA—National Association to Promote Library and Informa-
    tion Services to Latinos and the Spanish Speaking
www.reforma.org

SALALM—Seminar on the Acquisition of Latin American Library
    Materials, Tulane University
http://www.salalm.org/

Televisa
www.esmas.com

Univisión
www.univision.com

Chapter 3

Public Library Services and Latino Children: Getting it Right in the 21st Century

Oralia Garza de Cortés

> Many things we need can wait. The child cannot. Now is the time his bones are formed, his mind developed. To him we cannot say tomorrow, his name is Today.
>
> —Gabriela Mistrál

Historical Antecedents

From its inception, the American public library has served to enhance the Americanization of new immigrants with the aim of helping them to adjust to life in a new country. From Cleveland to Brooklyn, the library literature is replete with examples of how public libraries enhanced the socialization process by providing immigrants with reading materials and information designed to guide them on the pathway to citizenship and full participation in the civic process. Jones's illuminating history of the role that librarians played in literacy development and citizenship provides our profession with a vivid look at the librarians' role in helping immigrants to preserve their own culture as they adapted to the values of a new country. Librarian Eleanor Edwards Ledbetter stands as an inspiration and role model for her exemplary outreach services and diligent work on behalf of immigrants. Ledbetter and others like her worked both locally and nationally with the American Library Association's (ALA) Committee on Work with the Foreign Born (CWFB), helping to shape immigrant library service as immigrants made their transitions from their native Czech, Polish, or other European homeland to their new American home to be found in Cleveland and other cities of the Midwest (Jones, 1999).

While the public library did not initially serve children, when it did, its first experience with them was when they were over the age of eight. It was not until children's services pioneers, principally the legendary Ann Carol Moore, were instrumental in creating children's rooms and providing programs to help shape and develop the literary needs of young children (Walters, 2001). Working at the New York Public Library, Moore is credited with inventing children's library services and the children's room as we know it. She also believed strongly that children of immigrant parents should know the country and culture from whence their parents emanated, making sure that cultural holidays were celebrated and that books in foreign languages were made available to them (Lepore, 2008).

Documented evidence of public library service to Spanish-speaking children dates back to the 1920s: when Pura Belpré became the first Latina hired by the New York Public Library. Her extraordinary talent as a storyteller and puppeteer as well as her remarkable outreach service and commitment to children and their families touched young and old alike, particularly as she told the beloved folktales of her native Puerto Rico. In 1996, The National Association to Promote Library Services to Latinos and the Spanish Speaking (REFORMA), an ALA affiliate, in partnership with the Association for Library Services to Children (ALSC), which was the children's division of ALA, honored Belpré's memory with a children's literature prize that bears her name. The award honors Latino authors and illustrators for books that best reflect the Latino cultural experience in works for children. Noted children's librarian and author Lucia Gonzalez provides a vivid portrait of Belpré in the picture book biography *The Storyteller's Candle / La velita de los cuentos* (Children's Book Press, 2007).

For all the unparalleled precedent set by these institutions in the early part of the 20th century, particularly the New York Public Library in its efforts to reach out and serve the newly arrived families from Puerto Rico as they transitioned from the island to the mainland, there exists a glaring gap in library literature that shows the extent to which public libraries have provided library services to Spanish-speaking children. The gap is striking precisely because it spans a 70-year period, or more aptly put, a significant part of the 20th century: a period that includes the birth and development of the Library Services and Construction Act of 1962 (LSCA), the precursor of today's Library Services and Technology Act (LSTA). Established in 1964 at the height of the civil rights movement, this source for federal grant money morphed into the LSCA, focusing, in turn, on public library funding to outreach services, with a focus on serving the underserved and disadvantaged citizens. With funding infused by President Lyndon Johnson's War on Poverty, other federal projects such as the Model Cities Program provided additional funding. Some of these funds were used to purchase books such as was done in San Antonio's predominantly Mexican American community.

It was the passage of the Bilingual Education Act of 1968, however, that sparked libraries to pay closer attention to addressing the reading needs of the Spanish-speaking children, then centered primarily in the states of Texas, California, Arizona, New Mexico, Colorado, and Nevada, with a sprinkling of other Hispanics in the states of Florida, New York, New Jersey, and Illinois serving smaller populations of primarily Cuban, Puerto Rican, and Dominican Americans. In response to challenges to the Bilingual Education Act of 1968, which fell under the jurisdiction of Title VI of the Civil Rights Act of 1964, many school districts refused to comply with the mandates of the law. It was not until 1974 that the U.S. Supreme Court, in *Lau vs. Nichols*, ruled that the San Francisco Unified School District was in violation of the Fourteenth Amendment to the Constitution and Title VI of the Civil Rights Act of 1964. "There is no equality of treatment merely by providing students with the same facilities, textbook, teachers and curriculum, for students who do not understand English are effectively foreclosed from any meaningful education" (Lyons in Cazden & Snow, 1990). *Lau vs. Nichols* clearly outlined the legal responsibilities of schools to provide public education for limited English proficient children in the child's native language.

While the law specifically addressed the issue of language discrimination in schools, the same argument could also have been made about the public library's responsibility, given that the LSCA then fell under the jurisdiction of the Department of Education. For Mexican Americans and other Latinos, however, segregated practices in library usage were not as overt. In large cities like San Antonio, Texas, for example, Mexican Americans, unlike blacks who were prohibited from using the public library, were allowed to check out books, if they dared. But more often than not, library services to Mexican Americans, confined primarily to San Antonio's west side and to some extent to the south side of the city, much like other vital city public services such as drainage or sewer, were last in the allocation of needs and services. When library services were finally extended to these impoverished communities, services were, more often than not, confined to buildings such as storefronts or other temporary structures and with less-than-modest budgets. Austin, Texas's first branch in the predominantly Hispanic east Austin was not built until 1976, some 50 years after the first Mexican American families settled there, at the very site where the Faulk Main Library today stands.

Research about school librarians' attitudes about Spanish language materials and the dearth of reading materials for Spanish-speaking children is well documented through the research studies conducted by Dr. Isabel Schon in California (Schon, 1987). Lacking, however, are comprehensive statistics about programs and services, as are kept for public schools, as well as national surveys conducted by governmental agencies, or even solid research studies or evaluations conducted by national associations within the ALA or graduate library school programs. Without comprehensive documentation, it is difficult to assess the quality of programs and services for children and families in public libraries, much less the extent to which services were offered—or whether these services were culturally and linguistic relevant to meet the needs of this population group—if these services existed at all for Latino children and their families.

Since its founding by Dr. Arnulfo Trejo in 1971, REFORMA, the National Association to Promote Library Services to the Spanish Speaking, has been the library profession's leading advocate for services to the Spanish-speaking community. In 1994, REFORMA conducted a random general survey of public libraries to investigate the extent to which libraries were providing services to the Spanish-speaking patrons in their communities. While children's services were not the main or only focus of the survey, it noted the lack of qualified bilingual and bicultural librarians who could adequately serve the needs of Latino children. Overall, library services for Spanish-speaking children were rated as a "C" (Ayala & Ayala, 1996).

Preschool Door to Learning

While the public library long considered itself a key player in helping preschool children to develop the early literacy skills necessary for success in school, it was not until 1987 that the Public Library Association (PLA), a division of the ALA, formalized its commitment to preschool children's services by establishing the "preschool door to learning" as one in a menu of eight major roles that a public library could select when determining the scope of service within a community. These goals were clearly laid out in the *Planning and Role Setting for Public Libraries: A Manual of Options and Procedures* (McClure et al., 1987) and served as a framework for determining what type of public services libraries would provide in a community. Individual libraries, however, were free to choose which eight major roles they wished to implement in their library systems or branches. This meant that if library branch managers or library directors chose to focus on other goals, then they were free to do so, leaving the large unmet preschool needs for the very children who could benefit the most from the services of the public library. Yet for all of its limitations, PLA did away with these roles in 1998, opting instead to streamline the previous role-setting goals in favor of a more responsive public library tuned to community needs, thereby erasing any focus geared specifically to the needs of young children (Walters, 2001).

Every Child Ready to Read @ Your Library

In 2000, two divisions within the American Library Association—the Public Library Association and the Association for Library Service for Children—partnered with the National Institute of Child Health and Human Development (NICHD) to initiate Every Child Ready to Read @ your library (ECRR), an early literacy program for children ages 0–4 and their parents and caregivers. This program is designed to promote the essential preliteracy skills needed for children's success in reading (Ghoting & Martin-Diaz, 2006). ECRR is a program that more closely connects the public library with its role as a preschool door to learning. Notably missing from the decision-making table, however, were leading linguists and early childhood professionals as well as Latina/o librarians qualified to inform the project directors of the necessity to incorporate key components of bilingual literacy: in essence, to mediate on behalf of the needs and interests of children who hail from families where the mother tongue is one other than English. These highly specialized educators and early childhood experts understand the complexities of second-language learning and can best serve as advisors and program evaluators. At best, the key principals that should have been in place from day one is that very young children (ages 0–3) who hail from families where the primary language spoken is one other than English need a firm foundation in their home language. Additionally, best practices for young children learning English requires a culturally and linguistically responsive curriculum that takes into account the linguistic needs of English learners. Lamentably, it was not until ECRR was well underway that handouts or online materials for the program were translated into Spanish, as if translating the entire program into Spanish would suffice to meet the complex linguistic and socio-emotional needs of these young learners.

Language Matters

Research conducted by linguistics, bilingual educators, and child development experts all point to the importance of a child's home language and culture as key elements in early learning. "A child's home language is a crucial foundation for cognitive development, learning about the world, and emerging literacy," say language development experts (Working Group, 2005). During this crucial development stage of learning, parents should be speaking to their child at home and reading to them in their native language. It is a time when children should be sung to and talked to by their parents and family members, a time when they are learning new words at a very rapid pace. But for so many parents who want to do the right thing by their children—and what parent doesn't want their child to learn English and be successful?—there are some considerations. It is also a time of great confusion, particularly in states where English-only ideology permeates school and other public policy. Throughout, parents are hearing conflicting messages from schools and government agencies, including public libraries, particularly where there are no visible signs to welcome families from Spanish-speaking communities; when story-hour programs and other children's programs are conducted only in English; and when Spanish children's collections are small, rarely visible, and ill kept.

Such messages go against the grain of what the research says is how children best acquire language. In addition to trying to get parents to understand the six basic skills that all children need for successful reading in school, ECRR programs need to also focus parents' attention on how they can help their children accelerate language development by encouraging and promoting early literacy in their native, or first, language. But in order for librarians to impart such valuable information, they must first understand it. They must first know that language skills transfer and that a child's stock of language, no matter the type, will help the child to build on the knowledge that he or she already has.

When children come from homes where the parents or other adults speak only Spanish, then this is the language from which language development will occur: where a child's stock of words will be built up from. Thus, librarians who work with parents of preschoolers should be become well versed in the language and understand the process of second-language acquisition.

During the early preschool years, children are building up their vocabulary of words. A child's first vocabulary serves as his or her "store of knowledge" (Proctor et al., 2006). During this period, a child's brain is storing up the words that she is learning. REFORMA's Children and Young Adult Services Committee (CAYASC) member Dr. Patricia Montiel Overall says it best when she describes how knowing more than one language "adds more RAM to your hard drive" (de la tierra, 2006, p.1).

Effects of English-only Policy on Library Services

Since 1981, 28 states have passed some form or version of an English-only law (Crawford, 2008). Such propositions go against the grain of over 40 years of solid research in the field of bilingualism since the passage of the Bilingual Education Act. Based on nativism and a fear of the "other" and fear of foreigners, these laws have created an ambience of confusion and doubt, particularly about whether libraries should be providing preschool and school-age children with story times and programs in a language other than English. Such highly politicized efforts, coupled with embedded English-only ideology that drove education policy at the federal level primarily through the No Child Left Behind Act of 2001 (NCLB) has unfortunately diminished the public library's capacity to more adequately respond to the linguistic needs of preschool and school-age children. This is evidenced in the decreased number of bilingual or Spanish language story times, particularly at a time when more, not less, are needed to adequately keep up with the increased needs of the community based on the demographics.

One need only review a library's monthly program and compare that to the number of English language learners in a given city school district of English learners to recognize the disjoint between the need and the services actually being provided. In Pasadena, California, for example, 90 percent of the identified English learners, or 3,000 children in the school district, speak Spanish. Yet there are no bilingual or Spanish story times offered by the public library. One branch offered a Dutch story time, yet no bilingual or Spanish story time was offered to the 163 English learners, whose home language is Spanish, who could have been served from the elementary school that sits directly across the street (PUSD, 2008). The obvious inability of the public library system to address the needs of these children through its program offering is appalling. But Pasadena is not alone here. More and more, the libraries that do offer Spanish or bilingual story times are fewer and far between. More often than not, they are the rare exception rather than the rule, particularly at a time when the population growth of Latinos in the United States and cities like Pasadena has never been greater. Clearly there is a disjoint between the public library's recognition of community needs and the system's ability to meet the needs of the young English language learners (ELLs) in their communities.

The preponderance of evidence from the solid research garnered over the past 40 years by leading educators, linguists, and scholars from the fields of linguistics, bilingual education, and child development—leading figures such as Alma Flor Ada, Ellen Bialystok, James Crawford, Jim Cummins, Linda Espinoza, Lily Wong Filmore, Eugene García, Tatiana Gordon, Kenji Hakuta, Stephen Krashen, Laurie Olsen, Catherine Snow, Patton Tabor, and the internationally renowned linguist Tove Skutnabb-Kangas—all firmly upholds that the foundation for early literacy development is rooted in a child's culture and language. Nurturing a child's social-emotional growth not only affirms a child's culture and language, it is crucial for full participation as well as for healthy identity development (Working Group, 2005).

Impact of NCLB on Public Libraries

NCLB, while well intentioned in its origin of ensuring an equitable education for all, relies heavily on a "drill-and-kill" curriculum that ties the results of a test-driven curriculum to public school funding. The results for public libraries in Latino communities has been devastating, primarily because teachers pressured to raise test scores rely heavily on more "drill-and-kill" techniques, using up time that would normally be devoted to field trips to the public library. Additionally, the infusion of books in the classroom, while a welcome necessity for children's learning, has oftentimes served to undermine the school library collection, particularly as school districts scramble to balance their budgets during tough economic shortfalls. The classroom collections are also a challenge for many teachers who presume that now the children have access to books in their classroom libraries, there is no longer the urgency to take them to the public library.

Reading Scores of Latino Students

Is it any wonder, then, that given the current climate of the testing regime, coupled with the rhetoric and ideology of the English-only movement, that Latino students continue to fall behind in reading achievement? The 2005 figures released by the National Center for Education Statistics (NCES) demonstrated Latino students are lagging far behind their peers in reading proficiency. Released as the *Nation's Report Card*, the national assessment of students measures the full proficiency of reading comprehension at fourth- and eighth-grade levels. Anglo students ranked 41 percent proficiency in reading at the fourth grade level, compared to 16 percent for Latino students. Put another way, Latino students are a full 26 points behind their Anglo peers. While Latino students, as all students, continue to show improvements with each test, their improvements are not significant enough to close the achievement gap between Anglo and Latino students (NCIS, 2007). Scores over time have remained steady since 1983. Even more alarming is the degree to which researchers Gandara and Contreras have noted students' continued "disengagement" of learners from their schools as they move through the grade levels. They note that this process begins at kindergarten and progresses through the elementary years and into their middle and high school years. By the time Latino students are tested in the eighth grade, they demonstrate, on average, a 15 percent proficiency rate (Gandara & Contreras, p. 21).

Given these dismal reading scores, librarians can do two things: We can either throw up our hands in desperation, as the task at hand is much too mind boggling and overwhelming to get a handle on; or, we can think strategically of ways to work with schools, parents, and the community at large to engage students in the requisite homework centers, after-school reading clubs, story times, readers' theaters, and any other literary enrichment program that will engage students in literature that provides meaning for the students through year-round programs made available to children and young teens at the public library.

Leadership from Within: Pathways on the Road to Equality

Within the American Library Association, REFORMA has promoted the use of Spanish language materials for the population of readers who have a need for this type of materials since its founding in 1971. In more recent years, the organization has advocated for the rights of Spanish-speaking populations, primarily immigrants, to read in their native language through a Resolution on Language Rights (REFORMA, 1985). This resolution, championed by ALA Councilor Salvador Güereña, passed in ALA Council, and it went on record opposing English as the official language of the United States. In 2007, REFORMA sponsored a resolution before ALA Council on the rights of immigrants to access information provided by the public library, a resolution that was effectively passed by ALA Council at the ALA Annual Midwinter Meeting in Seattle, Washington, in 2007 (REFORMA, 2008). More recently, since the events of 9/11, the growing anti-immigrant sentiment in this country has escalated, fueled by the former Bush administration policy of labeling all undocumented workers as "terrorists" and a threat to America's security. Such fears have helped to turn the tide against providing "illegal" immigrants with taxpayer-supported public dollars. As Latino immigrants are besieged by attacks from fringe right-wing elements such as the Arizona Minutemen, REFORMA continues to speak out and effectively address immigration issues, particularly the need to continue providing reading and information services to all immigrants regardless of their citizenship status. In 2011, REFORMA initiated and championed a resolution before ALA Council (Document #39, 2011) in support of asking Congress to reintroduce the Development, Relief, and Education for Alien Minors (DREAM) Act, which gives eligible students the opportunity to continue their studies while they await reform-minded changes to current immigration laws.

Several major programs and initiatives of note have been sponsored by REFORMA with cosponsorship from other ALA divisions and round tables. Additionally, programs for children's professionals during the ALA Annual Conference and REFORMA National Conferences organized by CAYASC have helped guide the profession in the areas of bilingual literacy.

The REFORMA-initiated Pura Belpré Award, officially established in 1996 by the ALA, recognizes Latino authors and illustrators of books on the Latino cultural experience. The award was created to recognize Latino authors and illustrators of books for children that reflected the Latino cultural experience. At the time, the award creators were concerned about the low numbers of books being published by Latino authors and illustrators, as well as the need for children to see themselves and be seen reflected positively in American children's literature. Recognizing the voluntary nature of the REFORMA organization, yet recognizing the far-reaching effect that partnering with others can provide, REFORMA partnered with ALSC to jointly sponsor the award. As mentioned earlier, the Belpré Award is named after Pura Belpré, the first Latina librarian in the United States who pioneered Latino children's librarianship working with her native Puerto Rican community in New York City. The *Celebración* is the award ceremony held at the ALA Annual Conference to honor the winning authors and illustrators who are given an opportunity to tell librarians who they are, why they write and/or illustrate their stories, and how the award honors and validates their commitment to writing their stories and/or painting them. This festive event, held in conjunction with ALA's Annual Conference, provides these professionals with an opportunity to experience a "multicultural moment," especially for librarians who may not have opportunities to experience Latino culture on a daily basis. Open to all, the *Celebración* provides opportunities for all librarians to learn about Latino culture, particularly when they hear the authors and illustrators—many who are speaking to the library association for the first time. The biennial award became annual in 2008.

Since 1997, CAYASC has actively promoted efforts to spearhead national efforts within the library profession that lead REFORMA chapters and members to successfully organize the grassroots literacy campaign first introduced by Pat Mora, *El día de los niños/El día de los libros*. Today the children's division of ALA supports the *El día de los niños/El día de los libros* and, in fact, has served as the official home for *Día* since 2002.

The Children's and Young Adult Services Committee in 1995 was formally established for the explicit purpose of addressing issues related to library services and programs affecting Latino children and families. New librarians into the profession, Oralia Garza de Cortés and Sandra Rios Balderrama, first discussed the idea for a children's services committee within REFORMA. The year was 1988; the place was Dallas, Texas: the place of REFORMA's founding 17 years earlier. Liz Rodriguez Miller was president of REFORMA at the time, and the foci of leadership attention centered on a strategic plan for services to Latinos in general. At the time, "at risk children" was the buzz throughout the country, and everyone was talking about the needs of children in poverty: everyone, that is, except REFORMA. As we saw it, REFORMA needed to take charge in leading the profession in this area; after all, who knew better about the needs of Latino children than two children's librarians who both worked with children in public libraries in Texas and California? Knowing, too, that the Belpré Award would need a place within REFORMA where all issues related to the award could be worked out, Belpré cofounders Sandra Rios Balderrama and Oralia Garza de Cortés petitioned REFORMA for the development of a CAYASC within REFORMA that could focus its attention and energy specifically to addressing those issues pertinent to Latino children's LIS needs. CAYASC was conceived as the Pura Belpré Award was being developed. While CAYASC is responsible for the *Celebración* of the Pura Belpré Award, it has also simultaneously continued to lead the profession through its sponsorship of programs at the ALA Annual Conference such as the one in 1998. That one was held in San Francisco, when leading bilingual scholars Alma Flor Ada and Lily Wong Filmore addressed a group of librarians on the issue of bilingual literacy and the importance in children's biliteracy development.

Through venues such as ALA Annual Conferences; the REFORMA National Conference I, II, and III; and the first Joint Librarians of Color Library Conference (JCLC) held in Dallas, Texas, in 2004, library issues affecting Latino children have consistently been addressed. These professionally organized programs led by leading Latina and Latino library professionals and practitioners from throughout the country serve as mini-learning laboratories designed to introduce, educate, and deepen librarians' understanding of library issues, services, and best practices relating to Latino children—including collection development, bilingual and bicultural literature and programs, and services for immigrant children and families. In 2008, a REFORMA CAYASC-initiated program, "The Bilingual Mind: How Children Acquire and Use Language," featured leading researchers in the area of linguistics and early childhood literacy. The program was cosponsored by other divisions of the ALA, including the ALSC, the Public Library Association, and the Ethnic Materials Information Exchange Round Table of ALA (EMIERT).

El Día de los Niños/El día de los libros

The REFORMA Children's and Young Adult Services Committee has also been instrumental in working with REFORMA chapters in developing children's and family programs in celebration of *El día de los niños/El día de los libros* (*Día*), celebrated on April 30. As REFORMA saw it, Pat Mora's idea of establishing a day of literacy that honored children's language and culture and also their families to books and libraries was brilliant. The idea took off because it was a concept that families understood in a very personal way, particularly those who hailed from countries like Mexico where *El día del niño* is standard fare for all children who have ever grown up there. Like the popular children's song "Make New Friends," librarians could sell families on the idea that it's wonderful to honor traditions from childhood past, but if children are going to be successful in this country, then books and reading are crucial tools for their success. Most importantly, *Día* worked because it was developed from the bottom up, and it utilized a grassroots approach, developed by Latino librarians who knew best what was in the interest of the families they served.

CAYASC worked closely with ALSC to promote *Día* as ALSC found its official home in the children's division of ALA. REFORMA members served on the ALSC *Día* advisory board, including chairing the *Día* national advisory board for one term, as well as providing the knowledge content for the workshops conducted at ALA, PLA, and at the ALSC children's institute.

The work in these areas of Latino children's librarianship has brought REFORMA recognition and praise from other ethnic caucuses within ALA, as well as the praise and respect from other committees within REFORMA. The work of *Día* has garnered REFORMA national visibility within ALA as well as within the Latino community. CAYASC members have recently begun working with the Young Adult Library Services Association (YALSA) to develop the relationship necessary to work more effectively with each other.

Latino Children Today: Statistical Realities

The population of Latinos in the United States today is 46.7 million people, or 15 percent, of the entire U.S. population. Yet in spite of the worst economic downturn since the Great Depression, with rising unemployment, fierce anti-immigrant sentiment and xenophobic scare tactics and ruthless government-sanctioned raids, and detentions and deportations, the numbers of Latinos in the United States is projected to nearly triple to 132.8 million for the 2008–2050 period. Its share of the nation's total population is projected to double from the current 15 percent to 30 percent. Thus, nearly one in three U.S. residents will be Hispanic (U.S. Census, 2008). The projections for Latino children are one that should certainly concern librarians. Latino children today comprise 22 percent of all children less than five years of age (Cohn & Bahrampou, 2006). By 2023, more than half of all children in the United States will be minorities. By 2050, minority children will comprise 62 percent of the population, up from today's 44 percent. Of these, 39 percent are projected to be Hispanic, up from the current 22 percent in 2008 (U.S. Census, 2008).

While these numbers are significant, librarians, too, must recognize yet another subset of these figures that includes undocumented persons.

Since 2006, the population of them has remained steady since 2006 at about 10.4 million adults and 1.5 million foreign-born children. By contrast, the number of children born in the United States to undocumented immigrants rose from 2.7 million in 2003 to 4 million in 2008. These American-born children from "mixed-status" families, that is, families where one or more members is a U.S. citizen while one or more members lacks documents sufficient for citizenship—comprise 73 percent of the children of undocumented families and account for approximately 1 in 15 elementary and secondary school students nationwide, or 6.8 percent of the total student enrollment. Of these, more than 1 in 10 students reside in one of the five southwestern states of Arizona, California, Colorado, Nevada, and Texas.

Preschool Latino Children's Use of the Public Library and Levels of Literacy Participation

The most recent study conducted by the Tomas Rivera Policy Institute (Flores & Pachon, 2008) places the frequency of library use among Latinos surveyed at 49 percent. It may appear that Latinos are doing much better statistically than one would think, given the many obstacles and barriers that they have historically endured. The reality is that when it comes to services for children and families, the overall outlook is not as bright. Researchers Schneider, Martinez, and Owens's analysis of the data gathered for the National Household and Education Survey from 1993 to 1999 finds that three- to five-year-old Latino children are less likely to be read to as compared to their non-Hispanic peers of the same age. Moreover, they have also found that where Spanish is the primary language spoken at home, the level of participation in literacy activities is particularly low. Additionally, researcher data from 1999 reveals that children who live in homes where both parents speak Spanish trail white families whose parents read to them three or more times per week, by as much as 50 percentage points. Latino families in which both parents spoke English at home had participation levels that trailed whites by 15 percentage points. Overall, Hispanic homes are less likely than white households to participate in prekindergarten activities that promote literacy, such as visiting the public library or telling stories to their children (Schneider, Martinez, & Owens, p. 181). The findings from a research study of low-income and Latino immigrant parents from 31 Head Start programs in Los Angeles reveals that 70 percent of the total sample (N = 218) of moms interviewed took their four-year-old preschooler to the public library less than once per month. Equally alarming is the 90.3 percent of children's lack of involvement in any form of reading program or activity sponsored by the public library (Davis, 2008). The sobering statistics paint a much more realistic view of the extent to which public libraries are failing to reach out and meet the needs of Latino children in low-income communities, particularly those from predominantly Spanish-speaking households.

Core Competencies and the Training of the Culturally and Linguistically Competent Library Youth Specialists

Within the library profession, core competencies have been developed in many areas of librarianship to mean a set of skills required for proficiency. ALSC's core competencies, first developed in 1997, clearly spelled out all those skills required of an excellent children's librarian. From knowledge of children's literature to programming and administration, the excellent librarian is highly skilled in all areas, including the ability to lead, plan, and collaborate. The competencies were revised in 2008 with language that helps to explicitly "recognize the needs of an ethnically diverse community" (ALSC, 2008). While such statements are noble efforts at recognizing the need for librarians to know their user group, the expressed competencies are far from comprehensive. The groundbreaking research by Dr Patricia Montiel, a REFORMA CAYASC member, spells out a conceptual framework that introduces three domains or spheres through which cultural competence can be developed: the cognitive, interpersonal, and environmental domains (Montiel, p. 175). Each one of these domains is complex and requires a set of skills that serves as building blocks or next steps toward acquiring the depth of understanding and knowledge that librarians need to inform their thinking in order to be more responsive to the service needs of others.

Library School Education

Regrettably, the library profession has failed to produce sufficient library professionals from Latino communities to keep up with the growth of its population. The most recent figures maintained by the Office of Research and Statistics (ALA, Office of Research and Statistics, 2006) reveals that Latino librarians comprise a mere 3 percent of all credentialed librarians spread across the wide range of library institutions that include school, academic, and public libraries. Library education programs must consider institutes and other training programs that will open the doors to library workers that can earn their credentials as trained undergraduates working with diverse children and families. Specially designed library courses that provide introductions to children's literature, multicultural literature, language development and language acquisition, outreach, and basic library training would go a long way in credentialing the staff that currently serves Latino children and families. In places like San Diego, North Carolina, Oregon, and Minnesota, the demand for library services far exceeds the profession's ability to increase the numbers of professionals from the Latino population needed to produce the qualified staff needed to serve this group. While no statistics are kept on the number of proficient Spanish-speaking certified children's professionals, it is important that the profession think about keeping these numbers so as to encourage more librarians to become proficient and thus be able to better communicate and provide excellent service. But even more than a mere survey instrument, a massive national program geared to train students to work with underserved populations of children would indeed bolster excitement for the profession and for the work of serving children and families through library services. Creating these types of pathways to librarianship will go a long way in crating the next generation of Master of Library Science (MLS) professionals to carry out the enormous work ahead.

A large cadre of qualified children's librarians is essential to mitigate against the historic inequities as well as the new barriers such as restrictive language policies; we need them to be a support for second-language learners. For children's librarians to be more effective in working with Latino children and families, their knowledge base must reach beyond skills rooted in technology and other virtual information-seeking skills to also include knowledge about a community's culture and language and the ability to communicate with their clientele. Given the "Crisis of Leadership" articulated in ALA's Diversity Counts! Report (ALA, Office of Research and Statistics, 2008), the profession will be hard pressed to adequately meet the staffing needs of Latino children if the task at hand is not addressed today. Since by 2050 Latino children will comprise 39 percent of all children in the United States, they will soon become the workforce and leadership in our communities and in our nation, and the decision makers on public policy issues. If tomorrow's Latino leaders do not have the emotional connection to libraries that is nurtured and developed as youth, it is doubtful they will fully understand the importance of libraries and will be less inclined to vote for funding for these public institutions.

Ten Principles for Providing Comprehensive Library Services to Latino Children and Families

Unless Latino children experience the rituals and practices associated with a public library tradition, and unless libraries do more to provide for family programs that engage them to read aloud in the home and to avail themselves of the services and programs of the public library, it is difficult to expect the children to rise above the ever-increasing literacy and education gaps. Whether we like it or not, Latino children today will be America's future leaders. How these leaders decide the future of public libraries in America will depend to a large extent on whether we nurture and inculcate the love of stories, books, and the public library. The following principles serve as a guide for the transformation needed for more effective and responsive delivery to the library needs that Latino children and families require.

1. Hire Bilingual Specialists

Barring drastic measures needed to hire culturally and linguistically competent, knowledgeable children's librarians who can serve Spanish-speaking children and their families, interim measures are needed, include the retraining and development of the professional children's librarian. Concurrent with that change is the need to reconfigure staff needs and bring professionally trained bilingual educators onboard who have the skills needed to work with Spanish-speaking children and their families. The San Diego County Library and the Multnomah County Library are both examples of libraries that have responded to the growing needs of their communities and recognized that their diverse clientele requires a different set of skills than present library staffers are equipped to provide. But the skills of the bilingual specialists should not solely be based on their ability to speak Spanish. Rather, they must also have a core training background in either early childhood development, bilingual or language development, and/or language acquisition. Such staff persons should also have the ability to understand the complexities and issues surrounding second-language learners and be able to mediate on behalf of parents and advocate for and with parents to ensure that their children are receiving the proper Spanish reading-aloud support if they are in families where the adults speak a language other than English. Such staff persons should be teamed up with and mentored by the children's librarians to ensure best training practices in the use of nursery rhymes, songs, and story-time reading conducted in the most professional manner possible. Additionally, it is important to use culturally relevant materials that children and parents can identify with. These materials or a culturally responsive program or curricula is crucial for children's identity development. It also serves to bridge the gap between a child's home culture and the culture to be found in the stacks and shelves of the public library's children's section.

2. Establish Spanish Story Hour Programs in Libraries with Significant Numbers of Preschool Children

Young children as well as elementary age children learning English have a right to and deserve to listen to stories read to them in their own language. The needs of young children are crucial as they are acquiring vocabulary, and story times do that, particularly if longer stories that cleverly engage their interest are introduced. For children learning English, they too are in the process of mastering the language, and it does not hurt them to enjoy stories in their own language. Stories in a bilingual format are excellent choices here, as the child is introduced to the story in their own language. And once they know the context of the story, they are more apt to be motivated to read the story in English. Besides, there is no harm in reading the story in their own languages. Reading for pleasure in one's own language is valid reading and contributes to a child's reading practice as well, regardless of the language read.

3. Establish Bilingual Story Times in Neighborhoods Where Significant Numbers of Elementary School Students Are Enrolled in Schools as English Language Learners

Children's librarians have a great opportunity to help a child make the transition from one language to the next while still retaining that main or home language. While bilingual story times have been around for well over 40 years, conducting a good bilingual story time is indeed an art as much as it is a science. Children's librarians must act as public performers, carefully conducting a delicate balancing act between the written texts and the audience response to that text. Beyond the mere act of reading, a good bilingual children's librarian must interpret the text for the child audience from one language to another, while at the same time ensuring that it is exciting and the accompanying translation is conducted with style and grace. Keeping in mind the need to dialogue with the audience about the text, bilingual librarians must ensure that the spoken language is sufficient in the new language (English) while retaining the gist of the story in the native or Spanish language. Remember, too, that the purpose of story time is not all didactic but rather designed for literary enjoyment and fulfillment. As such, it is important that whatever happens, children's experiences with bilingual storytelling are meaningful and delightful. Because children are transitioning from one language to the other, it is important to retain the cultural flavor of a story. Bilingual, bicultural stories are important in this regard, as they offer context and meaning through familiar words, characters, or images.

4. Provide Culturally Based Staff Development and Training

The quality of children's programming depends on the extent to which the staff receives professional development training during staff in-house training, through regional trainings offered by the library cooperative systems throughout the year, as well as by workshops offerings at the state library and annual conferences of the library associations.

Staff working with young English language learners must receive research-based professional development training on issues and topics that range from "What's culture got to do with it?" to "Why can't they just learn English?" Additionally, all staff should recognize an important tenet of children's learning: a child's social, emotional, and cognitive and language development must be consistent at home; at school; and, by implication, at the public library. Additionally, all staff working with English language learners must understand that when one is learning a new language, there are distinct skills that surface: what noted Canadian linguist Jim Cummins calls Basic Interpersonal Communications Skills (BICS) and Cognitive Academic Language Proficiency Skills (CALPS) or the surface level versus the cognitive skills needed for complex thinking. The library profession and any staff member who works with young people would do well to heed the advice of the National Association for the Education of Young Children (NAEYC), whose position statement reads in part: "For the optimal development and learning of all children, educators must accept the legitimacy of children's home language, respect (hold in high regard) and value (esteem, appreciate), the home culture, and promote and encourage the active involvement and support of all families, including extended and non-traditional family units" (NAEYC, 1995). If library frontline staff is to be called upon to conduct bilingual story times, lead craft activities or group games with children, then they too need additional training in working with children and be attentive to their learning styles and language needs. More importantly, they must develop cultural competencies that will enable them to better understand and work with Latino children and families.

Finally, staff attitudes and actions that reflects negative feelings and biases toward others is unacceptable behavior for anyone, be it frontline staff or the children's librarian. In fact, it is a significant factor, even more important than the Spanish collections, that determines whether Latinos will frequent a public library or not (Flores & Pachón, 2008). Professional conduct must extend to these areas of socialization as well and should be a part of any rules for staff conduct and inappropriate behavior and a method for staff evaluation.

5. Establish Literacy-based Preschool Programs in Libraries with Large Concentrations of Preschool ELLs

While there is not much hope that the PLA's Preschool Door to Learning will revert to its role-setting model anytime soon, the public library must recognize its responsibility to play a leading role in the development of young ELLs' preliteracy skills by establishing literacy-based preschool centers that provide essential experiences to young children with limited or no access to formal preschool programs. By carving out play spaces at designated times during the day (Tuesday and Thursday mornings, for example), the public libraries can be a place where children can socialize and learn with their peers and with their families—much like many have done with the network of libraries that are part of Family Place, a network of libraries project funded by the now-defunct Libraries for the Future. But such programs must have a more focused approach to helping ELLs to develop their early literacy language skills through book-related activities such as story times, read alouds, puppetry, and music and theater arts-based learning experiences that utilize parents' talents and creativity to help them further develop those literacy practices in the home.

6. Redesign Every Child Ready to Read @ Your Library, or Design a Reading Program that Meets the Linguistic and Cultural Needs of Children

Every Child Ready to Read @ your library is designed to meet the emergent literacy needs of English-speaking children. In its present form, however, it fails to adequately address the emergent literacy needs of children whose home language is one other than English. Unless ECRR incorporates practices that center on the primacy of home language and culture in language development, the program remains ineffective in meeting the cultural and linguistic needs of children who are not English speakers. This is not to say that Spanish-speaking parents cannot benefit from the basic core skills that ECRR espouses. *Al contrario*, the information about emergent literacy is very useful and some that every parent and child care provider should know. But without adequately addressing the development and acquisition of second-language learning and the benefits of dual language learning, parents are likely to be confused about how they can help their own child develop language. Children's librarians must work more closely with Latino parents and families to hone the six core skills of ECRR within the context of second-language learning and learn to value the importance of home culture when working with Spanish-speaking Latino families.

Most importantly, however, children's story-time programs and the books and stories that we select must more adequately reflect the child's culture and everyday practices and traditions. Researchers make the case for a culturally responsive curriculum that they say is critical for a child's healthy identity development. "Cultures shape who children are and how they experience the world. Through participation in everyday cultural practices and family traditions, children learn meaning systems, social identity, language, values, beliefs, behavioral norms, and roles intended to develop the competencies appropriate to their culture" (Ray & Aytch, 2007). As professionals working with young children at crucial developmental stages in their life, we are challenged to learn about and implement these best practices that more adequately reflect a child's own world. Traditional nursery rhymes and songs as well as literature that reflects a child's own cultural experience is vital for the success of any program involving young Latino children or children of other cultures, for that matter.

7. Develop Collections that Reflect Cultural and Linguistic Diversity of the Community

English, Spanish, and bilingual children's book collections are needed. Particularly important are materials in these languages and formats that reflect one's cultural stories, traditions, and everyday experiences. Moreover, English, Spanish, and bilingual parent collections are needed in order to ensure that the community has sufficient books that can help them to better understand pertinent issues and help them to nurture their children's growth and development as learners.

Book budgets, too, should also reflect the population served as well as the language needs of the community. Such collections should be proportional to the percentage of children and adults in the community. Spanish-language policies that reflect the community's language needs as well as the library's commitment to Spanish and bilingual collections should be firmly in place. Such policies can be used as leverage, if needed, when defending challenges to Spanish-language acquisition of books and other materials. Additionally, libraries with low circulation rates should consider in-house circulation statistics that take into account the materials used while a patron is in the library.

8. Restructure LIS Education Training and Development of Children's Librarians to Meet Community Needs

With Latino children projected to become 39 percent of all children in the United States by 2050, library education must act quickly to embrace the changing demographics. Excellence in library services cannot be accomplished if graduate library school programs fail to respond to the realities of a changing America. With phenomenal growth of the Latino population in major cities throughout the United States, the responsibility for ensuring that the literacy needs of this country's Latino children are met falls to a greater extend on traditional immigrant states. Such states include Texas, California, Florida, and New York. These states have the largest numbers of Latino populations, as well as library schools in the new immigrant destinations in areas like the Carolinas and Nevada where the Latino population has grown exponentially in the last decade. Library education programs must heed the call for change and learn from leading scholars and professors such as Dr. Patricia Montiel-Overall (University of Arizona), Dr. Loreinne Roy (The University of Texas at Austin), and Dr. Jamie Naidoo (The University of Alabama) and reprioritize their teaching agendas to focus on the teaching and training of the next generation of children's librarians who can meet the needs of this large user group.

9. *Work with Parents to Develop Children's Bilingual Literary Development*

Nationally, while 57 percent of all children are enrolled in some form of preschool program, the rate for Latino children ages three–five is 43 percent (Gándara & Contreras, 2009, p. 89). Many factors account for this lower rate. The most commonly assumed one is that Latino parents do not want their children enrolled in these programs. The reality is that high-quality affordable preschool programs for children are just not readily available in Latino communities. Additionally, Bruce Fuller's insightful chapter analyzing the research on early learning attitudes and practices among Latino families illuminates many other factors at work, such as socialization practices and parents' value systems about schooling, language, and culture that are oftentimes in direct conflict with formal preschool practices (Fuller, 2007, pp. 227–270).

Library professionals working with children have a tremendous opportunity to work with parents and extended family members in nonschool formal settings like the public library so that children can participate in the enrichment practices that preschool story times and other young children's activities provide. In so doing, however, they also recognize the value in honoring the parents' role as "First Teachers" and must be more deliberate in finding ways to engage them in early literacy, particularly through parent training and other parent support programs. Establishing literacy circles and parents' club at public libraries as well as the local elementary school, where many of the Latino parents are to be found, can go a long way in developing trust and the long-term relationships with parents that is needed if we are to partner more effectively with them to believe that their active support in their children's learning really does matter and make a difference in their lives. Finally, family book clubs where parents and their children can read and participate in discussions about the books they are reading is critical in developing the practices that families need for reading aloud at home. These mothers' clubs are forms of social and civic engagement for Latino parents who may feel isolated and disconnected from the world of education. Giving them a voice, power, and the opportunity to participate in the shaping of their young children's cognitive development goes a long way not only in developing parents' own abilities and skills, but also leadership and a newfound way of children who can see their parents as actors in their own leadership development—particularly if they are connected to advocacy groups who can create the groundswell of support needed to keep these parent and children's programs funding.

10. Work with the Community to Develop a Culture of Literacy

The work of developing literacy in the community cannot be relegated to the schools alone. The public library can play a leading role in early literacy development, but only if it is central to the lives of children and families in the community. Developing English story times, Spanish-language story times, bilingual story times, and play spaces or centers would go a long way in providing much needed literacy-based early childhood programs. In developing programs that require parent engagement, the library is developing the long-needed relationships that must be built within the community if it is ever going to gain the much-needed trust and respect of the community. Only when parent trust and respect is earned will the public library be in a position to sell itself to the parents and community leadership who can, in turn, work to develop the support among the business community, elected officials, and other parties to ensure continued and expanded funding for community-based libraries. To do otherwise is to develop a culture of experts that diffuses the community's voice, power, and ability to speak for itself and to take ownership: to own the "people's university" that public libraries were once meant to become.

Conclusion

At the heart of library work within the American Library Association is that of working with children and families: this work lays the foundation for the literacy development of the person as a lifelong learner. ALA has worked vigorously over the last century to ensure that all persons have access to the library and the services and programs it provides. While the foundation for literacy development in the early part of this century was accomplished with great missionary zeal by devoted librarians, libraries in the last half of the 20th century have, for the most part, spent their energy and time developing the public library as a model for a middle class readership, catering to the reading and information and technology needs of them, unfortunately at the expense of poor communities. However, the public library track record of reinvesting itself to become more relevant in the global age of technology and information proves that libraries are capable of changing programs and services to be more responsive to the changing norms of society.

The "little committee that could"—REFORMA's Children and Young Adult Services Committee—has worked vigorously within ALA over the years to provide the direction and leadership for the library profession about issues and concerns related to Latino children. However, by establishing the Belpré Award, by promoting and the developing *El día de los niños/El día de los libros* as a national day of literacy, and by providing models for outreach and community development, an affiliate like CSYASC, either by itself or in conjunction with another ALA division, cannot bear the burden of responsibility for ensuring the successful delivery of library service to a fast-growing user group of children. With Latino librarians comprising a mere 3 percent of all credentialed librarians (Davis & Hall, 2007) and the profession remaining overwhelming white at 89 percent, it is indeed undergoing a "crisis of leadership" (ALA, 2007), to put it mildly. There are two clear choices: either we prepare for what USC urban planner Dowel Myers calls the " demographic tsunami" (p. 2) by developing a comprehensive library reform effort in LIS education as well as a reform in the design of public libraries services to meet the linguistic, cultural, and information needs of Latinos; or we continue on the same collision course, transforming libraries into virtual information centers with no regard for the human and social needs of a unique social group in need of more than information pathways for success. With 50.3 percent of the ALA membership belonging to the baby boomer generation, the association, in partnership with the Urban Libraries Council, PLA, and LIS graduate programs, as well as with the leadership of REFORMA, has a limited window of opportunity with which to reinvent the design, type, and delivery of services so as to more accurately reflect the changing face of America. This window of opportunity spans the next 40 years, a time period that denotes the halfway mark for the 21st century, a substantial one where we can gauge the full impact of the extent to which we have transformed library services to meet the needs of yet another generation. Will we enable this generation of Latinos to grow and develop as successful, full participants in a democratic society with the capacity to wield their socioeconomic and intellectual capital and develop into a vibrant democratic citizenry, or will we contribute to and enable the development of a marginalized society living on the fringe of American society? Failure to "get it right" will only result in haphazard efforts that will do little to provide for the complex needs of Latino children and families in this 21st century.

References

American Library Association. (2006). *Diversity Counts*. Office of Research and Statistics. http://www.ala.org/ala/aboutala/offices/diversity/diversitycounts/Diversity_Counts_CORS_Diversity_Aug07.pdf

American Library Association. (2007). *ALA Demographic Survey*. Office of Research and Statistics. http://www.ala.org/ala/aboutala/offices/ors/memberdemographicssurvey/ALADemographics03250.pdf. Revised, 2009.

American Library Association. (2008). *Competencies for Librarians Serving Children in Public Libraries*. Revised. http://www.ala.org/ala/mgrps/divs/alsc/edcareeers/alsccorecomps/index.cfm

Ayala, Reynaldo, & Marta Stiefel Ayala. (1996). *Report Card on Public Library Services to the Latino Community: Final Report*. June 1994. Austin: Texas State Library and Archives Commission Library Development Division.

Cohn, D'Vera, & Tara Bahrampou. (2006). Of U.S. Children Under 5, Nearly Half Are Minorities: Hispanic Growth Fuels Rise, Census Says. *The Washington Post*, p. A01. http://www.washingtonpost.com/wp-dyn/content/article/2006/05/09/AR2006050901841.html

Crawford, James. (2008). *Language Acquisition in the U.S.A. Issues in U.S. Language Policy*. http://ourworld.compuserve.com/homepages/JWCRAWFORD/langleg.htm

Davis, D. M., & T. D. Hall. (2006) (revised January 2007). Slide. Percent Credentialed Librarians. Census ACS 2001–2005 and ALA Membership 2007, by Race/Ethnicity. In *Diversity Counts*. American Library Association. http://www.ala.org/ala/aboutala/offices/diversity/diversitycounts/Diversity_Counts_CORS_Diversity_Aug07.pdf

Davis, Helen M. (2008). *Cultural Practices of Early Literacy among Low-income and Latino Immigrant Parents*. Presentation delivered for ALA Conference Program, The Bilingual Mind: How Children Acquire Language.

de la tierra, tatiana. (2007). English Only and the Right to Read in Spanish. *REFORMA Newsletter*. Vol. 25, No. 1/2, Spring/Summer.

Flores, E., & H. Pachón (2008). *Latinos and Library Perceptions*. Tomas Rivera Policy Institute. http://www.webjunction.org/c/document_library/get_file?folderId=10860985&name=DLFE-2520003.pdf

Fuller, Bruce. (2007). *Standardized Childhood: The Political and Cultural Struggle over Early Education*. Stanford, CA: Stanford University Press.

Gandara, Patricia, & Frances Contreras. (2009). *The Latino Education Crisis: The Consequences of Failed Social Policies*. Cambridge, MA: Harvard University Press.

Ghoting, Saroj, & Pam Martin-Diaz. (2006). Every Child Ready to Read @ Your Library. Chicago, ALA Editions.

Gonzalez, Lucia. (2008). *The Storyteller's Candle/La velita de los cuentos*. San Francisco: Children's Book Press.

Gonzalez, Lucia. (2008). *The Storyteller's Candle/La velita de los cuentos*. San Francisco: Children's Book Press.

Hispanic PR Wire. (2007). *Signa Foundation Provides Grant to Close Early Literacy Gap Among Young Children*. http://www.hispanicprwire.com/news.php?l=in&id=9726&cha=6

Jones, Plummer Alson, Jr. (1999). *Libraries, Immigrants and the American Experience*. Westport, CT: Greenwood Press.

Lepore, Jill. (2008). The Lion and the Mouse: The Battle that Re-shaped Children's Literature. *The New Yorker*. July 2008. http://www.newyorker.com/reporting/2008/07/21/080721fa_fact_lepore/

Lyons, Jim. (1990). The Past and Future Directions of Federal Bilingual-Education Policy. In *English Plus: Issues in Bilingual Education*. Courtney B. Cazden & Catherine E. Snow, editors. Vol. 508, pp. 66–80; *The Annals of the American Academy of Political and Social Science*. Richard D. Lambert & Alan W. Heston, editors.

McClure, Charles R. et al. (1987). *Planning and Role Setting for Public Libraries: A Manual of Options and Procedures*. Chicago: American Library Association.

Montiel-Overall, Patricia. (2008). Cultural Competence: A Conceptual Framework for Library and Information Science Professionals. In *Library Quarterly*. April, 2009. Vol. 79, No. 2, pp. 175–204.

Myers, Dowell. (2008). Old Promises and New Blood: How Immigration Reform Can Help America Prosper in the Face of Baby Boomer Retirement. In *Reform Brief*. Reform Institute. http://www.reforminstitute.org/uploads/publications/Old_Promises_New_Blood_Final_11-21-08.pdf

National Association for the Education of Young Children (NAEYC). (1995). *Responding to Linguistic and Cultural Diversity: Recommendations for Effective Early Childhood Education. A position statement of the National Association for the Education of Young Children*. http://www.naeyc.org/about/positions/pdf/PSDIV98.PDF

National Center for Education Statistics. (2007). The Nation's Report Card: Fourth Grade. http://nces.ed.gov/nationsreportcard/pdf/main2007/2007496_2.pdf

Pasadena Unified School District. (2008). R-30. Language Census Report Summary. http://manila.pasadena.k12.ca.us/ladd/

Ray, Aisha, PhD & Lynette Asch, PhD. (2007). *Kids Like Malik, Carlos and Keana: Culturally Responsive Practice in Culturally and Racially Diverse Schools*. First Schools Symposium. Early School Success: Equity and Access for Diverse Learners, Chapel Hill, NC. www.fpg.unc.edu/~firstschool/resources.cfm

Schon, Isabel, et. al. (1987). Books in Spanish for Young Readers in Schools and Public Libraries: A Survey of Practices and Attitudes. *Library and Information Science Research*. Vol. 9. No. 1, 21–28.

Schneider, Barbara, Sylvia Martinez, & Ann Owens. (2006). *Barriers to Educational Opportunities for Hispanics in the United States in Hispanics and the Future of America*. Marta Tienda & Faith Mitchell, editors. Committee on Transforming Our Common Destiny. National Research Council. Los Angeles: National Academies Press.

U.S. Census Bureau. Public Information Office. August 14, 2008. *An Older and More Diverse Nation by Midcentury*. http://www.census.gov/Press-Release/www/releases/archives/population/012496.html

Walters, Virgina A. (2001). *Children and Libraries*. Chicago: American Library Association.

Working Group of Southern California Comprehensive Assistance Center COE EL Service Providers & COE School Readiness Educators. 2005. *Six Research Based Guiding Principles Serving the Needs of English Learners in Preschool "School Readiness" Programs*. September 30, 2005.

Chapter 4

Academic Libraries: Pathways to Transforming Teaching, Learning, and Relationships in Chicano and Latino Studies

Susan C. Luévano, Tiffini A. Travis, and Eileen Wakiji

Lo que bien se aprende, nunca se pierde.
[What one learns well will never be lost.]

What are the best methods used to integrate information fluency skills into ethnic studies department curricula? What are the theoretical applications used to maximize success in higher education of underrepresented students? Can the proficiencies garnered from information literacy instruction be sustained after graduation? Starting in 2003, these were some of the research questions addressed by a California State University, Long Beach (CSULB) librarian learning community. The learning community began with a shared interest in exploring a collaborative faculty/librarian model as promoted by the California State University Information Competence Initiative (California State University, Information Competence Initiative, 2007). The formal study, research, and action relationship allowed for structured readings, intense dialogue, and writing that promoted tremendous professional growth in understanding how the scholarship on learning could be utilized in an ethnic studies information literacy context. Each member brought some special expertise and energy to the table that made this community of practice a more interesting and dynamic process.

The group had an opportunity to put the theory into practice with the creation of an information competence pilot project aimed at the Black Studies Department faculty (Luévano, Travis, & Wakiji, 2003). The theoretical knowledge and practical success gained on how to implement a faculty-centered information fluency course was a great boost for the learning community. The discipline librarian for the Chicano and Latino Studies Department (CHLS) was soon thereafter initiating a solo effort without the learning community but in conjunction with a Chicano Studies faculty at CSULB that became the *Seeds of Change/Semillas de Cambio* Information Competence project.

Basically, *Seeds of Change/Semillas de Cambio* developed a California State University (CSU) grant and funded an eight-session course targeting Chicano and Latino Studies faculty that was implemented in spring 2005 (Luévano, 2005). The goal of the course was to reinforce the importance of information literacy and illustrate how to integrate its main tenets into selected core curriculum. However, the key component of the course was the actual restructuring of class curriculum to include assignments aimed at honing competency (Delgado & Luévano, 2007). In this way, faculty were empowered to become more directive in the students' research development. This framework established a faculty-led pathway for the effective development of an increasingly more complex battery of information retrieval and critical thinking skills in CHLS majors and minors.

Directed by CHLS faculty Grace Peña Delgado and librarian Susan Luévano, the CHLS faculty participants integrated information competency skills in four courses: CHLS 101, 104, 150, and 300. Faculty met on eight occasions to discuss the application of information competency theory and applications. Their homework required the review of five online tutorial modules, written reflections, readings and infusion of information literacy skills, and assessments into target classes for specific assignments.

CHLS faculty went beyond the scope of the originally stated grant goals. In an effort to focus current restructuring of the CHLS major and minor, learning outcomes of all information literacy-targeted courses were linked to CHLS department goals. This was a crucial step as it ensured the maintenance of diverse learning experiences even as the department embarked on significant curricular change. It occurred because faculty understand that students' self-directed learning requires conscious and deliberate integration of information literacy skills in course content and structure.

Background

Information literacy is a conceptual framework that guides librarians and instructional faculty in teaching students how to find, identify, and apply information. This translates into the ability of students to recognize the need for information and to possess the knowledge and skills to obtain it; choose the proper sources and successfully retrieve appropriate information and then to organize, analyze, and synthesize it (Rockman, 2004). Information literacy, information competence, and information fluency are used interchangeably in this article to describe the acquisition and application of the aforementioned skills. The goal of information literacy is to make the student a critical thinker who is an independent lifelong learner and problem solver.

California State University, one of the largest higher educational systems in the nation, has maintained a firm commitment to information literacy since 1995. It has encouraged librarian and instructional faculty collaboration in teaching students information literacy skills through a series of information competence grants. Given this support structure, it is not surprising that the university library at CSULB proactively adopted their own set of minimum information literacy standards in 1996, a full four years before the Association of College and Research Libraries (ACRL) approved their own. As an academic community, CSU, Long Beach has embraced the importance of Information Literacy at the university level. In 2006, the CSULB college catalog (2006–2007 graduate and undergraduate catalog) included 10 general education learning objectives, and information literacy was one of them:

> Information Literacy
> Students will be critical users of the Internet and print information resources and will demonstrate the abilities to use and to apply what they learn constructively.

Also in 2006, CSULB and five other CSU campuses participated in the beta testing of the ICT (information and communication technology) Literacy Assessment developed and administered by the Educational Testing Service (ETS). This encouraging information competency climate within the CSU provided the backdrop for the faculty/librarian collaborations noted in this article.

Faculty's Role in Information Literacy Instruction

Among most of the Latina/o CHLS majors and minors at CSULB, a combination of poor academic preparation, low socioeconomic status, language minority status, and Latina/o identity sets them apart as a distinctive group as compared to other populations within the general student body. Self-identified Hispanics comprise 25.1 percent (7,132) of the CSULB undergraduate student body of 30,605 (Institutional Research, 2008). In a recent survey and community dialogue of CHLS students, it was documented that they continue to deal with cultural, linguistic, and social isolation (Chicano and Latino Studies Learning Community Survey, 2007; Latino Dialogues, 2006). Unfortunately, this is not an exceptional incident. This sense of alienation continues to be a common experience for many Latina/o students in higher education (Castellanos, Gloria, & Kamimura, 2005).

The CHLS department majors and minors at CSULB are a microcosm of the Chicana/o and Latina/o studies students in the United States. The majority of CHLS majors served by the department are first-generation Latino college attendees from low-income immigrant backgrounds who come to the university with a distinctive Latina/o cultural framework. Both the instructional faculty and the discipline librarian are constantly attempting to address the complex learning variability of Latina/o student demographics that influence student success, including immigrant versus nonimmigrant status, language development, familial support, learning style differences, educational preparation, acculturation factors, and the history and experiences of various ethnic groups beyond the predominant Mexican American community including, but not limited to, Salvadorans, Guatemalans, Dominicans, and Puerto Ricans. The department faculty and lecturers are all Latina/o. Most are Mexican Americans, but Caribbean Latinos are also represented. These faculty view the university as a critical space to develop concrete solutions to combat racism, poverty, and educational marginalization. The department promotes deep feeling of cultural pride premised on the reaffirmation of culture and Latina/o identity. Furthermore, they consistently attempt to create a sense of *communidad* among student scholars through clubs, cultural events, and mentoring.

The *Seeds of Change/Semillas de Cambio* model discussed here is based on the premise that teaching faculty are the most effective persons to provide course integrated information literacy instruction to Latina/o CHLS students. This approach assumes that CHLS faculty will be coached by a discipline librarian or faculty/librarian team beyond the essential key components of research and critical thinking development. In addition to faculty fluency on the finer points of information competence, the success of the faculty-led instruction is dependent on collaboration with the discipline librarian as a codeveloper in curricular assignments and assessment. This method requires the librarian to spend more time working with faculty to incorporate information literacy tenets into course outlines, not just individual course assignments.

Latino Research on Student Success and Chicano Studies

Much of the research on Latina/o student success in higher education continues to describe less-than-ideal experiences (Montero-Sieburth & Batt, 2001; Quijada & Alvarez, 2006). Gloria and Segura-Herrera (2004) indicate that this unfortunate situation has not changed much in the last 30 years. Factors that contribute to this state of affairs include the juggling of home and school responsibilities, indifferent curriculum and alienating pedagogy, unfriendly campus climate that does not reflect the cultural identities of Latina/o students, and lack of mentors and support systems. These negative factors color the university as an unwelcoming and often discriminatory learning setting that often cause Latina/o students to suffer distress, cultural incongruity, and withdrawal from classroom interactions. It is interesting to note that the research of Gloria and Segura-Herrera indicates that Latinas/os experiences of alienation have been documented even in students that persist and graduate from the university with degrees in their desired majors.

Current educational literature that analyzes Latina/o educational advancement focuses on the persistence or resilience of students who do well academically as opposed to earlier studies that focused on conditions that prevented student success (Gándara, 1995). For example, Arellano and Padilla (1996) explore the positive aspects of resilience; Solberg and Villareal (1997) look at the role of self-efficacy; Torres (2004) cites ethnic identity; and Gloria, Castellanos, and Orozco (2005) look at psychological well-being as a measure of projected academic matriculation. These studies and others have redirected research from just looking at cognitive issues to exploration of environmental and support systems.

Gloria and Rodriguez (2000) designed the Psychosociocultural (PSC) framework that details optimum factors contributing to academic success and persistence. These factors include the following areas:

- Psychological (e.g., self-beliefs, attitudes, perceptions).
- Social (e.g., networks, connections, role models, mentors).
- Cultural (e.g., cultural values, meaningfulness of experiences).

The premise of this theoretical model is that when Latina/o undergraduates have more positive personal experiences on campus, they are better able to learn and will develop coping skills that help them productively navigate the university structure that helps them persist to graduation. These scholars also suggest that students who are part of a learning setting that validates their cultural values and practices will learn more effectively and develop a more grounded sense of connectedness and well-being. Gloria and Rodriguez's research indicates that these conditions lead to persistence toward graduation.

There are few other academic disciplines other than Chicano and Latino Studies that so closely create the optimum learning conditions described by Gloria and Rodriguez. Certainly the conditions described in the PSC framework appear to depict the environment that exists in the CSULB, CHLS department. Ensuring culturally relevant classes, mentorship opportunities, peer support, and connections between learning objectives and the student's lives that validate and provide sustenance for student scholars is part of the department's mission. Scholarship that is directly tied to community action such as service learning that greatly enhances ethnic exploration and educational experiences in the classroom is a growing component of the CHLS curriculum. Latina/o students may still encounter demoralizing situations on campus, but if Gloria and Rodriguez are correct, the well-being and support that they receive in CHLS classes should assist them in developing coping skills that lead to persistence and ultimately graduation. This research supports Bemphechat (1998) who notes that the degree in which academic achievement is experienced among Latinos depends on their beliefs about learning that include their degree of confidence in their abilities to learn, their expectation and opportunities for experiencing success, and the degree to which they are invested in academic tasks. Also, rarely mentioned is the need for ongoing rich language environments where bilingualism is seen as an asset. This is an environment that contributes to the comfort of the student and his willingness to buy into the educational process. While instruction at the university level is English, the added ability of many CHLS faculty to provide for bilingualism is an important learning condition (García, 2001).

Given the positive outcomes of the PSC model, it is evident that CHLS classes provide an excellent academic environment to promote the transition of information literacy skills. Various other factors support the faculty as primary teachers of information fluency. For example, this case is made stronger by the studies that point to the increased transition of knowledge among Latino students when there is a sustained personal relationship (García, 2001; Griego Jones & Fuller, 2003). The importance of the instructional faculty who see the student for the duration of a semester/quarter cannot be overemphasized. This extended interaction allows time for the student/teacher relationship to be established and blossom as opposed to the library faculty who may provide one or two lectures or active learning activities during the same period. However, this arrangement should not diminish the role of the discipline librarian as part of a multilayered instructional team (e.g., librarian, faculty, graduate assistants) who remains a critical player in working with individual students during research consultations or at the reference desk; overseeing or leading student research sessions; providing targeted instructional sessions and workshops; the creation of class specific research guides; or the curriculum development role that is integral to this faculty-led framework. Nor does it negate the discipline librarian as another role model and mentor who contributes to the PSC model in collaboration with the faculty department.

General Research

In addition, the best practices literature on Latina/o success that the library literature provides numerous examples that support the usage of the faculty-centered model. Conteh-Morgan, for example, outlined a similar effort in the discipline of English as a Second Language (ESL) at Ohio State University. The author established a clear role for the librarian in course development and evaluation as well as an assessment of learning outcomes but allowed the instructor of record to teach the tenets of information literacy within the context of the class. Conteh-Morgan notes that the collaborative situation required a recognition and respect for the shared "knowledge, skills and constituencies" of librarians and faculty (Conteh-Morgan, 2002, p. 31). The author argues that because language instruction and information literacy instruction have common goals, theories, and practices, they can be easily combined.

Samson and Millet (2003) implemented a comparable instructor-focused model at the University of Montana. In this first-year student effort, teaching assistants who were also graduate students provided the primary instruction for writing and research classes. Librarians taught the teaching assistants who thereafter taught information literacy skills in English composition, public speaking, freshmen interest groups, and the freshman seminar. A librarian shortage and an increasing instructional workload made this an attractive model. Additionally, it assisted the teaching assistants by honing their own information literacy skills. Training occurred at a three-day teaching assistant camp. Half of a day was allotted to the information literacy instruction, which included teaching specific resources, adjusting teaching methods and research assignments to a freshman level, and acquainting them with the physical layout of the library as well as services and resources. The *Semillas de Cambio* course is similar to the University of Montana effort in that faculty were trained in intensive structured instructional sessions with the expectation that they would use these new skills in future course design and to further their own research pursuits.

Miller and Bell also make a strong argument for faculty as the primary purveyors of information literacy. They suggest that librarians should be more involved in "developing tools and resources that faculty would use to integrate information literacy skill building into their courses" (Miller & Bell, 2005, p. 1). For example, faculty can integrate tutorials developed by librarians as an integral part of the syllabus. Librarian-created research guides can be linked to electronic learning software such as Blackboard. Librarians and faculty might work collaboratively to develop a tiered approach to instruction in which specific classes are targeted for skill development. The authors suggest examination of on-line tutorial reviews in MERLOT (Multimedia Educational Resource for Learning and Online Teaching) or PRIMO (Peer Reviewed Instruction Materials Online).

Smith (1997) supported this position in a paper presented at the ACRL conference in Nashville simply on the basis of very practical realities. He cites the inadequate number of instructional librarians as part of the vali-dation for this approach. Who has not seen a decline in the number of librarians serving increasingly larger numbers of students and faculty? Smith deemed faculty development and collaboration a more realistic and instructionally effective scenario for librarians responsible for in-struction in academic libraries.

Some librarians are able to develop intense student relationships over extended periods of time when they work collaboratively with the fac-ulty on individual courses or teach a stand-alone course on information literacy. Porras and Miller (2004), a faculty/librarian team at California State University, Fullerton, provide an excellent example of this collab-orative arrangement in a Chicano studies class using a family history as-signment. Another ideal model is the stand-alone research methods class taught by the discipline librarian and offered for credit within the Chi-cano Studies Department. This model is used at California State Uni-versity, Northridge. Karin Durán, the Chicana/o Studies librarian at the Oviatt Library, is an adjunct professor in the Chicana/o Studies Depart-ment. She teaches a research class that is part of the regular curriculum. As the discipline librarian and an adjunct professor, she attends depart-ment meetings and is a member of the curriculum committee (Durán, 2008).

However, for most academic librarians, these ideal situations are not easily replicable on a large scale. The collaboration model requires inten-sive faculty and librarian planning, and the stand-alone model requires an even greater time commitment for the intellectual development of course content, lectures, assignments, grading, office hours, and related student interactions. These situations become a rarity rather than the norm due to all the competing demands on a librarian's time such as instruction responsibilities for large numbers of classes, and other discipline assign-ments, along with traditional duties such as reference, collection develop-ment, and shared governance.

Assessment/Defining Educational Success

When discussing Latina/o academic success, assessment is a key factor in documenting student learning. The current trends in academe suggest that librarians and faculty are under increasing pressure to indicate the measurable results of their teaching efforts. National and regional accreditation agencies and even some state legislatures are demanding more concrete accountability that educational dollars are being used in ways that improve quality education. The responsibility for measurement of learning outcomes falls directly in the sphere of instructional faculty. The faculty of record designs and controls the assessment of classroom assignments, research projects, or portfolio development.

Nash (2004) acknowledges this reality and suggests that instructional librarians consider the four levels of assessment delineated by Donald Kirkpatrick in his book *Evaluating Training Program: The Four Levels* (1998). Kirkpatrick's four levels can best be described as follows:

1. The first level simply assesses the student's reaction to the instruction (e.g., Was the teaching clear and logical? Was it too long or short?).
2. Kirkpatrick cites the measurement of formative learning as the second level (e.g., Did the student learn the concepts presented in the lecture?).
3. The third level evaluates the application of learning outcomes. Can students create and complete assignments/research using learned information literacy behaviors? Can they create a thesis statement? Can they use research databases to retrieve information? Can they analyze and synthesize information?
4. Level four attempts to measure the end product. Did the coursework incorporate superior learning outcomes due to information literacy training? Did the bibliography identify appropriate and varied resources? Did the final project reveal critical thinking and intellectual development?

Nash argues that librarians could easily assess the first two levels. However, faculty are in a better position to determine whether students appropriately applied information literacy concepts and skills and whether they have created a higher quality research paper, which is the learning measure that most faculty will use to determine effectiveness of the process. For example, level three assessment can only be achieved by having students actually complete an assignment that incorporates a specific learning outcome. Students submit these assignments in writing and send the results to the professors. The level four analysis attempts to measure the end product. The faculty evaluates the quality of the completed assignment as a stand-alone assessment and assigns a grade.

Nash states that when librarians teach information literacy skills, level one and two evaluations are easy for librarians to accomplish. For example, what did the student think of the training/lecture? What was the formative measurement of learning? Formative assessment provides immediate evidence of student learning usually after attending a library instruction session. Various methods are used by librarians to conduct this type of appraisal including short surveys or having the student write down two or three things he learned after the "one-shot" lecture or active learning workshop. More recently, personal response system technology, which actually allows testing and immediate assessment after any segment of class instruction, has become a popular measure of formative learning.

Nash emphasizes that instructional faculty are best situated to evaluate the other two levels. This includes the evaluation of applied learning and measurement of the final product. These two stages of evaluation are best suited to the professor because they are teaching the class for an entire semester or quarter. This long-term summative assessment allows her to fairly grade the student's intellectual development during the research process and the final research assignment. Only the professors will see how the learned skills are actually applied and whether or not the final research project was enriched by the information literacy instruction.

Kirkpatrick's theories of assessment further support the premise that faculty are best suited to pass judgment on the intellectual growth and development of a student in a specific class. Librarians can and do evaluate formative learning steps, but they are simply not positioned to provide a final appraisal on the student's achievement of learning outcomes. Often the faculty of record will share evaluative information with the instructional librarian after the end of the semester in a general discussion about the success or failure of an entire class. Individual student assessments are rarely provided. Suggestions for improvement or enhancement of information literacy instruction may follow.

Conclusion

Each of the theories discussed in this article adds to the understanding of the issues and establishes a rationale for acting on this awareness. These supporting concepts, the California State University information literacy vision, and the discipline librarian's applied experience working on a Chicano studies faculty-centered training course support the supposition that Chicano studies faculty are best situated to do intensive information literacy training that fosters concrete skill development and critical thinking. This situation is desirable only when departments engage in the PSC framework.

Given this analysis, the role of the instructional librarian must shift. Academic librarians must be more involved in faculty and curriculum development. These partnerships with individual faculty and departments should evolve into proactive relationships that further inform the discipline regarding the need for fluency development. Faculty/librarian relations must not only be more collaborative, but the librarian must become both a faculty coach and an assignment consultant. To encourage faculty education, librarians must spend more time developing active learning and critical thinking activities that can incorporate information literacy into course outlines, not just individual course assignments.

This shifting role should not in any way limit the discipline librarian from being a full player in the academic success of Latino students. Reference, research consultations, mentoring, creation of online research guides, instruction, and collection development are traditional librarian duties that can be creatively structured to provide a knowledge base of activities and programs that affirm cultural congruence. Using the PCS model as a guide, librarians, whether they are of Latina/o heritage or not, can create rich culturally based learning environments that enhance learning and foster Latino persistence.

As the Mexican *dicho* states: *"Lo que bien se aprende, nunca se pierde"* (What one learns well will never be lost.). Information literacy skills once learned will not be forgotten. Critical thinking and research skills taught in the most advantageous context that is socioculturally, linguistically, and cognitively presented will contribute to the high performance of Latina/o student scholars and their persistence to college graduation.

References

Arellano, Adele R. & Amado M. Padilla. 1996. "Academic Invulnerability Among a Select Group of Latino University Students." *Hispanic Journal of Behavioral Sciences* 18, no. 4 (November): 485–507.

Bemphechat, Janine. 1998. *Against the Odds. How "At Risk" Children Exceed Expectations*. San Francisco: Jossey-Bass.

California State University. 2007. Information Competence Initiative. http://www.calstate.edu/LS/infocomp.shtml

California State University, Long Beach. 2006. *Graduate and Undergraduate Catalog. 2006–2007*. Long Beach: California State University, Long Beach.

California State University, Long Beach. Institutional Research. 2008. *Beach Facts, 2007–2008*. Long Beach: California State University, Long Beach.

Castellanos, Jeanett, Alberta Gloria, & Mark Kamimura, eds. 2006. *The Latina/o Pathway to the PhD: Abriendo Caminos*. Sterling, VA: Styllus.

Chicano & Latino Studies Learning Community Survey. Spring 2007. Long Beach: Chicano & Latino Studies Department, California State University. Unpublished report.

Conteh-Morgan, Miriam E. 2001. "Empowering ESL Students: A New Model for Information Literacy Instruction." *Research Strategies* 18, no. 1: 29–38.

Delgado, Grace Peña, & Susan Luévano. 2007. *Semillas de Cambio*: Collaborative Approaches to Teaching Information Literacy in the Discipline of Chicano and Latino Studies. In *Information Literacy Collaborations That Work*, ed. Trudi Jacobson & Thomas P. Mackey, 95–108. New York: Neal Shuman Press.

Durán, Karin. March 22, 2008. "Critical Reflections on Information Literacy: Meeting Chicana/o Studies Student/Faculty Research Needs for the 21st Century." National Association for Chicana and Chicano Studies Conference, Austin, TX.

Gándara, Patricia. 1995. *Over the Ivy Walls: The Educational Mobility of Low-Income Chicanos*. Albany: New York State University.

García, Eugene E. 2001. *Hispanic Education in the United States: Raíces y Alas*. Lanham, MD: Rowman & Littlefield.

Gloria, Alberta M., & Ester R. Rodriguez. 2000. "Counseling Latino University Students: Psychosociocultural issues for consideration." *Journal of Counseling and Development* 78, no. 2 (Spring): 145–154.

Gloria, Alberta M., Jeanett Castellanos, & Veronica Orozco. 2005. "Perceived Educational Barriers, Cultural Congruity, Coping Responses and Psychological Well-Being of Latina Undergraduates." *Hispanic Journal of Behavioral Sciences* 27, no. 2 (May): 161–183.

Gloria, Alberta M., & Theresa M. Segura-Herrera. 2004. Ambrocia and Omar Go To College: A Psychosociocultural Examination of Chicanos and Chicanas in Higher Education. In *Handbook of Chicana and Chicano Psychology*, ed. Roberto J. Velasquez, Brian McNeill, & Leticia Arellano, 401–425. Mahwah, NJ: Lawrence Erlbaum.

Griego Jones, Toni, & Mary Lou Fuller. 2003. *Teaching Hispanic Children*. Boston: Allyn and Bacon.

Information Literacy Minimum Standards. 1998. University Library, California State University, Long Beach. http://www.csulb.edu/library/guide/infocomp.html

Kirkpatrick, Donald L. 1998. *Evaluating Training Programs: The Four Levels*. San Francisco: Berrett-Koehler.

Latino Dialogues—Factors Impacting Latino Success at CSULB, Meeting Proceedings. Fall 2006. Chicano and Latino Studies Department. Long Beach: California State University, Long Beach (unpublished report).

Luévano, Susan. 2005. *Semillas de Cambio/ Seeds of Change*: Information Competence in Chicano & Latino Studies. http://www.csulb.edu/~sluevano/seeds/

Luévano, Susan, Tiffini Travis, and Eileen Wakiji. (June 2003). Information Competence for the Discipline of Black Studies. PRIMO: Peer-Reviewed Instructional Materials Online, Site of the Month. Association of College and Research Libraries, Emerging Technologies Committee. http://www.ala.org/ala/acrlbucket/is/iscommit tees/webpages/emergingtech/site/june2003.cfm

Miller, William, & Stephen Bell. 2005. "A New Strategy for Enhancing Library Use: Faculty-Led Information Literacy Instruction." *Library Issues* 5 (May): 1–4.

Montero-Sieburth, Martha, & Michael Christian Batt. 2001. An Overview of the Education Models Used to Explain the Academic Achievement of Latino Students: Implications for Research and Policies into the New Millennium. In *Effective Programs for Latino Students*, eds. Robert E. Slavin & Margarita Calderón, 331–368. Mahwah, NJ: Lawrence Erlbaum Associates.

Nash, Mary. 2004. "Information Literacy and the Learning Community." *Nebraska Library Association Quarterly* 35, no. 4 (Winter): 18–24.

Porras Hein, Nancy, and Barbara A. Miller. 2004. "¿Quien Soy? Finding My Place in History: Personalizing Learning Through Faculty/Librarian Collaboration." *Journal of Hispanic Higher Education* 3, no. 4 (October): 307–321.

Quijada, Patricia Del Carmen, & Leticia Alvarez. 2006. Cultivando Semillas Educacionales [Cultivating Educational Seeds]. In *The Latina/o Pathway to the PhD: Abriendo Caminos*, ed. Janette Castellanos, Alberta M. Gloria, & Mark Kamimura, 13–17. Sterling, VA: Styllus.

Rockman, Illene F. 2004. Introduction: The Importance of Information Literacy. In *Integrating Information Literacy in Higher Education Curriculum: Practical Models for Transformation*, ed. Illene F. Rockman, 1–28. San Francisco: Jossey-Bass.

Samson, Sue, & Michelle S. Millet. 2003. "The Learning Environment: First-Year Students, Teaching Assistants, and Information Literacy." *Research Strategies* 19, no. 2: 84–98.

Smith, Risë. April 11–14, 1997. "Philosophical Shift: Teach the Faculty to Teach Information Literacy." Academic, College and Research Libraries Conference, Nashville, TN http://www.ala.org/ala/acrl bucket/nashville1997pap/smith.cfm

Solberg, V. Scott, & Pete Villareal. 1997. "Examination of Self-Efficacy, Social Support, and Stress as Predictors of Psychological and Physical Distress among Hispanic College Students." *Hispanic Journal of Behavioral Sciences* 19, no. 2 (May): 182–201.

Torres, Vasti. 2004. "Familial Influences on the Identity Development of Latino First-Year Students." *Journal of Student Development* 45, no. 4 (July/August): 457–469.

Chapter 5

Special Libraries and Collections: "Invisible as Night, Implacable as Wind" California Ethnic and Multicultural Archives (CEMA): The First 20 Years

Erica Bennett

"Vendido!" (sell out) shouted one of the 20 Chicano college students. The students were attending a January 15, 1988, lecture by playwright Luis Valdez at the University of California, Santa Barbara (UCSB). The demonstrators had filed in and stood menacingly along the walls of the Lotte Lehman Concert Hall, heckling Valdez's talk. "You cannot fight racism with racism," Valdez shouted back, countering, "Get out there and fight for your people any way that you can!"[1] The renowned playwright was the object of the students' wrath. They accused Valdez of leaving the cause of farm workers, "going Hollywood" by casting an Italian-American actress in the role of Mexican artist Frida Kahlo. Earlier in the afternoon, Valdez had concluded negotiations to bring his historic papers and the archives of the theater company he founded in the 1960s to the UCSB Library's *Coleccion Tloque Nahuaque* (CTN).[2] Perhaps it was lost on them that UCSB's university librarian, Dr. Joseph Boissé, and then-CTN librarian Salvador Güereña, strove for three years to bring these collections to UCSB for these students and for future students like them.

While the significance of what had occurred earlier that day was not on their minds, the prescience of Boissé and Güereña forever changed the nature of developing ethnic archival and manuscript collections. Their efforts, aptly illustrated by the story above, characterize the conflicts and contradictions, as well as perseverance through antipathy during their process of birthing the California Ethnic and Multicultural Archives (CEMA) out of the loins of the CTN. This article elucidates the journey that CEMA has taken, from its earliest beginnings through its evolution, into one of the nation's premier multicultural archival institutions.

Introduction

"Tloque Nahuaque, Lord of the Close and the Near, is the Aztec dual god-above-all. Named for this powerful god, the CTN was one of the country's preeminent collections of resources on the historical and contemporary Chicano experience."[3] According to Güereña, UCSB was the first university in the country to establish a comprehensive Chicano Studies collection within a university library rather than as an attachment to an academic department.[4] The collaboration between Boissé and Güereña began in 1984 when Boissé, the newly hired university librarian, called Güereña into his office to discuss implications of the population shift that was underway in California.[5] Boissé pointed out that while the East Coast university archives were "filled with the papers of the white male elite," few institutions on the West Coast were dedicated to collecting the papers and the work of the "leading edge" of Chicano/Latino literature, arts, and politics.[6]

Güereña and Boissé began developing the Chicano/Latino archives program to meet the scholarship needs of a growing Chicano/Latino academic community, dedicated to the principle of providing a permanent facility to document the social, cultural, and political history of California's Chicano communities.[7] The CTN achieved a major coup in 1986 by gaining the trust of and signing agreements with the *Ralph Maradiaga* estate, *La Galeria de la Raza*, *El Teatro Campesino*, *Royal Chicano Air Force (RCAF)*, and *Self-Help Graphics & Art*. Three years later, Boissé and Güereña conceived of CEMA, in a drive to direct and build the collection into a multicultural archive of national significance. Beginning in February of 1989, Boissé and Güereña met with librarians Stella Bentley, associate university librarian (AUL) for Collection Development; Connie Dowell, head of the Reference Department; Sylvia Curtis, Black Studies Library; and Ruben Rey, development officer in the Office of Institutional Advancement. They revised the original scope of the program to build upon the Chicano/Latino archives program by including the papers and works of members of the Asian American, Native American, and African American communities.[8] However, they were also determined to limit the geographic scope to include only collections created by "people born in

California, based in California, or who have made an important impact in California . . . given the serious under-representation of California-based ethnic groups and individuals in the repositories of this state."[9] Additionally, they developed a documentation strategy that sought to stem the tide of the pointless destruction of historic items that document California's heritage by "gathering and indexing significant records as they are created and discovered."[10]

The first Advisory Board meeting was held on November 2, 1991. Statistics from that meeting reveal that between 1984 and 1991, approximately 30 collections were identified; 25 of those were considered viable, and of those, 15 were secured. State Archivist John Burns stated unequivocally, "For ethnic communities there has been no paper trail—this is an area where CEMA can provide a real service . . . everyday working men and women who have no working papers, from whom oral histories would be valuable."[11] Committing to collect, protect, and provide access to the cultural heritage of the underserved and underheard populations of California is what gives CEMA its national significance. For while the United States National Archives and Records Administration "enables people to inspect for themselves the record of what government has done," and in the process protect the democracy in which we live, who is protecting our cultural heritage, if not organizations like CEMA?[12]

History and Development

UCSB was established on July 1, 1944. The third campus in the University of California system after UC Berkeley and UCLA, UCSB's enrollment had doubled by 1947.[13] The post-WWII era of growth and prosperity grew more complicated in the 1960s with American discontent over the Vietnam War and the rapidly escalating civil rights movement. Disenfranchisement led to a more assertive student body politic, whose frustration came to the boiling point in 1970 when rioting student protesters burned down the Isla Vista branch of the Bank of America.[14]

The forerunner to CTN was instituted in 1969. That year, 16 black students barricaded themselves in the North Hall Computer Center. They made eight demands that led to the founding of the black studies department, research center, and library. Also that year, the UCSB's Mexican American Youth Organization (MAYO), in support of Chicano/Latino students, demanded a corresponding Chicano studies department, research center, and library. They met with the library director, and as a result of their discussions, several library collections were created.[15] The two libraries began with one collection in the research center, to support its work; and a reading room collection in the main library. The two were later consolidated and renamed the MECHA collection, and in 1977, it was moved into a dedicated space in the newly constructed south wing of the main library.[16]

As with the rest of the nation, UCSB experienced a racial cooling during the 1970s and by 1982 had a student body of over 15,000.[17] A now flourishing medium-sized academic institution, the library held approximately 1,416,100 books, 18,800 serials, and 1,582,000 microfilm items, as well as the Chicano Studies Collection, Black Studies Collection, and Oriental Collection.[18] By this time, UCSB had "a handful of registered campus organizations that could be labeled protest-oriented or pseudo-radical."[19] However, minority enrollment was up 0.3 percent, representing over 17 percent of the total student population by 1983.[20]

Into this mix came the efforts and expertise of Güereña and Boissé. Güereña, the son of lemon packers, is a native Santa Barbaran. He received his MLS from the University of Arizona in 1979 and then managed one of the branch libraries of the Santa Barbara Public Library; he lead a multicultural outreach program for the system before his career move into academia in 1983. That year he accepted a UC Santa Barbara appointment as head of the Chicano Studies Library.

Boissé is of French Canadian and American Indian descent.[21] He received his MSLS from Simmons College and his EdD from Temple University, where he was director of libraries from 1979–1983.[22] When Boissé became university librarian at UCSB in 1983, the *Daily Nexus* reported that he had hopes of making the library more accessible as a learning tool for students and faculty. Boissé remarked, "UCSB offers an outstanding opportunity for developing the library."[23] In the 15 years of his tenure at the UCSB library before his retirement in 1998, he did not take that opportunity lightly.

Demographics

Where *Nationalism* rejects the "Chicago school" theory of *assimilation*,[24] in 1987 Professor Elliott Butler Evans, the director of UCSB's Center for Black Studies, announced a new motivation:

> California adds a whole different audience that stresses a kind of multicultural approach to things, and in that kind of context, if you are going to play a viable role in the community in the larger community, then you have to find a way to make your efforts include as many diverse groups as possible.[25]

Young people were beginning to show signs of increasing involvement in multicultural protests when in November of 1987, in excess of 2,500 students staged a "Week of Protest" to advance ethnic representation in California colleges and universities.[26] UCSB students did not participate in the protest. UCSB Associated Student Body President Curtis Robinson attributed it to "the demographic makeup of UCSB . . . Our campus is different. We don't have the makeup and strength."[27]

So what were the "demographic changes that were occurring in California," to which Boissé was referring in his 1984 meeting with Güereña? Schmittroth cites Camarota, who notes that "between 1970 and 2000 the immigrant population [in the United States] grew from 9.6 million to 28.4 million."[28] A 1989 Review of the California Master Plan for Higher Education went even further, recognizing that "early into the 21st Century, California will be the first mainland state with a majority of non-white persons," predicting the following demographics:

> Sometime between 2000 and 2010 Latinos will constitute over 30 percent of the general population, Asians 13 percent, Blacks 8 percent, Whites less than 49 percent. By the end of the following decade one of three Californians will be Latino; one in seven will be Asian. At the same time, 3/4 of our retirees will be white, and approximately 60 percent of our work force will be persons of color.[29]

Boissé was right on target. However, the demographics were also significant in that it they mark a rapid decline in the educational achievement of immigrants. In 1970, established immigrants lacking a high school diploma lagged behind native Californians a mere 7.1 percent. However, the gap widened to nearly 25 percent by the year 2000.[30] Yet immigrants were not the only minority group in the United States showing an academic achievement gap. In 1986, only 5.0 percent of Latino graduates were eligible for admission into the University of California, compared to 4.5 percent of black high school graduates.[31] In 1987, UC spokesman Ray Colvig referred to a UC study that compared white and black student graduation rates; 65 percent of white students graduated within five years compared to 27 percent of black students.[32]

The California Ethnic and Multicultural Archives (CEMA)

University of California, Santa Barbara had a dramatic 1989. In January of that year, Chancellor Barbara Uehling avowed her commitment to representative ethnic diversity on campus.[33] On February 9, Boissé and Güereña met with Bentley, Dowell, Curtis, and Rey to discuss the formation of CEMA.[34] However, less than two weeks later, a group of 40 UCSB students began a hunger strike that they vowed would continue until the university took substantive action to put an end to "institutional racism and increase ethnic diversity on campus." They decried the now 24.4 percent minority student population yet 14.1 percent minority ladder-rank faculty on campus. Their demands included the establishment of a two-course ethnicity requirement, elimination of the existing two-course American history and institutions requirement, and the creation of a taskforce to study the possible development of a gender studies requirement. Additionally, the group stipulated for the development and implementation of an Asian American studies department and a Native American studies program.[35] Gabriel Guiterrez's comments were particularly poignant: "We aren't just striking for ethnic studies, (but to) bring attention to institutional racism, cultural disrespect, student disempowerment. This action is for those who are to come after us . . . (so they) won't have to go through the shit I've had to go through."[36] Another hunger striker, Lucia Palacios, added:

> I believe the ethnicity requirement is necessary in order for students to learn about contributions made by ethnic groups to American history. I'm tired of learning about the white man. Education is my right, not my privilege, and I pay enough for them to teach me what I want to know.[37]

Before long, the students' demands spread through all of the UCs.[38] On Day 9 of the hunger strike, UCSB political science department Chair Cedric Robinson and black studies Professor Gerard Pigeon began their own three-day fast in support of the students.[39] Güereña spoke to the rally. He said, in part:

> The students have made a great sacrifice to call attention to the issues of institutional racism and to their proposals for solutions . . . In short, there must be a much more tangible commitment to diversity, a commitment to producing leaders who understand and respect the ethnic experience . . . The University simply must develop new and effective strategies to better sensitize all members of the academic community and improve opportunities and participation of under-represented groups.[40]

Finally, on Day 10, Chancellor Uehling responded to the hunger strikers, officially agreeing to create an overarching committee to answer the students' demands.[41] On Day 11, a statement was issued by the black, Chicano, and Native American faculty and staff, announcing their support for the hunger strikers.[42] On Day 12, with the promise of negotiations to begin five days later, the hunger strikers ended their fast.[43] The following month, black studies librarian Sylvia Curtis was interviewed by the *Daily Nexus*, the UCSB student newspaper. She remarked that "as a result of the discussions initiated by the now-suspended hunger strike, minority faculty has increased their interaction with other minority professors from different ethnic backgrounds."[44] It appears that the students were more successful than they had even imagined. However, on April 12, negotiations between students and administration collapsed.[45] Students decided to take more militant actions, such as "guerilla-theater, take-over's of buildings and disruptions of other kinds," when unexpectedly UC Berkeley agreed to initiate an ethnicity requirement.[46] Finally, on June 1, 1989, the UCSB College of Letters and Science faculty approved 250–241 a one-course general education ethnicity requirement.[47]

> The requirement [would] go into effect Fall Quarter 1989, mandat[ing] that students entering the university take one course studying either the historical experience of Blacks, Chicanos/Latinos, Native Americans or Asian-Americans: or take a class "providing a comparative or integrative context for understanding the experience of oppressed and excluded racial minorities in the United States."[48]

Minority enrollment grew in the fall quarter of 1988 from 29 percent to 32 percent the following year with 1,040 out of 3,250 new freshman identifying themselves as minorities.[49] Boissé believes the choice to create a multicultural archive that included various ethnic groups was one of the reasons for CEMA's success; certainly the decision was supported by the campus and administration.[50]

CEMA's line of authority was admittedly awkward at first. Operationally, CEMA initially reported to the head of the Reference Department but concerning its development answered directly to the university librarian. In regard to acquisitions, CEMA reported to the AUL for Collections Development. This chain of command was streamlined later, and by 2004 CEMA reported directly to the head of Special Collections.[51]

As the CEMA emerged from the CTN's orbit, the next step toward becoming a multicultural archive was to institute a collections development plan. Boissé recognized that many research library archives collected in a haphazard or accidental fashion. They were often approached by a grieving family who sought to gift the papers of their well-known family member to the repository upon his or her death. What Boissé sought to do, instead, in establishing CEMA was to "identify individuals who were playing an important role in their communities and to arrange to collect their papers even while they were still producing them."[52] This proactive approach prevents the loss of potentially significant works, and CEMA was the first institution in California systematically attempting to build a collection of this kind.[53]

Yet how did that decision affect CEMA's ability to remain viable in light of the budget retrenchments that were looming ahead? In April of

1991 the library was facing a cut of $225,000 from its $13 million annual budget, a decision made official in June when the California State Assembly cut $12.5 million from the UC-system budget.[54] Boissé went on to cut $250,000 from the library's budget but spared CEMA. Clearly, Boissé considered CEMA a priority unit within the library.

According to Boissé, it was Güereña who actually developed the archives.[55] CEMA's annual reports reveal a substantial number of goals for each subsequent year: in acquiring collections, creating finding aids, processing multiple collections, grant writing, creating and maintaining the CEMA website, following potential leads for donors, launching exhibits, and making conference presentations, as well as participating in collaborative work with professional associations.[56]

Güereña's initial work took him on the road to California's ethnic communities. In his 2001 talk to the University Library Colloquium at the University of Illinois, Urbana Champaign, Güereña reminisced about the trips that he and Boissé took "through the rural farmlands to meet with Cesar Chavez at the UFW compound at La Paz, and through East L.A. to win the hearts of Chicano artists at Self-Help Graphics & Art."[57] In a 1986 planning memo, Güereña reported that he would travel to the Bay Area to not only retrieve remaining materials for the *Ralph Maradiaga* collection but also to visit *La Galería de la Raza* and the *El Teatro Campesino* to discuss their collections.[58] These efforts paid off several years later when CEMA secured the performing arts archives of *El Teatro Campesino*, as well as the papers of Chicano author and lawyer Oscar Zeta Acosta.

> There are two categories of materials that are collected by CEMA. The first consists of personal papers of individuals including correspondence, diaries, speeches, photographs, manuscripts, and memorabilia. The second type consists of organizational records. These document the history of an institution, and include reports, minutes of meetings, agenda, memoranda, and publications.[59]

CEMA made great strides in collecting the works of visual artists, "including many thousands of silkscreen prints and posters, tens of thousands of slides and photographs, printed files, artifacts, and ephemera."[60] The acquisition by CEMA of the Self-Help Graphics & Art archives collection allows researcher to see how the artists "functioned to build community, how they stimulated political action and made an impact on social and cultural consciousness."[61] Additionally, Güereña developed a K-12 initiative and created a workshop for fifth graders built around the Self-Help Graphics & Art print collection, bringing important issues of cultural iconography, segregation, and racism into the classroom.[62]

A prolific writer, Güereña's publications include books and articles on library studies, bibliography, and archives. Additionally, Güereña taught

Documentary Research in Chicano Studies through the Department of Chicano Studies. He encouraged students to develop their competencies in library research, online database searching, Internet proficiencies, and to gain a familiarity with oral and family history research.[63]

Güereña is recognized on the national stage through his leadership in REFORMA. He was its president from 1984–1985, and in 1992 he was honored as "Librarian of the Year." He also served on the governing Council of the American Library Association and chaired numerous committees. Next, he turned his attention to the Society of California Archivists, serving on its board of directors. He continues his leadership in the field by speaking at conferences and organizing programs on such topics as ethnic studies and manuscripts, library services to Latinos, library cultural diversity, community analysis, and digitizing for diversity.[64]

Güereña's handwritten notes begin on February 9, 1989, recording CEMA's planning meeting, giving evidence to its goals. Attended by Boissé, Güereña, Bentley, Hammes, Dowell, Curtis, and Rey, among others, the notes offer poignant reminders of their concerns.[65] They develop their future actions, as well as identify potential donors, including Valdez, Willie Brown, and California Secretary of State March Fong Eu. Eu was instrumental in introducing CEMA to the Asian American community. She recognized that "so much of the early documentation of our California heritage was lost forever simply because the importance of the materials was not considered when they were available."[66]

CEMA in the 21st Century

By 2004, Güereña's collection inventory checklist reported 98 total collections. Of those, 49 were processed. Fifty-two collections were unprocessed, although 41 of those had a preliminary guide. It is important to note that all of these acquisitions were made through gifts of collections: none were purchased. Lacking in endowment support, Güereña had to present a convincing case to potential donors to place their confidence in the CEMA program. Among Güereña's strongest arguments was the permanent institutional investment in CEMA, such that it was funded by real money from the library budget, and not dependent on grants.[67] According to Güereña, "Latino archives in general [had] a history of uneven priorities and shoestring budgets that were subject to the changing whims of whoever happened to be in charge."[68] The promise of a permanent program with guaranteed funding not only provides a better foundation for growth but also alerts potential donors that CEMA is a stable organization.

Nevertheless, Güereña is among the first to admit that sometimes it take years to build trust before a donor is willing to make that first step to donate a collection. This is best illustrated by CEMA's acquisition of the papers of Lalo Guerrero, now considered the father of Chicano music.[69] It took many years of phone calls before Güereña finally developed a trust relationship with the family, and that persistency convinced Guerrero's son Dan Guerrero, that CEMA was the repository best suited for his father's works.[70] The collection was inaugurated at a December 4, 2000, ceremony and is considered part of a new initiative of the Library's Performing Arts Collections and CEMA to document the legacy of Mexican American music in California.[71]

Of particular significance to any archives is the use of the collections. In 1971 it was reported that for the 1985–1986 academic school year, researchers used the materials in the CTN more than 9,000 times,[72] while in 2004, Güereña reports that the CEMA website was visited several hundred thousand times per month.[73] In the case of CEMA, use by the students and faculty of UCSB is of particular concern.

Güereña began his pursuit of Asian American collections by securing, in 1991, the archives of the Chinese American Political Association; the Asian American Theater Company archives followed in 1993. However, it was not until 2003 that CEMA finally acquired the papers of renowned Asian American playwright and writer Frank Chin. A graduate of UCSB, Chin also founded the Asian American Theater Workshop in San Francisco, which evolved into the Asian American Theater Company.[74] Claire Conceison, a UCSB assistant professor of dramatic arts, assigns students to study Chin's plays, requiring them to work with the CEMA archives.[75] There is no better validation for an archive than to acquire a collection that is developed into the curriculum.

Güereña embraces current archival traditions, conforming to the principles and guidelines of the Society of American Archivists, Association for Recorded Sound Collections, Research Libraries Group, California Digital Library, and the Visual Resources Association, as well as the Intermuseum Conservation Association. He also utilizes current OAC-EAD finding aid and METS compliant digital objects standards. CEMA does more item-level processing of visual arts materials than many institutions in order to "prevent the loss of cultural memory and the historical context through which these objects were created."[76]

CEMA cannot do all of its work alone. Collaborations are an important part of the equation. Working with partners such as the L.A.-based former national leaders of the Comision Femenil Mexicana Nacional, CEMA took on the challenge of the California State Library to encourage libraries to "break out of their traditional insular mode and begin working with community groups and community based organizations to work together to develop more relevant services to meet their needs."[77] Güereña works closely with the librarian, faculty, and community partnerships at UCSB to develop relationships between the archives, the campus curriculum, and research requirements.[78] For example, collaboration between CEMA and the University Art Museum resulted in a three-year national touring exhibit entitled "Just Another Poster: Chicano Graphic Arts in California."[79]

Güereña is also a leader in the field of digital access, influenced by the work and writings of Clifford Lynch, Anne Kenny, and Oya Rieger.[80] It is in this area that CEMA received several grants. Working with the Online Archive of California (OAC), CEMA's goal is "to provide online access to CEMA collections, whether they are archives and manuscripts, posters, slides, or photographs."[81] In 2001 Güereña took the initial steps to create an Asian American performing arts digital collection, with the intent of presenting images, sound graphics, and play scripts from the Asian American theater collections.[82] In 2003, CEMA received a $100,000 grant for *CARIDAD II* from the California Digital Library, as part of the California Cultures Project of the OAC, to add over 8,000 Latino cultural arts images to their already extensive Chicano visual arts digital image collection.[83] This developed from the work of an earlier project, *Proyecto CARIDAD* (Chicano Art Resources Development and Dissemination). *Proyecto CARIDAD* was founded in 1990 to preserve the visual arts resources created by the nation's leading Chicano art collectives in California, including the *Centro Cultural de la Raza* (San Diego), *Galeria de la Raza* (San Francisco), the *RCAF* (Sacramento), and *Self-Help Graphics & Art* (Los Angeles).[84]

The CEMA website lists three additional projects. Through a grant from the University of California Institute on Mexico and the United States (UC MEXUS), the *Proyecto Aeronaves* project funded the processing of the archives of the RCAF and the production of an online finding aid.[85] UC MEXUS also provided a grant for the *Border Arts Cultural Heritage project*, that processed the papers of Salvador Torres, Victor Ochoa, and the *Centro Cultural de la Raza*, with online finding aids posted to both the CEMA website and the OAC.[86] *Proyecto RESCATE* (Reconstituting Selected Chicano Archives for Transitioning into Electronic Format) funded the digitization of nearly 1,400 visual arts images that were selected from the vast slide collections in the archives of the four cultural centers (listed above), including images of silk screen art, murals, installation art, *cajas* and *nichos*, paintings, drawings, sculptures, and cultural processions as in *Dia de los Muertos*.[87] Additional items of interest located on the CEMA website are the extensive guides to collections. It should be noted that Güereña not only posted online EAD finding aids for the OAC but also mirrored them on the CEMA website because at that time the EAD finding aids were not discoverable on the open Web.

While Boissé admits that it was Güereña who developed CEMA into the success that it is today, clearly, the final success is due to the talents of both men, who both inspired and created it, who worked from within the community and outside it, mindful of both the institutional and racial politics surrounding it. CEMA was established to accomplish eight goals: (1) enable and enhance research efforts to study the ethnic and racial diversity of the state and nation and attendant demographic and social issues; (2) support study and research in many disciplines; (3) enrich the academic work of the ethnic studies departments in the University of California; (4) enhance the recruitment of underrepresented faculty and students; (5) serve as a site for graduate-level internships in history, archives management, and ethnic studies; (6) organize exhibitions, conferences, and symposia on various topics related to the archival holdings; (7) develop monographs, exhibition catalogs, and other publications; and (8) ensure, by preserving the materials, that future generations have access to the important historical documents.[88] CEMA is an unusual accomplishment: a prize that benefits the past, present, and future of all students of the state of California, and through them, the nation and the world.

Notes

1. Staff, "Luis Valdez: American Original," *Daily Nexus*, January 14, 1988, 7A; Doug Arellanes and Jess Lerma, "Controversial Lecture by Luis Valdez Turns into Fervid 'Verbal Free-for-all,'" *Daily Nexus*, January 19, 1988, 3, 5, 14.

2. Doug Arellanes, "Luis Valdez Library Coleccion," *Daily Nexus*, January 21, 1988, 4A.

3. Staff, "Wealth of Cultural Riches," 2A.

4. Cory Anne Azumbrado, "Several Resources at UCSB Available to Educate Students in Chicano Culture," *Daily Nexus*, September 28, 1987, 3, 7.

5. Salvador Güereña, *Plenary Address: An Archival Call to Action for "Memoria, Voz y Patrimonio."* Draft August 13, 2003: 1.

6. Ibid.

7. Ibid., 5.

8. Salvador Güereña, e-mail to author Re: More files on CEMA history. April 27, 2004.

9. Salvador Güereña, e-mail to author Re: Revised CEMA proposal and interview questions. October 8, 2004.

10. Connie V. Dowell, "Collecting Primary Materials of Major Ethnic Groups: The California Ethnic and Multicultural Archives Project," *College & Research Libraries News* 53(3) (March 1992), 157.

11. CEMA Advisory Board Meeting Notes: Status of collections. November 2, 1991.

12. The National Archives. Our Vision Statement, http://www.archives.gov/about/info/mission.html (April 5, 2006).

13. John Krist, "UCSB's History At Goleta Point," *Daily Nexus*, September 17, 1982, 1.

14. Ibid., 15.

15. Salvador Güereña, *Delivering or Dabbling: Diversity Initiatives in a University Library Setting*. For the University Library Colloquium, University of Illinois, Urbana Champaign, delivered April 18, 2001. See also *Political Tolerance in Higher Education: Identifying the Threshold of Support for Diversity Policies*, Marisela Marquez dissertation, 2002.

16. Salvador Güereña, e-mail to author Re: CEMA Conceptual Essay. October 12, 2004.

17. John Krist, "Growth and Change: A History of UCSB," *Daily Nexus*, August 27, 1982, 1.

18. Jane Musser, "Library Offers Research Help," *Daily Nexus*, September 17, 1982, 11A.

19. Vanessa Grimm, "UCSB Haunted by Ghosts of Protest," *Daily Nexus*, September 16, 1983, 10C.

20. Kim Hansel, "Enrollment Figures At UCSB Increase," *Daily Nexus*, October 18, 1983, 1; Keith Ross, "UCSB Minority Enrollment Reaches All-Time High," *Daily Nexus*, December 1, 1983, 1.

21. Güereña (2001).

22. *Directory of Library and Information Professionals* (Woodbridge, CT: Research Publications, 1988), 111.

23. Anthony Salazar, "Joseph Boisse: Librarian Will Increase Collection," *Daily Nexus*, November 15, 1983, 6.

24. Ibid., 14–16.

25. Brent Anderson, "De-Centering the Center: Moving the Center for Black Studies Toward an Era of Multi-culturalism," *Daily Nexus*, April 27, 1988, 7, 10.

26. Michael Berke, "'Week of Protest' Draws Attention to College Minority Representation," *Daily Nexus*, November 11, 1987, 4.

27. Ibid., 5.

28. Steven A. Camarota in Linda Schmittroth, *Immigration and Illegal Aliens: Burden or Blessing?* (New York: Thomson Gale, 2004), 92–93; Steven A. Camarota, *The Slowing Progress of Immigrants: An Examination of Income, Home Ownership, and Citizenship, 1970–2000* (Center for Immigration Studies, *Backgrounder*, March 2001).

29. Joint Committee for Review of The Master Plan for Higher Education. *[1989] California Faces... California's Future: Education for Citizenship in a Multicultural Democracy*, 1989, http://dynaweb.oac.cdlib.org:8088/dynaweb/uchist/public/cahighered/masterplan1989/ (June 8, 2004).

30. Camarota in Schmittroth, 92–93. Established immigrants are defined as those who have lived in the United States for 11 to 20 years.

31. Joint Committee for Review of The Master Plan for Higher Education (1989).

32. John Lynn Smith, "Students Seek Solution to Campus Racial Problems," *Daily Nexus*, October 19, 1987, 3.

33. Staff Reports, "Chancellor Talks of Expansion Enrollment," *Daily Nexus*, January 9, 1989, 1.

34. Salvador Güereña. Handwritten notes from CEMA planning meetings. 1989.

35. Chris Ziegler, "Hunger Strikers Fast to End UCSB Racism: Student Fasters Hope to Publicize Demands for Implementation of Ethnicity Requirement," *Daily Nexus*, February 22, 1989, 1.

36. Chris Ziegler, "Ethnic Studies Voting Integrity Questioned," *Daily Nexus*, February 27, 1989, 7.

37. Ibid.

38. Heesun Wee, "Ethnicity Demands Spread to All UCs," *Daily Nexus*, February 28, 1989, 1.

39. Amy Collins, "2 UCSB Professors Hold Three-day Fast," *Daily Nexus*, March 1, 1989, 1.

40. Salvador Güereña, e-mail to author Re: CEMA Conceptual Essay. Remarks to 1989 Hunger Strike Rally, October 11, 2004.

41. Amy Collins, "Chancellor Formally Responds to Strike: Fasting Students Nix Uehling's Offer, Gain Added Support From UCSB Staff, Faculty," *Daily Nexus*, March 2, 1989, 1.

42. Amy Collins, "Hunger Strike Support Snowballs; Professors to Speak During Rally Today at Cheadle Hall," *Daily Nexus*, March 3, 1989, 1.

43. Amy Collins, "Strikers, Uehling Meet, 12-Day Fast Suspended: Negotiations to Start by Friday; Students Insist on 'Meaningful Dialogue' with Uehling," *Daily Nexus*, March 6, 1989, 1, 5.

44. Heather Davis, "Portrait: Sylvia Curtis: Black Studies Librarian Uses Job to Shorten Cultural Gap," *Daily Nexus*, April 6, 1989, 3.

45. Chris Ziegler, "Protest Resumes as Negotiations Collapse: Students Complain Administration Does Not Take Their Demands Seriously," *Daily Nexus*, April 19, 1989, 1.

46. Amy Collins, "Hunger Strikers Switch Strategy; Threaten More Militant Measures," *Daily Nexus*, April 26, 1989, 1; Heather Jones and Michelle Ray, "UC Berkeley Accepts Ethnicity Requirement," *Daily Nexus*, April 27, 1989, 1, 3.

47. Chris Ziegler, "L&S Faculty Approves Ethnicity Requirement: One-Course Option Squeaks by, 250–241, with Most Ballots Ever," *Daily Nexus*, June 2, 1989, 1.

48. Ibid.

49. Jennifer Ogar, "Minority Enrollment Level Surpasses Record Set Last Year." *Daily Nexus*, September 15, 1989, 1.

50. Dr. Joseph Boisse, e-mail to author Re: CEMA. October 12, 2004.

51. Salvador Güereña, e-mail to author Re: more files on CEMA history. April 27, 2004.

52. Boisse (2004).

53. Boisse (2004).

54. Joanna Frazier, "Library to Trim Staff, Shorten Hours Due to State Budget Shortfall," *Daily Nexus*, April 15, 1991, 5; Bonnie Bills, "New State Budget Cuts $12.5 Million From UC," *Daily Nexus*, June 26, 1991, 1–2.

55. Boisse (2004).

56. Salvador Güereña, CEMA Annual Reports, 1993–2003.

57. Güereña (2001).

58. Salvador Güereña, Memo to Olga Ignon, AUL, Collection Development Re: Review of follow-up assignments, Chicano archives," Santa Barbara: Office of the Librarian. November 20, 1986.

59. Salvador Güereña, *California Ethnic and Multicultural Archives brochure*, Department of Special Collections Donald C. Davidson Library University of California Santa Barbara (undated material).

60. Güereña (2001).

61. Ibid.

62. Salvador Güereña, interview with author. June 11, 2004. Description of the project is located at the CEMA website at http://cemaweb.library.ucsb.edu/k12.html.

63. Ibid.

64. Salvador Güereña, "Professional Biography," *CEMA*. April 15, 2004. http://www.library.ucsb.edu/people/guerena/ (June 8, 2004).

65. Güereña (1991).

66. Dowell (1992), 157.

67. Güereña (2001).

68. Salvador Güereña, "Draft: Plenary address: An Archival Call to Action for "Memoria, Voz y Patrimonio." Delivered August 13, 2003.

69. Ibid.

70. Ibid.

71. Güereña (2000).

72. Connie V. Dowell, "Art in the Library," *Coastlines 17*(2) (Winter 1987): 4.

73. Salvador Güereña, e-mail to author Re: CEMA use statistics. October 25, 2004.

74. Jon Bartel, "Home Again: The UCSB Libraries Acquire the Papers of Alumnus and Author Frank Chin," *Coastlines 34*(2) (Fall 2003): 9.

75. Dowell (1992), 159.

76. Güereña (October 14, 2004).

77. Güereña (2003).

78. Ibid.

79. Ibid.

80. Güereña (October 14, 2004).

81. Güereña (2001).

82. Ibid.

83. Salvador Güereña, "Chicana/o Art Digital Initiative [CARIDAD II]," *CEMA News 1*(1) (August 2003), 1–2.

84. Salvador Güereña, "Proyecto Caridad: Chicano Art Resources Information Development and Dissemination," CEMA website, March 4, 2002, http://cemaweb.library.ucsb.edu/caridad.html (October 19, 2004).

85. Salvador Güereña, "Proyecto Aeronaves," CEMA website, April 10, 2002, http://cemaweb.library.ucsb.edu/aeronave.html (October 19, 2004).

86. Salvador Güereña, "Border Arts Cultural Heritage Project," *CEMA News 1*(1) (August 2003), 2. For images, see the CEMA web page at http://cemaweb.library.ucsb.edu/bach.html (October 19, 2004).

87. Salvador Güereña, "Proyecto Rescate," CEMA website, March 6, 2002, http://cemaweb.library.ucsb.edu/rescate.html (October 19, 2004).

88. Salvador Güereña, "The Lalo Guerrero Collection," Inaugural Ceremony The Lalo Guerrero Collection University Libraries, UCSB brochure (December 4, 2000).

89. Richard Chabran, "Notes on the History and Future of Major Academic Chicano Libraries," in *Biblio-Politicia: Chicano Perspectives on Library Service in the United States*, ed. Francisco Garcia-Ayvens (Berkeley: Chicano Studies Library Publications Unit, University of California, Berkeley, 1984), 97.

References

Anderson, Brent. "De-Centering the Center: Moving the Center for Black Studies Toward an Era of Multi-Culturalism." *Daily Nexus*, April 27, 1988: 7, 10.

Arellanes, Doug. "Luis Valdez Library Collection." *Daily Nexus*, January 21, 1988: 4A.

Arellanes, Doug, & Jess Lerma. "Controversial Lecture by Luis Valdez Turns into Fervid 'Verbal Free-for-all.'" *Daily Nexus*, January 19, 1988: 3, 5, 14.

Azumbrado, Cory Anne. "Several Resources at UCSB Available to Educate Students in Chicano Culture." *Daily Nexus*, September 28, 1987: 3, 7.

Bartel, Jon. "Home Again: The UCSB Libraries Acquire the Papers of Alumnus and Author Frank Chin." *Coastlines 34*(2) (Fall 2003): 8–9.

Berke, Michael. "'Week of Protest' Draws Attention to College Minority Representation." *Daily Nexus*, November 11, 1987: 4, 5.

Bills, Bonnie. "New State Budget Cuts $12.5 Million From UC." *Daily Nexus*, June 26, 1991: 1–2.

Boisse, Joseph A. E-mail to Erica Bennett re: CEMA. October 12, 2004.

CEMA Advisory Board Meeting Notes: Status of Collections. November 2, 1991.

Chabran, Richard F. "Notes on the History and Future of Major Academic Chicano Libraries." In *Biblio-Politica*, ed. Francisco Garcia-Ayvens, 89–106. Berkeley: Chicano Studies Library Publications Unit, University of California, Berkeley, 1984.

Collins, Amy. "Chancellor Formally Responds to Strike: Fasting Students Nix Uehling's Offer, Gain Added Support from UCSB Staff, Faculty." *Daily Nexus*, March 2, 1989: 1, 4.

Collins, Amy. "Hunger Strikers Switch Strategy; Threaten More Militant Measures." *Daily Nexus*, April 26, 1989: 1.

Collins, Amy. "Hunger Strike Support Snowballs; Professors to Speak During Rally Today at Cheadle Hall." *Daily Nexus*, March 3, 1989: 1, 12.

Collins, Amy. "Strikers, Uehling Meet, 12-Day Fast Suspended: Negotiations to Start by Friday; Students Insist on 'Meaningful Dialogue' with Uehling." *Daily Nexus*, March 6, 1989: 1, 5.

Collins, Amy. "2 UCSB Professors Hold Three-day Fast." *Daily Nexus*, March 1, 1989: 1, 8.

Davis, Heather. "Portrait: Sylvia Curtis: Black Studies Librarian Uses Job to Shorten Cultural Gap." *Daily Nexus*, April 6, 1989: 3, 10.

Directory of Library and Information Professionals. Woodbridge, CT: Research Publications, 1988.

Dowell, Connie V. "Art in the Library." *Coastlines 17*(2) (Winter 1987): 4–6.

Dowell, Connie V. "Collecting Primary Materials of Major Ethnic Groups: The California Ethnic and Multicultural Archives Project." *College & Research Libraries News 53*(3) (March 1992): 157–159.

Frazier, Joanna. "Library to Trim Staff, Shorten Hours Due to State Budget Shortfall." *Daily Nexus*, April 15, 1991: 5.

Grimm, Vanessa. "UCSB Haunted by Ghosts of Protest." *Daily Nexus*, September 16, 1983: 10C.

Güereña, Salvador. "Border Arts Cultural Heritage Project." *CEMA News 1*(1) (August 2003).

Güereña, Salvador. *California Ethnic and Multicultural Archives Brochure*. Department of Special Collections Donald C. Davidson Library University of California Santa Barbara. (Undated material).

Güereña, Salvador. CEMA Annual Reports, 1993–2003.

Güereña, Salvador. "Chicana/o Art Digital Initiative [CARIDAD II]." *CEMA News 1*(1) (August 2003).

Güereña, Salvador. *Delivering or Dabbling: Diversity Initiatives in a University Library Setting*. For the University Library Colloquium, University of Illinois, Urbana Champaign, speech delivered April 18, 2001.

Güereña, Salvador. Draft: Plenary Address: An Archival Call to Action for "Memoria, Voz y Patrimonio." Delivered August 13, 2003.

Güereña, Salvador. E-mail to Erica Bennett re: CEMA Conceptual Essay. October 12, 2004.

Güereña, Salvador. E-mail to Erica Bennett re: CEMA Conceptual Essay. Remarks to 1989 Hunger Strike Rally. October 11, 2004.

Güereña, Salvador. E-mail to Erica Bennett re: CEMA use statistics. October 25, 2004.

Güereña, Salvador. E-mail to Erica Bennett re: more files on CEMA history. April 27, 2004.

Güereña, Salvador. E-mail to Erica Bennett re: Revised CEMA proposal and interview questions. October 8, 2004.

Güereña, Salvador. E-mail to Erica Bennett re: UCLA GSEIS research project on CEMA. October 14, 2004.

Güereña, Salvador. Handwritten notes from CEMA planning meetings. 1989–1991.

Güereña, Salvador. Interview with Erica Bennett. June 11, 2004.

Güereña, Salvador. "The Lalo Guerrero Collection." *Inaugural Ceremony The Lalo Guerrero Collection University Libraries*, UCSB brochure. December 4, 2000.

Güereña, Salvador. "Memo to Olga Ignon, AUL, Collection Development re: Review of Follow-Up Assignments, Chicano Archives." *CEMA*. November 20, 1986.

Güereña, Salvador. "Professional Biography." *CEMA*. April 15, 2004. http://www.library.ucsb.edu/people/guerena/ (accessed June 8, 2004).

Güereña, Salvador. "Proyecto Aeronaves." *CEMA*. April 10, 2002. http://cemaweb.library.ucsb.edu/aeronave.html (accessed October 19, 2004).

Güereña, Salvador. "Proyecto Caridad: Chicano Art Resources Information Development and Dissemination." *CEMA*. March 4, 2002. http://cemaweb.library.ucsb.edu/caridad.html (accessed October 19, 2004).

Güereña, Salvador. "Proyecto Rescate." *CEMA*. March 6, 2002. http://cemaweb.library.ucsb.edu/rescate.html (accessed October 19, 2004).

Hansel, Kim. "Enrollment Figures at UCSB Increase." *Daily Nexus*, October 18, 1983: 1.

Hunter, Gregory S. "Filling the GAP: Planning on the Local and Individual Levels." *American Archivist* (Winter 1987): 114.

Joint Committee for Review of the Master Plan for Higher Education. [1989] California Faces . . . California's Future: Education for Citizenship in a Multicultural Democracy. March 1989. http://content.cdlib.org/ark:/13030/hb2r29n7hc/ (accessed January 13, 2009).

Jones, Heather and Michelle Ray. "UC Berkeley Accepts Ethnicity Requirement." *Daily Nexus*, April 27, 1989: 1, 3.

Krist, John. "Growth and Change: A History of UCSB." *Daily Nexus*, August 27, 1982: 1, 34.

Krist, John. "UCSB's History at Goleta Point." *Daily Nexus*, September 17, 1982: 1, 14–15.

Lee, Joel M., ed. *Who's Who in Library and Information Services*. Chicago: 1982.

Musser, Jane. "Library Offers Research Help." *Daily Nexus*, September 17, 1982: 11A, 12.

The National Archives. *Our Vision Statement*. http://www.archives.gov/about/info/mission.html (accessed April 5, 2006).

Ogar, Jennifer. "Minority Enrollment Level Surpasses Record Set Last Year." *Daily Nexus*, September 15, 1989: 1, 15.

Omi, Michael & Howard Winant. *Racial Formation in the United States from the 1960s to the 1980s*. New York: Routledge & Kegan Paul, 1986.

Salazar, Anthony. "Joseph Boisse: Librarian Will Increase Collection." *Daily Nexus*, November 15, 1983: 6.

Schmittroth, Linda. *Immigration and Illegal Aliens: Burden or Blessing?* New York: Thomson Gale, 2004.

Smith, John Lynn. "Students Seek Solution to Campus Racial Problems." *Daily Nexus*, October 19, 1987: 3.

Staff. "Luis Valdez: American Original." *Daily Nexus*, January 14, 1988: 7A.

Staff. "Wealth of Cultural Riches." *Daily Nexus*, September 28, 1987: 2A.

Staff Reports. "Chancellor Talks of Expansion Enrollment." *Daily Nexus*, January 9, 1989: 1, 6.

State of California, Department of Finance. *E-4 Population Estimates for Cities, Counties and the State, 1970–1980.* http://www.dof.ca.gov/HTML/DEMOGRAP/E4call.htm (accessed October 19, 2004).

State of California, Department of Finance. *E-4 Population Estimates for Cities, Counties and the State, 1981–1990.* http://www.dof.ca.gov/HTML/DEMOGRAP/90e-4.xls (accessed October 19, 2004).

State of California, Department of Finance. *E-4 Population Estimates for Cities, Counties and the State, 2001–2004, with 2000 DRU Benchmark.* Sacramento, California, May 2004. http://www.dof.ca.gov/HTML/DEMOGRAP/HistE-4.htm (accessed October 19, 2004).

State of California, Department of Finance. *Race/Ethnic Population Estimates: Components of Change for California Counties, July 1970–July 1990.* Sacramento, California, July 1999. http://www.dof.ca.gov/HTML/DEMOGRAP/Eth70-90.htm (accessed October 19, 2004).

State of California, Department of Finance. *Race/Ethnic Population Estimates: Components of Change for California Counties, April 1990 to April 2000.* Sacramento, California, March 2003. http://www.dof.ca.gov/HTML/DEMOGRAP/RACE-ETH.HTM (accessed October 19, 2004).

Wee, Heesun. "Ethnicity Demands Spread to All UCs." *Daily Nexus*, February 28, 1989: 1, 3, 5.

Wee, Heeseun. "Retaining Minorities Is Persisting Problem." *Daily Nexus*, January 10, 1989: 1, 6.

Ziegler, Chris. "Ethnic Studies Voting Integrity Questioned." *Daily Nexus*, February 27, 1989: 1, 5–7.

Ziegler, Chris. "Hunger Strikers Fast to End UCSB Racism: Student Fasters Hope to Publicize Demands for Implementation of Ethnicity Requirement." *Daily Nexus*, February 22, 1989: 1, 11.

Ziegler, Chris. "L&S Faculty Approves Ethnicity Requirement: One-Course Option Squeaks by, 250–241, with Most Ballots Ever." *Daily Nexus*, June 2, 1989: 1, 7.

Ziegler, Chris. "Protest Resumes as Negotiations Collapse: Students Complain Administration Does Not Take Their Demands Seriously." *Daily Nexus*, April 19, 1989: 1, 14.

Chronology

1968–1983

1968

❖ October 14, 16 black students barricade themselves in the UCSB North Hall Computer Center

1969

❖ UCSB black studies department, research center, and library established
❖ UCSB Chicano studies department, research center, and MECHA library established

1971

❖ MECHA library becomes the *Coleccioń Tloque Nahaque* under the leadership of librarian Carlos Najera[89]

1977

❖ Librarian Roberto Trujillo named director of *Coleccioń Tloque Nahaque*

ca. 1980

❖ The Confederation of La Raza Organizations Collection (C.O.R.O.), 1975–1980; donated by the Center for Chicano Studies

1983

❖ Salvador Güereña receives a temporary six-month appointment as manager of the *Coleccioń* via the Target of Opportunity Program

1984–1993

1984

❖ Dr. Joseph Boisse becomes university librarian at University of California, Santa Barbara Donald C. Davidson Library
❖ Salvador Güereña hired as unit head of UCSB's *Coleccioń Tloque Nahaque*

1986

❖ Galería De La Raza Archives, 1969–1999; donated by Galería de la Raza
❖ The Self Help Graphics Archive, 1960–; donated by Self Help Graphics & Art, Inc.
❖ The El Teatro Campesino Archives, 1964–1988; donated by El Teatro Campesino

1988

❖ José Montoya Papers, 1969–2001; donated by José Montoya, May 6
❖ The Royal Chicano Air Force Archives, 1973–1988; donated by Royal Chicano Air Force

1989

❖ Acosta (Oscar Zeta) Collection, 1936–1990; donated by Marco Acosta, son of Oscar Zeta Acosta, June 1989
❖ February 9, first meeting to establish CEMA
❖ February 22, 40 UCSB students begin hunger strike to fight alleged institutional racism and increase ethnic diversity on campus

1990

❖ The Papers of Ana Castillo, 1953–1990; donated by Ana Castillo, June

1991

❖ First CEMA advisory board meeting held
❖ Bay Area Black Panther Party Collection, 1963–2000; donated by Douglas Daniels, November 1
❖ Chinese American Political Association

1993

❖ The Horace James McMillan Papers, 1946–1988; donated by Horace James McMillan, November
❖ Asian American Theater Company Archives; donated by Asian American Theater Company

1994–2004

1995

❖ Genny Lim Papers established

1996

❖ Chinese American Voters Education Committee
❖ Irby (Charles C.) Collection,1938–1987; donated by Gretchen M. Bataille, February 21
❖ Yolanda M. Lopez Papers, 1961–1998; donated by Yolanda Lopez, December 12
❖ Simón Silva Papers; Established October
❖ Ester Soriano-Hewitt Papers

1997

❖ Francisco Camplis Papers, 1967–2000; donated by Francisco Camplís
❖ The Chinese American Democratic Club Archives; deeded to the University of California and designated to become part of CEMA in July
❖ The William Downey Papers, 1922–1994; donated by Michael Downey, April 21
❖ Adelina Garcia Collection, 1939–1978
❖ Victor Ochoa Papers, 1962–2000; donated by Victor Ochoa, May 15

1998

❖ Salvador Roberto Torres Papers, 1934–2002 (bulk 1962–2002); donated by Salvador Roberto Torres, December 12
❖ Emigdio Vasquez Papers; Established on February 25
❖ Elizabeth Wong Papers, donated July 14
❖ The Nellie Wong Papers, 1972–2001; donated by Nellie Wong, July

1999

❖ Kearny Street Workshop Archives, donated May 21

2000

❖ Centro Cultural De La Raza Archives, 1970–1999; donated by CCLR, October 16
❖ Lalo Guerrero Collection, 1939–2002; donated by Lalo Guerrero, December 4
❖ Lucha Corpi Papers, 1958–2000; donated by Lucha Corpi, September 26

2001

❖ Comision Femenil Mexicana Nacional Archives, 1967–1997 [Bulk dates 1970–1990]; donated by CFMN, January
❖ The Esteban Villa Papers, 1974–2002; donated by Esteban Villa December
❖ Linda Vallejo Papers; donated

2002

❖ Nancy Hom Papers; donated March 16
❖ The Luis C. Gonzalez Papers; donated August 29
❖ Dan Guerrero Collection on Latino Entertainment and the Arts; donated November 14

2004

❖ Lawrence "El" Colacion Papers; donated April
❖ Don Tosti Papers; donated August

2005

❖ Don Tosti; Endowment for the Preservation of Mexican American Music Heritage established

Chapter 6

Special Collections: The Cuban Heritage Collection at the University of Miami Libraries

María R. Estorino

The Cuban Community in Miami

Sociologist Guillermo Grenier notes, "The most visible and recurring manifestation of the Cuban saga over the past four decades has been emigration."[1] Since Fidel Castro's revolution took hold in Cuba in 1959, over 700,000 Cubans have left the island, settling primarily in the United States and Puerto Rico. "Each wave [of migration] has a particular historical motivation for leaving the island and is received in a different socioeconomic and political context than the other waves."[2]

Between 1959 and 1973, approximately 550,000 Cubans arrived in the United States. The Cuban exodus trickled until the Mariel Boatlift of 1980, when almost 125,000 Cubans fled the island. The next major wave of migration followed the fall of the Soviet Union in 1989 and Cuba's *periodo especial* (special period), culminating in the rafter crisis of 1994. Subsequent migration has been shaped by the United States's current "wet-foot/dry-foot" policy, which orders that Cubans interdicted at sea are returned to Cuba while those who touch dry land are allowed to stay in the United States; and a subsequent increase in the illegal smuggling of Cubans to South Florida.

The 2000 U.S. Census indicated that approximately 1.2 million persons born in Cuba or of Cuban descent resided in the United States, with 65 percent of them living in Florida.[3] Over the last 49 years of exile, Cubans have had an immeasurable impact in Miami, the seat of the Cuban

American community. This community has grown dramatically over time and changed in ways that are still unfolding.

The experiences of exiles that arrived in the 1960s are dramatically different from more recent Cuban émigrés. The former group is defined by an unending and unwilling absence from their homeland, while the latter never knew a Cuba without Castro or the revolution and are increasingly driven to leave the island for economic rather than political reasons. Earlier exiles arrived in the United States during the Cold War. As refugees from communism, they were welcomed with federal welfare programs that provided financial aid, medical services, job training, and resettlement services. More recent arrivals still benefit from the Cuban Adjustment Act of 1966, which grants Cuban migrants a work permit after residing in the United States for one year and permanent residence after two years. The majority of Cuban migrants continue to settle in the Miami area, where the economic, political, and social infrastructures facilitate their transition to life in the United States.

The Cuban American community in South Florida maintains strong ties to Cuba, yet its identity, demographics, and role in American society continue to evolve as successive generations acculturate to life in the United States. How the future of Cuba will further impact the Cuban American community is highly anticipated yet difficult to predict.

The University of Miami and Cuba

Founded in 1926, the University of Miami faced several challenges in its early years. Shortly after the groundbreaking for the first building on its Coral Gables campus, a devastating hurricane hit South Florida, and the region faced an economic downturn due to the ensuing real estate bust. The university halted construction on its campus and moved into temporary headquarters for the next 20 years, operating at times on a year-to-year basis.

Despite these pressures, the university forged ahead with its programmatic and educational goals. Recognizing Miami's strategic location in relation to the Caribbean and Latin America, the university strove to develop a curriculum in Latin American studies and to promote cultural exchange with institutions in the region. It was perhaps most successful in carrying out this vision with the University of Havana in Cuba. In its first three decades, the university hosted faculty from Havana and awarded honorary degrees to leading Cuban political and educational figures. Student athletes competed against each other in football and swimming, and the university offered scholarships to Cuban students.

In support of the Latin American curriculum, the university's library began acquiring materials on the Caribbean and Latin America as early as

1930. When the university moved back to its Coral Gables campus after World War II, the library was allocated temporary space in a classroom building. As its collections expanded to keep pace with the rapidly growing university, the library moved into the new Otto G. Richter Library in 1962.

The university community immediately expressed both scholarly and humanitarian interest in the Cuban Revolution and the ensuing influx of exiles into South Florida. Cuban-born students enrolled at the University of Miami, joining together in the Federation of Cuban Students in the late 1960s. With federal support, the university instituted Cuban refugee training programs for doctors, lawyers, and teachers. The economics department formed the Cuban Economic Research Project in 1961 and hired seven exiled Cuban economists to carry out research. In 1965, the School of Continuing Studies established the Cuban Culture Center at its John J. Koubek Memorial Center to offer language classes and vocational training for Cuban refugees.[4]

Despite these historic programs and its place at the heart of Miami, the university has never instituted a Cuban studies program, and faculty engaged in research or teaching about Cuba or the Cuban experience outside the island can be found across academic departments. Many of these scholars participate in the Latin American studies program, while others are based at the Institute for Cuban and Cuban-American Studies (ICCAS). The institute administers the federally funded Cuba Transition Project, which makes recommendations about the reconstruction of Cuba post-Castro; sponsors lectures, and exhibitions at its Casa Bacardí; and hosts an academic summer program about Cuba for U.S. and foreign students.

Cuban Collections at the University of Miami Libraries

Along with the rest of the University of Miami, the Otto G. Richter Library responded to the changes brought about by the Cuban Revolution. Soon after opening its doors, the library hired two exiled Cuban librarians, the late Rosa M. Abella and Ana Rosa Núñez. With growing research interest in Cuba and the Cuban community of South Florida, and driven by their personal experiences, Abella and Núñez set out to document the dramatic changes both on the island and in Miami by reenergizing the library's Cuba collecting practices and putting new emphasis on the output being generated by Miami's Cuban community.

Abella and Núñez employed various tactics to grow Richter Library's Cuban collections, including traditional purchasing and subscription avenues as well as working with academic faculty to identify areas and resources of scholarly interest. With the support of other Cuban library staff, especially Lesbia Orta Varona and Esperanza Bravo de Varona, Abella and Núñez also reached out to the growing Cuban exile community to gather materials for the library. They attended meetings of exile organizations, visited Cuban markets and businesses to collect publications and ephemera, and reached out to fellow exiles for support in identifying and acquiring materials. They also worked with Cubans exiled in other parts of the United States and the world to document the Cuban experience in these areas. These outreach efforts have proven to be an important foundation for the continued growth of Cuban collections at the Otto G. Richter Library.

Throughout its history, the library collected and housed special collections, officially forming the Archives and Special Collections department in 1978. The primary collecting goals of this department was, and continues to be, the history and culture of Florida, the Caribbean, and Latin America. Both Cuba and the Cuban exile community in South Florida fit well within this collecting focus. The department immediately set out to document the impact of the Cuban community in Miami.

To grow and manage these Cuban materials in the department, Esperanza B. de Varona was named curator of the Cuban Archives in 1980. A librarian in Cuba, de Varona worked at Richter Library for 13 years as a library assistant before obtaining a library degree from Florida State University. The Cuban Archives that she was asked to lead were organized into the Cuban Collection and the Cuban Exile Collection. Because rare Cuban books formed part of the department's rare book section, the Cuban and Cuban exile collections focused on periodicals, ephemera, and manuscript collections. Among the first collections donated to the Cuban Archives were the records of the Truth About Cuba Committee, a Cuban exile organization that was established after the failed Bay of Pigs invasion in 1961 to disseminate information regarding the political and economic realities of Cuba after the revolution. Other collections were created by the archives based on the format of the materials, such as the Cuban Photograph Collection, the Cuban Map Collection, and the Cuban Poster Collection.

The Cuban Archives had grown dramatically by the 1990s. Recognizing the uniqueness of this collection, a group of individuals from the Cuban community formed the Amigos of the University of Miami Library Cuban Collection, in 1995, to support the work of the archives. This group was cochaired by Dr. Henry King Stanford, former president of the University of Miami; and Elena Díaz-Versón Amos.

Elena Díaz-Versón Amos studied at the University of Miami, where she met and married her husband, John B. Amos, the founder of the American Family Life Assurance Company of Columbus (AFLAC). She was the chairperson and founder of The John and Elena Amos Foundation.

Through this foundation and often through her own personal contributions, she supported various local and national organizations; humanitarian and Cuban causes; and institutions of higher education, including her alma mater. Her interests in higher education and Cuban issues were united in her support of the Cuban Archives. In 1994, she anonymously donated $1 million to the University of Miami to build a space for Cuban collections at the library. This vision was bigger than anything the library had planned for its Cuban materials at the time, and the university held the gift for several years.

Coupled with the growing interest from the exile community in the Cuban Archives was the proliferation of Cuban materials throughout the library. Collecting responsibilities for Cuban and exile materials were distributed among different departments. In 1994, the library adopted a new policy statement in an attempt to centralize Cuban collecting procedures, but these efforts still distributed Cuban materials in five different areas of the library. This statement did not alleviate the challenges for the library in administering Cuban materials or for the researcher in accessing such resources.

In response to these challenges and to the attention of the Cuban exile community, the library conceived of bringing together all Cuban resources housed in the archives and dispersed throughout the library into one department. In 1998, the library established the Cuban Heritage Collection (CHC) with the vision of creating a nationally and internationally recognized repository of research resources for the scholarly study of Cuba and the Cuban experience outside the island.

The Cuban Archives were separated administratively and physically from the Archives and Special Collections department and joined with the Cuban Permanent Reserve Collection to form the Cuban Heritage Collection. Headed by librarian Lesbia Orta Varona, the Reserve Collection included scarce books and periodicals that did not meet the criteria for inclusion in the Archives and Special Collections. This merger resulted in a collection of over 45,000 books, close to 400 titles of Cuban periodicals, over 1,000 titles of Cuban exile serials, and approximately 200 linear feet of manuscript collections and archival materials.

The library appointed Esperanza de Varona as head of the new Cuban Heritage Collection and Lesbia Varona its bibliographer and reference librarian, with responsibility for acquiring Cuban and exile materials for both CHC and the library's general collection. This has helped to ensure the cohesive growth of Cuban materials throughout the Richter Library. A library assistant in the Archives and Special Collections department was also transferred to CHC as support staff.

With these plans in place, the new Cuban Heritage Collection department moved into a section of Richter Library's Brockway Hall, a space on the first floor of the library's stack tower. From its inception, CHC set out to meet the research and teaching needs of the university's faculty and students. But it also recognized that it was serving other constituents, including scholars of Cuban and Cuban American studies from around the world and the Cuban exile community interested in preserving and promoting its cultural, historical, and social heritage.

To meet the needs of these various stakeholders, the CHC designed a comprehensive collecting policy to acquire exhaustive collections of published materials and extensive collections of manuscript and archival materials. This included resources in any language but primarily in English and Spanish; created currently or retrospectively from colonial times to the present, anywhere in the world; and in various formats including books, pamphlets, periodicals, maps, posters, ephemera, audiovisual materials, illustrations, photographs, postcards, personal papers, and organizational records.

The creation of the Cuban Heritage Collection opened the door to new possibilities. It demonstrated the library's commitment to preserving and providing access to Cuban and exile resources and served to attract new collections to the library. Manuscript collections, in particular, grew to include the papers of Cuban political leaders in exile; Cuban-born and Cuban American writers, musicians, and other artists; exiled political and academic organizations, and others.

In 1999, the Goizueta Foundation endorsed the library's commitment with a $2.5 million challenge grant to build a home for the CHC. This gift provided the impetus to finally carry out the vision of Amos's earlier donation; and in 2000, the Fanjul family supported the effort to build this new space with a pledge of $500,000.

Also in 1999, CHC received a directed grant from the Institute of Museum and Library Services (IMLS) to digitize selected materials. Along with a second grant from IMLS in 2000 and the support of Xerox, the library dedicated $1 million to digitization efforts of CHC materials. This was a strategic initiative to create broad access to and promote the collection and helped put CHC in a leadership position for digital projects at Richter Library.

In January 2003, the university opened the Roberto C. Goizueta Pavilion. Named in honor of Roberto C. Goizueta, the late Cuban-born CEO of Coca-Cola, and the gift made by his foundation, this 10,000-square foot addition to the second floor of Richter Library was built to house the Cuban Heritage Collection. By the time the pavilion opened, the CHC's staff had expanded to include an assistant to Esperanza de Varona, an additional library assistant, and an archivist.

The opening of the pavilion expanded the opportunities available to the Cuban Heritage Collection and gave it a more prominent position in the library and the university. These opportunities, in turn, created new challenges for adequately providing access to its quickly expanding holdings and for meeting the growing needs of researchers with innovation and agility.

Looking Back and the Road Ahead

I was hired as the director for the IMLS grant project in 2001 and was permanently appointed to the CHC faculty two years later as its archivist and digital projects librarian. After two years heading the Archives and Special Collections department, I returned to the Cuban Heritage Collection in 2007 as deputy chair and chief operations manager. I have had the privilege of working in CHC during a watershed period in its history. The Cuban Heritage Collection marks its 10th anniversary and five years in the Goizueta Pavilion in 2008, and this historical moment allows for reflection on the factors contributing to its success and the road ahead.

The importance of hiring Cuban-born and Cuban American librarians and staff cannot be overstated. The late Rosa Abella and Ana Rosa Núñez were part of intellectual and literary circles in Miami's exile community. In addition to serving as a reference librarian, Núñez was an accomplished poet and as such knew many other exiled writers. One of these was Lydia Cabrera, a leading scholar of Afro-Cuban religions and folklore. Cabrera knew both Abella and Núñez both personally and as library patrons. It was because of these associations that Cabrera decided to deed in her will to the Cuban Archives her manuscripts, correspondence, thousands of photographs, field notebooks, and other materials. The Lydia Cabrera Papers are today one of the most heavily used manuscript collections in CHC.

Building on the foundations laid by Núñez and Abella before there was even a centralized Cuban collection at the University of Miami Libraries, Esperanza de Varona, and Lesbia Orta Varona have been indispensable in developing the depth and breadth of the Cuban Heritage Collection. As exiles themselves, they have also been able to establish relationships and create networks built on commitment, trust, and their personal understanding of the Cuban experience.

With 40 years at the Otto G. Richter Library, Esperanza de Varona has excelled at cultivating donors by imparting the importance of preserving and providing access to scholarly resources. Her passion for documenting the Cuban experience can be credited for the acquisition of most of the Cuban Heritage Collection's manuscript collections. It was her leadership and vision that facilitated the major donations from Elena Díaz-Versón Amos and the Goizueta Foundation. In her honor, the University of Miami Libraries received an anonymous gift of $1.5 million in 2005 to endow its first chair, the Esperanza Bravo de Varona Chair of the Cuban Heritage Collection.

Lesbia Orta Varona's contributions are equally significant. With responsibility for developing CHC's books and periodicals holdings, she has exerted tremendous effort and innovation in acquiring materials by and about Cubans from around the world. Her knowledge of Cuban and Cuban American literature and theater arts has helped create strengths in our holdings in these subject areas, both of primary and secondary sources. Researchers seek out her reference assistance, knowing that she will help find pertinent resources whether held by the collection or not.

Her services have earned her many lifelong friends and partners who help identify materials for acquisition or who collect such items on behalf of CHC. Such partners have contributed significantly to the collection's ability to capture ephemeral and fugitive materials. Cuban exiles not only in Miami but also in Puerto Rico, New York, Paris, Madrid, and other locations continually send pertinent materials to us. One such associate is the writer William Navarrete, who along with other Cubans exiled in Europe founded the *Asociación Tercera Republica Cubana* (Association for the Third Cuban Republic) in Paris. Navarrete sends us the publications of this association as well as of other publications and ephemera related to Cuban exiles in Europe.

Faculty at the University of Miami have also been important partners for the Cuban Heritage Collection. A political scientist and former associate dean of the Graduate School of International Studies, the late Enrique Baloyra introduced several donors of manuscript collections to CHC. One of these was the *Directorio Revolucionario Estudiantil en el Exilio* (Revolutionary Student Directorate in Exile). The Directorio, or DRE, was a militant, revolutionary resistance student organization that fought against the government of Fulgencio Batista in the 1950s. In exile, the DRE continued operations against the Castro regime with the support of the U.S. government. The group disseminated anticommunist propaganda and conducted paramilitary operations in Cuba. The DRE gave their records to the Cuban Archives, thanks to the efforts of Dr. Baloyra and Ana Rosa Núñez. The collection includes the entire run of the DRE newsletter, *Trinchera*, and other publications such as position papers and circulars, correspondence, photos, letters from prisoners in Cuba, reports from chapters in Latin America, and a list of members executed in Cuba. It is an important collection for the study of the Cuban exile community and U.S.-Cuban relations during the Cold War.

We have also struck a fruitful collaboration with Dr. Lillian Manzor of the Modern Languages and Literatures department. Dr. Manzor is the founder and director of the Cuban Theater Digital Archive (CTDA), a cultural heritage digital initiative sponsored by the University of Miami Libraries and the university's Center for Latin American Studies. The CTDA (scholar.library.miami.edu/archivoteatral/) provides information and research on theater in Greater Cuba (on the island and in the diaspora) that focuses on the works, both written texts and live-art performance, of theater practitioners. The collection supports this project through collection development, digitization of materials, research support, and service learning and research opportunities for students. One of the results of this project has been the significant growth of theater materials in the collection's holdings of 20th- and 21st-century papers of theater artists in Cuba and the diaspora, principally the papers of playwrights, designers, performers, directors, and theater companies. The CTDA has directly contributed to the growth of the Cuban Heritage Collection's theater holdings, serving as the liaison for the acquisition of the INTAR Theatre, Eduardo Machado, Repertorio Español, and Caridad Svich papers, among others.

Established in 1995, the Amigos of the Cuban Heritage Collection has also contributed to our growth. Made up of bankers, lawyers, architects, and other professionals, the Amigos is a fundraising and outreach organization that supports the Cuban Heritage Collection. As previously noted, the founding cochair of the Amigos, Elena Díaz-Versón Amos, was the first major financial contributor to the collection. Other Amigos members introduced Javier Goizueta of the Goizueta Foundation to CHC, thereby helping to make possible the foundation's matching gift for the building of the Goizueta Pavilion. When the opportunity arose to acquire the papers and library of Gastón Baquero, a Cuban writer exiled in Madrid, the Amigos raised the funds necessary to obtain and transport the collection. Amigos members have also brought donors of manuscript collections and other materials to CHC.

Sometimes, they have donated materials themselves. One example is Francisco X. Santeiro, one of the first Amigos members who today serves on the organization's board. He came to know the Cuban collections as an undergraduate at the University of Miami when he worked in the library. Santeiro facilitated the donation to the Cuban Heritage Collection of the exile papers of Gerardo Machado, Cuba's controversial fifth president and Santeiro's great grandfather. He also brought his brother Luis's papers to CHC. Luis Santeiro was the head writer for ¿Que Pasa, USA?, the groundbreaking 1970s bilingual sitcom about three generations of Cubans living in Miami. He has won Emmys for his writing for Sesame Street and is the author of several plays, most notably Our Lady of the Tortilla.

The Cuban Heritage Collection would not exist without the support of the administration of the University of Miami or its libraries. CHC is operationally integrated into the libraries; and, as such, its holdings are included in the libraries' catalog (ibisweb.miami.edu), digital library (merrick.library.miami.edu), and website (library.miami.edu). The libraries allocate operating and acquisitions funds to CHC each year and assist in fundraising efforts. When Donna E. Shalala became president of the University of Miami in 2001, her first stop on campus was to the Otto G. Richter Library, specifically to the Cuban Heritage Collection. This represented recognition of the Cuban Heritage Collection as a significant university resource and invaluable community asset.

In 2009, The Goizueta Foundation again offered its support to the Cuban Heritage Collection with a five-year, $2.5 million grant to enhance and expand its reach. The grant supports a vision of the collection as a center for scholarly inquiry and the most comprehensive resource in the United States for research on Cuba and its diaspora.

We strive to fulfill this vision through:

- Targeted collection building, processing of materials, and digitization to increase breadth of holdings and uncover hidden resources
- Creating and supporting opportunities for research, teaching, learning, and the creation of new knowledge
- Cultivating a community of users through support for research
- Reaching a greater audience and increasing awareness through new media
- Adding value through educational outreach activities

The Goizueta Foundation grant supports activities in these areas by funding several existing programs: collection development, creating access to our resources, and digitization; and investing in the establishment of new initiatives and partnerships: a graduate fellowships program, an undergraduate scholars program administered by the College of Arts and Sciences, a lecture series run by the Institute for Cuban and Cuban-American Studies, and marketing and Web communications activities.

The undergraduate scholars and graduate fellowships programs have proven especially fruitful in fostering a community of users of the collection. The undergraduate scholars program offers funded research opportunities to University of Miami students. Through the fall 2010 semester, we hosted 11 undergraduates from a variety of disciplines. In the spring 2011 semester, the College of Arts and Sciences gave the program to the Center for Latin American Studies to administer, a move that will help advance the program through the center's network of faculty and students.

The Cuban Heritage Collection manages the graduate fellowships, a program that funds doctoral students from across the country to do research in the collection. In 2010, the first year of the program, we hosted 10 fellows. The majority of them work in history and literary studies programs, two disciplines we are particularly well prepared to support.

The marketing and Web communications activities are also notable in that grant funding supports a position dedicated to the collection's website and other efforts to communicate with various audiences in a more frequent and consistent manner. We relaunched our website in 2010 (library.miami .edu/chc/), a redesign that included a blog, a monthly newsletter, a video channel on Vimeo, and a Facebook page. These efforts have helped us reach new audiences and stay connected to our various communities through communications about everything from new acquisitions to new digital collections and profiles of graduate fellows and undergraduate scholars.

The grant has also allowed the collection to dedicate greater resources to creating and improving access to its collections of personal papers and organizational records and related archival materials. To maximize output in this area, we have adopted some of the recommendations put forth by Mark A. Greene and Dennis Meissner in their article "More Product, Less Process: Revamping Traditional Archival Processing" published in *American Archivist*'s Fall/Winter 2005 issue. These include making user access paramount and establishing acceptable minimum processing levels as benchmarks. In particular, we adapted practices developed at Princeton University's Seeley G. Mudd Manuscript Library for implementing More Product, Less Process (MPLP). When we started working with MPLP guidelines in 2008, only 15 percent of its manuscript collections were discoverable through finding aids made available online. Through the MPLP work plan, by the end of 2010, we were able to provide descriptive information for about 55 percent of its collections with a range of descriptions from collection-level records to finding aids. This was facilitated in part by the University of Miami Libraries' implementation of the Archon system for publishing archival descriptive information online. We continue to use MPLP guidelines to make decisions about arrangement and description levels for manuscript collections.

We have also grown our digitization efforts. Based on the results of previous endeavors and user demand, the Cuban Heritage Collection prioritizes the digitization of photographs and visual materials. Recently, the collection has also started digitizing books and periodicals in its holdings. Additionally, with the Libraries' Digital Scholarship and Programs department, we have dedicated resources to delivering video in the digital library. Efforts have focused on recordings of lectures and presentations hosted by the collection and interviews from our Luis J. Botifoll Oral History Project, an initiative funded by the Amigos of the Cuban Heritage Collection. By December 2010, we have shared almost 27,000 objects in the libraries' digital library.

All of this work rests on the foundation of our collection development. We need to be more proactive in addressing gaps in our holdings and identifying opportunities for growth. To do this, we must be cognizant of the teaching, learning, and research needs of our university faculty and students and the broader scholarly community; the changing nature of the Cuban American population; and the uncertainties of a post-Castro Cuba will impact how we continue to grow our holdings.

Any effort that improves our awareness of our users' needs will help direct our collecting activities. We work directly with faculty in different disciplines to create opportunities for instructional opportunities in the collection. These relationships are crucial to understanding how the collection can support curricular goals. We work one-on-one with researchers who use our holdings to understand their needs and how the collection does or does not meet them. Occasionally, we conduct user surveys to be able to explore these questions. It has also been important to stay connected to the scholarship being published in Cuban studies through reading and conferences.

We must also be sensitive to particular circumstances and interests of our potential donors and vendors. For example, collecting activities will be affected by the changing demographics of the Cuban American community. While Cubans continue to migrate from the island, second- and third-generation Cuban Americans are another major component of the community in Miami. We have been most successful in acquiring collections, related materials, and funds from Cubans of the earlier waves of exile from the 1960s and 1970s. We must find ways to connect with both more recent Cuban émigrés and the younger generations of Cuban Americans in order to continue and extend the important ties we have to the community.

Political changes on the island and their consequences will have significant impact on Miami. We will have to be diligent and nimble in documenting such changes and the reactions, responses, and effects of transition on the Cuban American community.

"Miami is the principal stage of the Cuban-American community, where most of the recurring dramas of exile have taken place," notes Guillermo Grenier.[5] We must keep pace with the changes in Miami and in Cuba to continue to be the premier collection for research on Cuba and its diaspora. We look forward to continuing to grow our collections and to developing dexterity in providing access to our rich resources.

Notes

1. Guillermo Grenier, "The Establishment of the Cuban American Community," Miami, FL: CubaInfo: A Project of the Cuban Research Institute, Florida International University, 2007. Available from http://cubainfo.fiu.edu/Documents/GrenierReport.pdf. Accessed January 2008.
2. Ibid., 3.
3. U.S. Census Bureau, "The Hispanic Population: Census 2000 Brief," Washington, DC: U.S. Census Bureau, 2001. Available from http://www.census.gov/prod/2001pubs/c2kbr01-3.pdf. Accessed January 2008.
4. See Charlton W. Tebeau, *The University of Miami: A Golden Anniversary History, 1926–1976* (Coral Gables, FL: University of Miami Press, 1976) and Lisa Sedelnik, "The Fabric of Friendship," *Miami Magazine* (Spring 1998). Available from http://www6.miami.edu/miami-magazine/spring98/cuba.html. Accessed January 2008.
5. Grenier, 5.

Chapter 7

Gay, Bisexual, Transgender, Lesbian, Queer: Being There: Queer Latin@ Representation in the Library

tatiana de la tierra

I have a queer dream
or should I say, a queer reality
I am in a circle of queers
We are queering in the rain
parading in a queer-nival
doing queer-gonomic things
drinking queer beer
bar-b-queering with our friends
playing A Street Queer Named Desire
publishing with Queer-laca Press
researching the Art of In-queery
documenting a Tale of Queer Cities
traveling to the Queer-ibbean
settling in Nova-squeer-tia
tucking our toddlers into bed:
Twinkle twinkle little queer[1]

An etching, an alphabet, a digital file, a birth certificate—all of these and more document our presence on earth. Each of us has proof of our existence on a personal level—the paper napkin neatly folded into a pocket with a lucky phone number written in ink; the black and white photograph of you on a big city sidewalk, your tiny hands clutched by your mother and father on either side; the 100-year-old dessert recipe book handwritten by your great grandmother. We have it on a broader social level as well—a myriad of Bibles and religious doctrines, huge dusty volumes of *The World Book Encyclopedia*, the infamous image of a hooded prisoner in Abu Ghraib. We have personal diaries, zines, online databases, academic texts, pulp fiction, and Cheech and Chong's *Up in Smoke*. At times lost and at times found, we have, somewhere (an attic, an archive, in the pages of a book) evidence of lesbian lust—from Sappho's lyric longings and Sor Juana's female-centered poetics to an aunt's correspondence with that childhood friend that invites you to read between the lines.

We have all of this stuffed in forgotten boxes. That which we have pitched decays in dumps. That which we prize and salvage is preserved in museums and archives. That which we have deemed the right stuff for the right population, within space and budget considerations, is in libraries.

But what ends up in a library or archive is identified and selected by inherently biased human beings. The collection and preservation of documents that represent our history and culture mirror the vision and values (and prejudices) of those who make the decisions. Archiving is an incomplete art—we will never know the full scope of sexuality if homosexual, bisexual, and transgender documents were obliterated by family members, rendered inaccessible by archivists or disregarded by researchers.

Likewise, the circulating collections of today's libraries are selected by librarians empowered to make judgment calls. Some, but not all, of these librarians are able to choose materials outside of their sociopolitical comfort zone. Librarians are schooled in a heartless and methodical way. They are trained to see books as objects prone to dust and mold. Electronic collections become "products," and the patrons are "users." While focusing on budget cuts and classification and call numbers, some librarians forget about the words, the authors, the miracle of a book's birth. They lose sight of the social movements anchored to a published work. They don't realize that the student in front of them has the vision and wherewithal to make an impact, the teenager muttering before them is freaking out about her sexuality, and she's got nowhere else to go.

Let us remember why we have libraries. Let us remember that books have the potential to save lives. Let us remember that libraries preserve the blood and bones, the poetry and politics, the history and herstory of the populations they serve. And that when groups of people are erased based on race, gender, ethnicity, sexuality, language, or spiritual affiliation, libraries and archives are not fulfilling their mission of attending to the needs of a diverse population. People who are ignored continue to exist regardless of how they're represented in a library. They continue to work, dance, pray, make family, and pay taxes. They will persist in searching for their roots, for their authors, for their community. And in the case of lesbians and gays, the coming-out phase often involves a deep searching for resources, identity markers, and inspiration. In the best of worlds, a library can be a place that people to turn to as part of their search.

Libraries today, especially public ones, are increasingly serving a Spanish-speaking public. Latinos from Mexico and from all over Latin America are now literally all across the country—from Fort Lauderdale and San Antonio to Birmingham and Omaha. It is a significant population of nearly 40 million people who have traversed oceans and transcended realities in order to be here.

It is a reality that almost always begins in Spanish and is marked by a lack of personal things. Documented or not, arriving by foot or boat or commercial airplane, here with family and a job or without either, new immigrants typically have a lot of hope and very little of anything else. It is a new world, a new start. It is time to go to the library. Not everyone gets there, though. It is a learned act, to walk through institutional doors and think that you belong there. Those who do so often do it on foot, close to home.

In 1968, I went to my first public library in the United States. We were new immigrants, my family and I, and our new American friend directed us to the downtown branch of the Miami Public Library. My mom, a dreamy 25-year-old, hungered for the Colombian authors she had left behind, but there weren't any. A Cuban library assistant told her she could request them, and she did, title by title. Books by Gabriel García Márquez, Gustavo Álvarez Gardeázabal, Hernando Téllez, and Rafael Pombo made it to the library's shelves in Spanish, thanks to my mom. Back then, when the Latino population in Miami was quietly transforming the neighborhoods, you couldn't find a word in Spanish on a billboard, in a local newspaper, or on the radio. On Sundays, I journeyed with my family on three city buses to get to La Fonda Colombiana, a restaurant that doubled as a community center. Those of us in that world of Spanish had a secret and separate existence that was rife with parties, politics, rumors, and survival tips about living in gringo-landia.

Like many other public institutions and businesses in the private sector, public libraries were clueless as to what to do about all the monolingual Spanish-speaking people like those in my family. Even with the best intentions, a realistic budget, and sound administrative backing, many libraries were at a loss at how to select, purchase, and process library materials for Spanish speakers or what types of programming and services to implement. Not only were there hardly any Spanish-speaking librarians around, Anglo Miamian culture was a world apart from Latino culture.

Today, we are much closer culturally, albeit still spiritually apart, than we were in those earlier days when the Latino population hit 9 million in 1970. By now, librarians have established significant networks and have access to resources for serving the Spanish-speaking public. REFORMA, as mentioned in an earlier chapter, was formed in 1971 as an affiliate of the American Library Association. Groundbreaking books and guides were published these past years—from early works such as *32 Ideas to Reach Your Spanish-Speaking Patrons*, published in 1977, to the revised 2007 edition of *Serving Latino Communities: A How-To-Do-It Manual for Librarians*, to more specialized resources such as the 2009 title *Read Me a Rhyme in Spanish and English*.[2]

We could use more culturally literate Spanish-speaking librarians and also benefit from greater resources, but there has been a marked improvement over the years. We can network within REFORMA and, for academic librarians, within the Seminar for the Selection of Latin American Library Materials. We can attend gatherings such as the Guadalajara International Book Fair and establish accounts with Spanish language vendors. We can provide services in Spanish, translate library information into Spanish, do bilingual story time, and plan celebrations for El día del niño/ El día del libro.

I think we're at a good place, but some people are missing from the process. The librarians who promoted services to Latinos and the Spanish speaking have not given much thought to Spanish-speaking gays and lesbians. I applaud the veteranos and veteranas who did the initial work—they are the ones who organized regional gatherings, founded groups such as REFORMA, and wrote initial guides for our field. It took vision and fortitude to get to where we are now. But I've looked over the books, guides, and journal articles that have been published with a focus on serving Spanish speakers within the last 30 years, and there isn't a queer query in there.

What about the gays and lesbians who exist within the Spanish-speaking communities that libraries serve? We are careful to select books in Spanish about health, parenting, cooking, computers, history, and heterosexual romance. But many libraries overlook queer culture, making it invisible on the bookshelves, in exhibits, and in the library's programming.

There are reasons for this: first things first. First the language, those foreign *palabras*, had to come on stage. These words and the ethnicities and cultures associated with them withstood the glare of the spotlight as culture clashes, racism, and all such forces of evil attempted to obliterate them. Then we had to deal with budgets, space issues, vendors, foreign language distribution rights, cataloging, call numbers, subject headings, diacritics, selections, and services. In fact, we are still dealing with all of this, and the Spanish language is still on stage. But no matter the arguments against these words, Spanish is not going back to where it came from; it is here to stay.

Here, also, is homosexuality and lesbianism, as it is everywhere, in all languages. Whether we know it or not, whether they show it or not, whether they identify or not, some percentage of the public we come into contact with is queer. At the same time, there is homophobia and lesbophobia. Where I come from, it's *Maricon* this, *Maricon* that. Pansies and pájaros. Horrid *jotos*. "Real" men are really straight, something I find incredibly boring, considering my personal penchant for the manliest *mujeres*. Family is the center of the universe, which is not so bad when your sense of family breaks through the blood barrier.

All things queer have gained some measure of visible standing in mainstream society here and in Mexico, Spain, Latin America, and the Caribbean. It took a while to get to the openness that there is today, but, as a broad social movement, Latino gay and lesbian culture is developing. The First Latin American Lesbian Feminist *Encuentro* took place in Cuernavaca, Mexico, in 1984. The *Encuentros* have also taken place in Costa Rica; Puerto Rico; Argentina; Brazil; and, most recently, Chile. Pride marches of lesbian, gay, bisexual, and transgender extraction have hit the streets in Lima, Peru; Boquerón, Puerto Rico; Bogotá, Colombia; Tijuana, Mexico; Buenos Aires, Argentina; Caracas, Venezuela; San José, Costa Rica; Madrid, Spain; San Pedro Soa, Honduras; Guatemala City, Santiago de Chile, and in many other Spanish-speaking places. There are gay and lesbian organizations all over, as well as a growing consciousness and debate about trans identities within. Some groups exist on a clandestine level, while others are out there, front and center. Queer websites, zines, music, books and films pop up sporadically, affirming the culture. But homophobia is also at play on multiple levels. In Cuba, in 2008, what would have been the island's first gay pride parade was canceled as government officials detained organizers; gay men were arrested in different occasions in 2009.[3]

In the United States, where same-sex marriage is currently legal in five states, violence against gays and people perceived as gay continues. In a highly publicized case that occurred in December 2008, Jose O. Sucuzhañay, an Ecuadorean immigrant, was beaten to death in Brooklyn in the middle of the night by three men who attacked him and his brother as the murderers spewed antigay and anti-Latino slurs. In July 2008 in Greely, Colorado, a transgendered Latina, Angie Zapata, was beaten to death with fists and a fire extinguisher. In both of these cases, the perpetrators were additionally charged with hate crimes.[4]

Yet hatred also takes form in bullying, with devastating results. After being bullied at school for being "gay," 11-year-olds Jaheem Herrera from Georgia and Carl Joseph Walker-Hoover of Massachusetts committed suicide in April 2009. As detailed in the *New York Times*, statistics and research show that homophobic bullying is widespread, black and Latino children are more likely to be affected by it, and there is a connection between bullying and suicide.[5] And Latinos report a greater number of serious suicide attempts at young ages, something that possibly correlates to the coming-out phase.

Clearly, homosexuality is relevant to Latino culture. The issues of marriage and immigration are particularly important as a number of queer Latino immigrants have domestic partnerships with U.S. citizens. While heterosexual immigrants are eligible to apply for U.S. citizenship, gays and lesbians are not. As organizers of the Queer Contingent of the annual May Day parade in Los Angeles wrote on the 2009 promotional flyer, "LGBTQ issues rarely figure significantly in any immigration reform discussions and policies . . . LGBTQ people's rights are violated in ICE detention daily." Whether mainstream society acknowledges it or not, topics such as immigration, marriage, adoption, and health care are of concern to queer immigrants.

Library holdings can do a great deal of good when they contain materials that reflect queer Latino identities. As Luz Caballero Rodriguez wrote in the introduction to *Entendámonos*, a Spanish language gay and lesbian guide published online by Gamá, Colectivo de Lesbianas, Gays, Transexuales y Bisexuales de Canarias, "Literature helps us know other worlds, other realities, other ways of feeling; if we ignore these realities they will seem distant or abnormal but reading about them enriches us and brings us closer"[6] (author's translation).

Lesbian and gay worlds, even in Spanish, are worlds apart from the heteronormative world we live in. But we must acknowledge the queers. We must cater to them. We must go out of our way for them. And it really does require extra steps. Because homophobia has silenced and muted our writers. It has blindsided publishers. It has given vendors the perfect excuse to not distribute our works. It has erased much of our herstory. It has wrecked our families; it has defiled our icons; and it has permitted, even encouraged, violence. As librarians, we can honor our Spanish-speaking patrons by supporting queer writers, by goading the publishers, by pressuring the vendors, by allowing sexual diversity and its cultural expression to flourish.

We must assume that queer patrons exist, even if we can't pinpoint who they are, even if they're not coming into the library in droves demanding queer resources in Spanish. In academic libraries, faculty and student research and courses dictate, to some degree, the libraries' holdings. But Spanish-speaking patrons in public libraries, especially recent immigrants who are organically disempowered by their status, are not prone to making demands on libraries. And in small towns in Latin America, speaking out about homosexuality is taboo; gays and lesbians typically migrate to larger cities, away from their families, to come out. It's our responsibility to stock the shelves with a little something for everyone in the community and to include Spanish language materials of interest to queer patrons. The stuff just needs to be there, on the shelf, ready for that moment to be plucked off the vine.

It's easy to justify not having *joto* Spanish language materials in the library. Few books get published, and many of those that do are translations (English to Spanish, some from the French, etc.). Some are novels and many are nonfiction, as queer theory has taken off in Spanish. Publishers in Spain, where gays and lesbians can legally marry, have been cranking out queer titles for years now. Gay and lesbian literature in Spanish also gets published sporadically in Mexico and Latin America, usually by small presses with tiny print runs and spotty distribution. Vendors may not want to promote gay and lesbian material, or they may think there is no market for it. Authors aren't likely to be visible in the literary circuit because public venues are not welcoming to blatant homosexuality.

Also problematic is that, along with book dealers, publishers, and the general public, librarians may classify queer books as pornographic adult materials by their very nature. But this isn't necessarily so. Published by EGALES in Spain, the 2008 lesbian anthology *Dos orillas: Voces en la narrativa lésbica* exemplifies a "lesbian" title practically devoid of lesbian sexuality. Edited by Minerva Salado, a Cuban writer who resides in Mexico, the anthology includes work by 20 self-identified lesbian writers from Spain and countries of the Americas; I am one of the authors featured in this book.[7] While most of the content is about love between women, the focus is primarily emotional. The "graphic" lesbian content is limited to two stories—one that I wrote and one written by Anna Lidia Vega Serova. And even in these two instances, the overt lesbian sexuality is scant.

A lack of graphic queer content is not surprising, though, considering decades of sexual repression. Most "homosexual" texts take place within a heteronormative world, something that requires a bit of maneuvering. A queer world has to be created on the page similar to how it gets created in reality. And this reality is complicated with closets, Catholicism, social repression, and generations of *la familia*.

So it is somewhat miraculous when Spanish language lesbian and gay literature and nonfiction does get written, published, and distributed. My favorite lesbian author is Cristina Peri Rossi, who was born in Uruguay and went into exile in Barcelona in 1972 after the military dictatorship banned *Evohé,* her Sapphic book of poetry.[8] While much of her work is not blatantly queer, a few titles, such as *Estrategias del deseo* (Strategies of Desire) and *Habitación de hotel* (Hotel Room) are steaming in lesbian drama.[9] My favorite gay author is the Cuban Reinaldo Arenas, whose autobiographical *Antes que anochezca* (Before Night Falls) came to be widely known after it was made into a movie.[10] In contrast to Peri Rossi's lesbian poetry books, a relative few of which have made it onto U.S. library bookshelves, Arena's memoir is all over the country, in both Spanish and English.

Personally, I appreciate lesbian and gay literature most when it is in my face. A book such as *Sol de mi antojo: Antología poética de erotismo gay* (Sun of My Fancy: Poetic Anthology of Gay Eroticism) is priceless (and in the case of this particular book, beautiful).[11] I don't have the patience to read between the lines for queer content, and I'm tired of sleuthing around for it. I hope that writers and everyone involved in the publishing process can cut to the chase and put out the goods.

Sometimes it takes an insider who's lived it to learn the history, to make the inroads into the communities and to the materials, to the breadcrumbs, to the stuff that represents us. Perhaps it is my job, and that of my queer colleagues, to work toward Latino and Spanish language queer bibliographic representation by using the tools of our profession. Yolanda Retter Vargas, a Latina lesbian activist librarian who died last year used her skills to develop archives and to document Latina lesbian herstory and culture. It is in her absence now that I feel her presence, when I come across references to papers she presented and to encyclopedia articles she researched and wrote, and when I remember those snide remarks she'd make and her not-so-subtle insistence that we must bring visibility to queer people of color in our libraries and archives. I am also grateful to Adán Griego, a colleague at Stanford University who frequently promotes queer titles among librarians and maintains the online Bibliography of Sexuality Studies in Latin America. Out librarian Mario A. Ascencio, 2007–2008 president of REFORMA, is notable for bringing gay visibility to the organization during the annual 2008 ALA conference via his "President's Program: Libraries and Justice for LGBT." Having queer librarian insiders come out within the profession is a valuable act that forces all librarians to recognize that gays really are everywhere.

It is up to us and to our allies to compile bibliographies, to scour for books across continents, to be homosexual hound dogs, to dyke out our hallowed holdings. We have to see to it that our special materials get critical reviews, that authors are featured, that vendors see dollar signs when they get a hold of a queer book in Spanish. We have to indicate the library's queer content to our patrons with signage. We have to educate people on how best to search library catalog for the queer materials. We have to ensure that our collection development policy covers us should queer materials be challenged. We have to think like librarians and like consumers. We can add queer titles to the romance section; we can have a well-rounded selection of books on sexuality, where a book such as Rinna Riesenfeld's *Papá, Mamá, soy gay* (Mom, Dad, I'm Gay) shares the space with books about orgasms and talking to teens about love and sex.[12]

We have to take social responsibility within our role as librarians and consider that the gay guy from Tijuana is as precious as the five-year-old from El Salvador. Having library materials of interest to Spanish-speaking queers is not about pride or political rhetoric. It is about justice and fairness for everyone, including *las jotas y los jotos*. But the work needs to be done by everyone, not just those of us comfortable in our queer skin. Librarians who purchase Spanish language materials should take it upon themselves to include queer titles, and those who purchase queer collections should take it upon themselves to purchase titles in Spanish. Every librarian, from her or his vantage point, can do something for the cause, however small, however visionary. Our work must continue, because, like the Spanish language, gay and lesbian Latinos are here and have always been here, and they're in our libraries.

> Write it
> so it doesn't die.
> Write
> against forgetting.
> Write
> to hold on to it.
> Set it down in words
> runes of desire
> an alphabet of love
> a palindrome: *love her*
> *love her love.*
> And once it's written
> once it's set down in ink
> on paper
> in calligraphy
> in a manuscript
> once it's fixed
> held there
> fastened with words
> read it.
> Then you'll understand
> it's all been in vain:
> life slipped away from us
> between the caresses
> and the kisses
> it slipped away from us, just like words.
> In memoriam.[13]

References

1. tatiana de la tierra, "Queer It Up" personal poem of the author, 2004.
2. Ernesto Mayans, *32 Ideas to Reach Your Spanish-Speaking Patrons* (New York: Santillana Publishing Company, 1977); Camila Alire and Jacqueline Ayala, *Serving Latino Communities: A How-To-Do-It Manual for Librarians*, 2nd ed. (New York: Neal-Schuman Publishers, 2007);

Rose Zertuche Treviño, *Read Me a Rhyme in Spanish and English* (Chicago: ALA Editions, 2009).

3. LGBT Cuba News Today, "Inside Cuba: Gay Life in Cuba," *Miami Herald*, December 7, 2009, Accessed December 12, 2009. http://www.miamiherald.com/1447/story/1260198.html

4. Kareem Fahim, "Two Indicted in Fatal Beating of Ecuadorean Immigrant," *New York Times*, March 3, 2009, Accessed April 17, 2009. http://nytimes.com; Dan Frosch, "Murder and Hate Verdict in Transgender Case," *New York Times*, April 22, 2009, Accessed April 22, 2009. http://nytimes.com

5. Charles M. Blow, "By the Numbers: Two Little Boys," *New York Times*, April 24, 2009, Accessed April 24, 2009. http://blow.blogs.nytimes.com

6. Luz Caballero Rodriguez, "Presentación," *Guía Entendámonos* (Gamá, Colectivo de Lesbianas, Gays, Transexuales y Bisexuales de Canarias). Accessed September 15, 2008. http://www.colectivogama.com/noticias/docs/guia%20v3.pdf

7. This title was subsequently translated and published in English by ELLES as Minerva Solado, *Two Shores: Voices in Lesbian Narrative* (Barcelona: ELLES, 2008); Minerva Salado, ed., *Dos orillas: Voces en la narrativa lésbica* (Barcelona: EGALES Editorial, 2008).

8. This book was later translated into English and published in the United States in 1994. Cristina Peri Rossi, *Evohé: Poemas eróticos/Erotic Poems*, trans. Diana P. Decker (Washington, DC: Azul Editions, 1994), 144.

9. Cristina Peri Rossi, *Estrategias del deseo* (Barcelona: Random House Mondadori, 2005); *Habitación de hotel* (Barcelona: Random House Mondadori, 2007).

10. Reinaldo Arenas, *Antes que anochezca* (Barcelona: Tusquets, 1992).

11. Victor Manuel Mendiola, ed. *Sol de mi antojo: Antología poética de erotismo gay* (Mexico: Plaza & Janés, 2001).

12. Rinna Riesenfeld, *Papá, Mamá, soy gay: Una guía para comprender las orientaciones y preferencias sexuales de los hijos* (Mexico: Grijalbo: Random House Mondadori, 2000).

13. Cristina Peri Rossi, "In Memoriam," *Estrategias del deseo* (Barcelona: Random House Mondadori, 2005), 12. Poem translated by author with permission.

Chapter 8

Recruiting and Mentoring: Proactive Mentoring: Attracting Hispanic American Students into Information Studies

Alma C. Ortega and Marisol Ramos

Even though Hispanic Americans[1] are the fastest growing minority in the United States—about 15 percent of the population and growing[2]—they are vastly underrepresented in the library and information science (LIS) field.[3] In 2009, the U.S. Department of Labor reported that 15.1 percent of all librarians were minorities: of those, 5.3 percent were black or African American, 6.8 percent were Hispanic or Latino, and 3 percent were Asian.[4] In terms of minority students' enrollments in LIS schools, the Association for Library and Information Science Education (ALISE) reports that:

> Among racial and ethnic minorities, LS [Library Science] attracts a disproportionately small number of Black, American Indian, Hispanic and Asian or Pacific Island students. Students identified as White constituted 70.8 percent of those receiving LS degrees. In contrast, students identified as Black and Hispanic collectively earned less than 10 percent of the total number of degrees conferred, while American Indians and Asian or Pacific Island students earned less than 5 percent of the total number of degrees conferred. (Wallace & Naidoo, 2010, p. 11)

Considering these numbers, this essay will try to answer the question of why efforts to recruit Hispanic students into the LIS field seems to have little or modest success and what can be done to increase these numbers in the near future. When we consider that Hispanics constitute over 15 percent of the U.S. total population, but only 3.4 percent of Hispanic students graduate from library sciences graduate programs,[5] we realize that new approaches need to be considered to create a more representative and diverse professional force in our field.

For this article, we reviewed what has been accomplished over the years in terms of challenges to achieve the goal of recruiting and retaining this underrepresented population and propose the idea of *proactive mentoring* as a way to complement current state and national recruiting and mentoring initiatives. Finally, this is also a personal account of the authors' efforts to create awareness of the field of information studies among Hispanic undergraduates. Examples were selected to illustrate how proactive mentoring helped several Hispanic students apply and then attend library schools in the United States.

A Look to the Past: The Elusive Goal of Recruitment

The issue of recruiting minorities into the information science field is not a new one and has been addressed by its professional organizations since the 1970s. Affiliate groups within the American Library Association, the oldest and largest library organization in the United States and the world, such as the Black Caucus, the Chinese American Librarians Association (CALA), and REFORMA were created in response to a perceived lack of support inside the ALA in dealing with the many issues affecting underrepresented librarians and users. Some mainstream groups inside the ALA, such as the Rare Books and Manuscripts Section (RBMS), have also joined the cause of diversity and equality, approving the 2003 RBMS Diversity Action Plan to recruit underrepresented racial and ethnic groups into RBMS and to promote special collection librarianship as a career option.[6] Since the 1990s, studies and articles have been published regarding the need to recruit and retain minority information professionals (both at library schools and information institutions). For example, in her master's thesis, completed in 1993, Jennifer Grady discussed at length the challenges, strategies, and methods that were used at the time to attract minority students and which ones seemed to have an impact: for example, scholarship targeted to minorities or official recruitment programs geared to minorities (Grady, 1993). More recent articles still address the same issues (Dewey & Keally, 2008; Love, 2010). The persistence of this topic highlights the fact that there is still much to be done to attract minorities in general into the profession. The fact that the library and information profession is disproportionately white when compared with the population boost of many minority groups in the United States, especially Hispanics at the end of the first decade of the 21st century, calls for the need to find more effective ways to increase diversity in our field to serve a more multicultural and multilingual society.

For Hispanics in the profession, attracting Hispanic students to the field has been an issue of high priority for many years. In the anthology *Latino Librarianship: A Handbook for Professionals*, edited by Salvador Güereña in 1990, Tami Echavarria's article discussed in detail the lack of success by the library profession to enlist Hispanic librarians to better serve the growing population of Spanish-speaking users, especially in the public library sector. She explained:

> Librarians, as well as paraprofessionals, with language skills and familiarity with the literature of Latino culture are needed. . . . Latino librarians are needed as collection development specialists, public service providers, cataloguers, role models and library administrators. (Echavarria, 1990, pp. 20–21)

She argued that the only way to solve this problem was by "attracting into the profession individuals from these linguistic and cultural backgrounds . . ." (Echavarria, 1990, p. 21). A decade later, the call to recruit Hispanic librarians continues. Isabel Espinal wrote an article in *Críticas Magazine* (Espinal, 2003), which discussed the same issues and concerns that Echavarria did in the early 1990s. They both suggested the same solutions for this crisis: recruiting bilingual Hispanic individuals into library science through the combined strategies of *recruitment* and *mentoring* by both Hispanics and officially sanctioned programs.

Our review indicates that this call for action did not fall on deaf ears and that, over the years, numerous professional groups, grants programs, and graduate school programs have been created to address these problems. For example, since its inception in 1971, REFORMA has actively worked to recruit and mentor bilingual and bicultural librarians. The ALA's Spectrum recruitment and scholarship program was established in 1997 to increase the diversity of underrepresented librarians within the profession. At the national level, the Institute of Museum and Library Service has provided millions of dollars in grants to recruit bilingual librarians in border towns through the Rio Grande Initiative, one of the grants under the Laura Bush 21st Century Library Program (Brezosky, 2007). Additionally, in the last 10 years, several information sciences school programs and university libraries have created minority recruitment programs or have added diversity policies that encourage the recruitment and retention of minorities into their programs. Such programs include the University of Arizona's Knowledge River,[7] UCLA's Information Studies Department Diversity Policy,[8] and University of Tennessee Libraries

Diversity Residency Program.[9] Bearing in mind all of these great efforts, why do we continue to have such trouble attracting Hispanic Americans into the field of information science?

Refocusing: What We Really Need to Do and How to Get There

For several decades, Hispanic information science professionals have focused on recruiting bilingual Hispanic students to the field but with little success. Why have we failed in our goal and continue to face a crisis in this area? There are two aspects to this dilemma. One is related to how many Hispanic students are actually entering higher education, and the second is the assumption that most Hispanics are bilingual.

The 2000 U.S. Census reported that although Hispanic students comprised about 13.5 percent of the total population, only 7 percent of college students in four-year programs are from this group (Bordes & Arredondo, 2005). Therefore, the main problem seems to be that not enough Hispanics are graduating from high school (Bordes & Arredondo, 2005; Chapa & De La Rosa, 2006; Lutz, 2007). Hispanic students have higher dropout rates compared to other racial and ethnic groups. As of 2008, the rate was 18 percent for Hispanic Americans compared to 9.9 percent for African American, 14.6 percent for Native American, 4.4 percent for Asian/Pacific Islander, and 4.8 percent for whites.[10] "The fact [is] that Latinos are seriously underrepresented in higher education programs and that the degree of underrepresentation increases as the level of education increases" (Chapa & De La Rosa, 2006, p. 207).

If the pool of Hispanic American students completing a bachelor's degree is already small, it follows that there will be even lower enrollment at the graduate level. One possible explanation is the economic burden of graduate education. Many Hispanic students come from low-income families, especially among Mexican Americans, the largest minority group in the United States. Dealing with the added pressure to join the workforce to support their families, they probably find it very hard to commit to graduate school, which is prohibitively expensive, even with financial aid. It is not surprising that these students might balk at dedicating two more years of their lives to a master's degree, much less four years toward a doctoral degree. Why take two more years of graduate school and incur (more) debt, to be what—a librarian? Worse still, the career of information specialist is unfamiliar to many of their families. Therefore, it is not unexpected that the percentage of Hispanic students earning doctoral degrees in the field is so low—2 percent in 1996 (Valverde & Rodriguez, 2002, p. 51) and 3.8 percent in 2000 (Chapa & De La Rosa, 2006, p. 204).

Added to the challenge of recruiting from an already small pool of candidates is the difficulty in finding bilingual Hispanic Americans. Bilingualism is a skill essential to serving Spanish-speaking library users. In reality, not all Hispanics are bilingual. Depending on the generation, the level of bilingualism varies from being fully bilingual to code-switching to being monolingual in English. As indicated in a 2003 report by the Pew Hispanic Center and the Kaiser Family Foundation (Suro & Passel, 2003), "Spanish-speakers make up most of the first generation [72%]. The second generation is substantially bilingual [47%], and the third-plus generations are primarily English speakers [78%]."[11]

Thus, we find ourselves in a paradoxical situation: although immigration has continued to increase the Spanish-speaking population over the last two decades, as time and social pressures move them away from their immigrant roots, the descendants of Spanish-speaking peoples may cease to speak Spanish after several generations (Portes & Schauffler, 1994; Veltman, 1990), rendering them incapable of helping address the needs of the growing population of Spanish-speaking migrants from Latin America and the Caribbean. Until now, the emphasis for recruitment into the profession has been on bilingual Hispanics. But how can we address the dual need of increasing diversity by recruiting Hispanic Americans and increase the number of bilingual librarians serving Spanish-speaking users?

We propose the need to refocus the effort and expand the pool of candidates for recruitment into the field of information science. We suggest targeting three very distinct groups: Hispanics (regardless of their level of bilingualism), recent immigrants (mono- or bilingual), and bilingual students (regardless of ethnic or racial background). We can begin by offering *new academic and professional opportunities* to Hispanic and immigrant students. Through these efforts they can use their abilities to deal with a largely underserved population. Secondly, we can *recruit and hire bilingual persons* (regardless of ethnic/racial background) who can serve the growing population of Spanish speakers: heavy users of libraries but mostly unable to take full advantage of all the services offered due to the language barrier.

As important as it is to recruit Hispanics into the profession (our original emphasis), it is equally important to attract young recent immigrants who are intimately involved with their communities. Ultimately, we should strive to attract anyone willing to acquire Spanish language skills and work with underrepresented communities. Ideally, we should have a librarian who is both Hispanic and bilingual, but to serve the growing Spanish-speaking population adequately we need to expand the search by including non-Hispanic bilingual individuals as well.

We will further advance the idea that efforts to recruit Hispanic students into college and the information profession should include promoting bilingualism among those students who are monolingual or limited bilinguals, as a means to improving their chances of both academic and professional success. We also need to make students aware that by learning Spanish they are honoring their immigrant heritage. Finally, *it is imperative* that we recruit Hispanics (regardless of Spanish proficiency) because they bring to the profession an awareness of the different cultures and traditions among Spanish-speaking groups through their connection to their countries of origin or their interactions with original immigrants such as grandparents. These experiences provide the understanding and empathy necessary to deal with recent immigrants, often overwhelmed by their new life and surroundings. Most importantly, Hispanic librarians present a friendly face to immigrant users; their presence invites interaction without fear of rejection.

Recommendations for Recruitment and Retention: A Multilevel Approach

How can librarians already in the profession create strategies to recruit and retain Hispanic or recent immigrant students? How can we refine current strategies, such as outreach, mentoring (personal or programmatic), and volunteers programs? What really works?

Unfortunately, at this point, there is not enough empirical data to determine which particular approaches or programs provide the best results to increase the recruitment of minorities into the field. Kyung-Sun Kim, a researcher at the School of Library and Information Studies, University of Wisconsin-Madison, explains:

> Although there is an abundance of literature suggesting effective recruitment/retention strategies, only a few of them are based on empirical research. Even among the empirical studies, most of them rely on existing statistical data or inputs from administrators and/or organizations, but not on the input from librarians and students of color who are actually from the target group of such recruitment/retention efforts. (Kim, 2007, ¶4)

Kim's study did not investigate any particular program. Instead, she performed a survey on how minority students in LIS programs perceived their institutions' recruitment and retention strategies such as satisfaction with recruitment efforts, suggestions for better recruitment/retention strategies, and how these perceptions varied among different minority groups. Nevertheless, her findings discovered that among all minority groups, Hispanic Americans were the most dissatisfied about the library school's efforts to recruit and retain minority students. These findings are extremely useful in reshaping current recruitment and retention practices and targeting them to meet the needs of minority students.

Current literature discusses a wide variety of strategies we can take advantage of: recruiting paraprofessionals in public libraries, recruiting and mentoring undergraduate students, promoting doctoral programs for Hispanic students, and reaching out and recruiting high school students (Bordes & Arredondo, 2005; Echavarria 1990; Espinal 2003; Kim, 2007; Reese & Hawkins, 1999; Santos & Reigadas, 2002; Valverde & Rodriguez, 2002; Winston & Walstad, 2006). An assessment of these efforts would allow us to create a mega-strategy to address these issues and to better target and recruit Hispanics, recent immigrants, and bilingual students into information science careers.

To address the recruitment challenge, we recommend developing a three-level strategy that can be used by individuals, organizations, or information studies schools and adapted to immediate needs. Because it relies heavily on collaboration among stakeholders, such as community colleges, public and university libraries, and national and state professional organizations for libraries and other information professions, this strategy is harder to implement, but we believe it is worth pursuing. Combined with proactive mentoring, it will allow you to apply a multilevel approach that can be adapted to any circumstance.

Bearing in mind that most Hispanic students enroll in Hispanic Serving Institutions (HSI)[12]—both community colleges and four-year institutions (Bordes & Arredondo, 2005, p. 115)—and that a higher rate of Hispanic students selects a community college[13] to acquire an associate of arts instead of a bachelor's degree (Chapa & De La Rosa, 2006, p. 208), the *first level of recruitment* should target students entering or already enrolled in two- and four-year programs at HSI colleges. At community colleges, outreach and mentoring programs should be created in collaboration with library and/or other professional organizations, both at the national and state levels. Community college librarians and career guidance counselors are key components. When targeting Hispanic and recent immigrant students, we need to emphasize these goals: encouraging students to enroll in honors programs so they can transfer to four-year colleges; providing financial aid information to encourage students not only to finish a bachelor's degree but to earn a graduate degree in library and information science; persuading students to take Spanish courses; and advertising and promoting employment in library and information science as a viable, long-term career opportunity. Recruitment can also begin while students work or volunteer at the college library.

Similarly, at the four-year college or university level, collaborative projects sponsored by library and/or other information professional organizations, academic librarians, and support staff can join forces with career counselors and the staff at cultural centers to create new ways to reach out and mentor these students (Love, 2010, p. 491). As in community colleges, student aides working in libraries can be recruited into the field.

When targeting Spanish-speaking Hispanics and recent immigrants, we need to emphasize the desirability of language and cultural skills—knowledge of a particular ethnic community or the ability to read and/or translate materials from Spanish to English and vice versa. Consider reaching out to students from ethnic studies programs such as Chicano Studies, Puerto Rican Studies, and Latino Studies. Establish a formal or informal relationship with the cultural center at your institution, and make yourself available to undergraduate students that may not be in ethnic programs but who use the center as a gathering place or study area. Also focus on Latin American and Caribbean Studies programs (that attract Hispanic students) through job fairs and any other library or school event that fosters research in these areas.

The *second level of recruitment* should target high school students, especially schools located in areas densely populated by Hispanic Americans and recent immigrants. If we truly want Hispanic students to consider information science as a career worth pursuing, we need to begin attracting them early, rather than later in their studies. As Reese and Hawkins explained:

> To spread the word about the library profession, we need to target outreach programs to the full range of the population, starting with junior high and high school students. The American Library Association in collaboration with local and state library organizations must initiate a program that encourages our minority students to pursue a college education and consider a career in library and information science. (Reese & Hawkins, 1999, p. 62)

Library and/or other information professional organizations should team up with school librarians[14] and counselors to advertise and promote careers in the information sciences, going beyond job fairs and finding ways to bring libraries into the classroom. School librarians can teach classes on how to do research using the Internet and how to properly cite print and electronic resources; there is no limit when advertising how information science is relevant to students. School librarians can also assist career counselors with finding financial aid information for minorities and potentially mentor these students. Another idea is to create a library club for students interested in libraries. A good model to follow would be the Louisiana Teen-age Librarians Association (LTLA), a group sponsored by the Louisiana Association of School Librarians section of the Louisiana Library Association.[15] Since the 1950s, their mission has been to promote librarianship among middle and high school students. Students run contests, help with the library and other related club work, and hold an annual convention. Because students, with the help of their school/media librarian, operate the organization, statistics are not available on how many students have gone on to become librarians, but anecdotal evidence confirms that some of them have. One example is Paula Clemmons, LTLA student relations chairwoman, who relates the following:

> I personally, am a former LTLA member from 1988–1990 from Lacassine High School in Lacassine, LA. I became a librarian in 1999 and soon after formed a local library club that joined LTLA.[16]

Another way to attract and recruit high school students is to establish collaborations between public libraries and middle schools and high schools. Most public schools have Young Adult (YA) librarians that specialize in connecting students with information. Internships for school credit might be established between junior high and/or high schools and their local libraries as a collaborative project between school/media librarians and their public library counterparts. This type of project increases awareness of the profession and helps to improve the performance of students who are failing academically. Encouraging the participation of minority students would increase interest in the profession. We should also mentor these students and help them overcome one of their greatest obstacles—graduating from high school. Creating a formal collaborative project between librarians and schools can lead to the possibility of applying for federal grants. For example, one of the funding categories of the Laura Bush 21st Century Librarian Program is *Pre-Professional Programs*,[17] specifically geared toward generating interest in careers in the information sciences among high school and college students.

The *third level of recruitment* should target the paraprofessionals who work in public libraries and other library settings. Many Hispanic individuals and recent immigrants can be found working as messenger clerks, at the circulation desk, as clerical staff, or as library assistants. They are prime candidates for recruitment because they have the practical knowledge of working in a library but might need encouragement to apply to library school. A good model to follow would be the Los Angeles Public Library (LAPL) system grant program. Janine Goodale, a former program coordinator at LAPL, explains how this program has been funded:

> The grant was a[n] Institute of Museum and Library Services award to the Urban Library Council.[18] We were one of the libraries then select[ed] by the ULC to receive monies as a pass through to students in local library schools who were our employees. There was an underlying intend [sic] to recruit from minority populations so we did track ethnicity. Altogether there were 25 students who began the program. Three withdrew. Nine graduated and are working for LAPL or interviewing to do so. One is at an academic library and two are at other public libraries. Of those employed or interviewing 3 are Hispanic, 1 is Caucasian, 1 Vietnamese, 3 Filipino, 1 Asian (Chinese

language). Those not yet graduated are Caucasian with the exception of 1 Hispanic.[19] (Goodale, 2007)

Although these numbers may seem small, the implications in terms of recruitment are enormous. This is a successful program that shows how a proactive approach can bring minorities to the field.

Librarians and other information specialists need to reach out and challenge mass media stereotypes regarding our profession. We believe that a key element for a successful targeted recruitment program is not only to promote and advertise why library and information sciences jobs are a good career move, but to make it clear to potential recruits that we WANT and NEED them. We can help counteract the trend of Hispanic Americans losing their Spanish language skills as they acculturate over time by conveying how much we value these qualities and by encouraging their retention. If we can influence this population to seriously consider the information sciences as a career, just as they might consider medicine or the law, we can truly begin noteworthy life transformations.

There are many ways to actively recruit Hispanic Americans and recent immigrants into the field, but they require much support from library administrators and our peers, regardless of ethnic or racial background. There are simply not enough minority information specialists to do the job. In the end, to create and ensure the success of these programs we need to recruit our superiors and our peers.

Finally, we need to start tracking and quantifying current and defunct programs to understand and identify the most successful and replicate them across the country. To increase the presence and participation of Hispanic Americans in the information science field, we cannot continue to work blindly or by intuition: we need to plan and execute the right approaches. Furthermore, we need to retain and mentor Hispanic Americans to successfully complete their programs and then actually incorporate them into the ranks of information specialists.

Proactive Mentoring—A Tool for the Resourceful Information Specialist

As important as it is to recruit these students into the field, retaining them and making sure that they earn their degree is equally important. Some library schools have programs in place to recruit and mentor minority students for an MLIS or a doctoral degree, such as the University of Arizona's Knowledge River and the University of Tennessee Diversity Libraries Residency Program. These are excellent models that should be emulated by library schools across the nation and adapted as necessary. Mentoring is an important element in these programs. When possible, a minority faculty member is matched with a similar minority student; but more commonly, faculty is matched with a student with similar research interests. These matches seek to create a nurturing relationship where a faculty member will support and advise the student. Recent research suggests that these mentoring models help to retain Hispanic students in higher education (Bordes & Arredondo, 2005; Kim, 2007; Santos, 2002; Valverde & Rodriguez, 2002; Winston & Walstad, 2006), though it does not provide enough empirical evidence to support the idea that having faculty of the same minority group increases the rate of success. However, what has been verified is that good mentoring increases the retention of Hispanic students (Bordes & Arredondo, 2005). Moreover, there is evidence that Hispanic students yearn to see more faculty and peers from their own ethnic group (Kim, 2007).

Now what if your organization does not have recruitment or mentoring programs? What can you do as an individual to recruit someone to the information sciences? This is where proactive mentoring comes into play. We define "proactive mentoring" as an individual (formal or informal) mentoring style driven by an individual's desire to attract, recruit, retain, and mentor a student into a particular career. It differs slightly from traditional individual mentoring in that it is not accidental, but something you choose to do proactively on a daily basis. It is a philosophy that goes beyond merely performing good deeds. It is not an unplanned process. It is a specific and targeted action by the proactive mentor to seek out individuals to recruit: in our case, Hispanic Americans, recent immigrants, and non-Hispanics interested in serving Spanish-speaking library users.

This mentoring approach, active engagement in the recruitment and mentoring process, can be used by librarians and any information specialist in any interaction with students and/or peers. It is a proactive philosophy that should be adopted by all those concerned with the current underrepresentation in our field of Hispanic Americans and other groups. More than ever we have the means to steer students into the field, even if one at a time. There is no better reward than the satisfaction of knowing we were instrumental in recruiting another student into our profession. If we could persuade our peers and supervisors to help us recruit minorities, then it would not be a lonely, thankless process but the beginning of a revolution. It is time to recognize that without commitment to this task, nothing significant will ever happen.

Proactive Mentoring in Action: Real Experience Examples

At the first-ever Joint Conference of Librarians of Color (JCLC) from October 12–15, 2006, in Dallas, Texas, the librarians at the awards reception were told that it was their personal responsibility to recruit two people to the profession. Of these two eventual librarians, one was to replace "yourself," and another was to replace a librarian who was about to or had already retired.[20] As long-time practitioners of proactive mentoring, the authors are proud to report that we have personally surpassed this recruitment challenge; however, we do not feel that our obligation to the profession has been fulfilled. We are going beyond finding replacements and continue to unabashedly share with our students, and anyone willing to listen, how much we enjoy our chosen profession.

Working in academic environments has really helped our recruitment endeavors. Since we both work in university libraries, we take advantage of every opportunity to promote our field of work among the students we serve. This enthusiasm for librarianship is passed on through information literacy sessions both in the classroom setting and in the library. We have open door policies, give out cards, and invite students to e-mail us. Students are invited to come to us not only for research consultations but also to vent and to help answer any questions they may have about their major.

We view these as opportunities to market the information sciences as a valid option for graduate school and a very gratifying career. Yes, we recognize libraries are not for profit, but a business approach is truly needed if we are serious about creating successful recruitment and mentoring opportunities. At every encounter with students, we can market what we do, share why we do it, and our love for doing it. An example of this occurred at an event on the existing job market for ethnic studies majors held by the university's ethnic studies program. Ortega attended to support the event, and when one of the four presenters did not show up, she offered herself as a presenter. The event organizer looked at her askance but realized that she must have a background in ethnic studies to have been assigned as the program's liaison. Her participation was accepted. Ortega took this opportunity to share with about 15 ethnic studies majors why she loved her job. She enjoys working with people, helping them find what they need as well, as help plan their research agendas. This came as a surprise to many students who had assumed she only gave "library tours" once a year!

Getting Down to Business: Proactive Mentoring Examples

All of the examples presented here are about Hispanics. Each represents a different type of student entering information studies as a career. In the first example, a recently graduated student entered a master's in library science and information studies program. Appropriately, the second one is about information studies as a second career option in life, as it is for a large number of librarians who gravitate to librarianship as a second or third career. The third example is about a Chicana pursuing her doctorate in information studies against all odds. Although recruiting minorities to the profession is very important, recruiting them to become information studies professors is imperative. Future librarians cannot easily be recruited if students never see themselves reflected in their professors or in the curriculum.

Example One: Sam's Story

A liaison librarian to the departments of history, Spanish, and ethnic Studies was in a privileged position to reach a diverse student population on a daily basis. It was through one of this librarian's information literacy sessions (aka library tours) for an ethnic studies class that she first met Sam. He shared, in a research paper library appointment, that he was a junior and was considering whether to continue to graduate school and, if so, in what field. The librarian mentioned to Sam that she became a librarian because she enjoyed the many aspects of the research process and that in addition to engaging in research projects of her own, it was part of her job to help others with their research as well.

She got to know Sam better when he was close to graduation. By then he had decided on graduate school and was curious about library school. He wanted to become a researcher some day. Sam had seen his liaison librarian "in action," as he put it, and thought it might be "cool" to help students research their desired topics. He really wanted to be sure that he could develop his passion for ethnic studies and wanted this field to be a part of his graduate school experience. The librarian told him that librarianship offers the flexibility of combining one's research interests within various methodologies.

Sam graduated, and before returning home (to California's Central Valley), he said he was starting to seriously consider librarianship but that he needed time to think about it and would be in touch. Four months after graduation, Sam sent his former librarian a tentative e-mail. He had some questions he wanted to ask. Did she mean it when she said she would guide him through the graduate school application process? Would she really take time to talk to him about his musings concerning library school? The librarian e-mailed him immediately to let him know that she had indeed meant what she said. They continued to e-mail, and she even called him several times to follow up on his progress. The next time they spoke, he said he was still interested in library science and that he was ready to apply. Would she really help him with this personal statement? She told him again, "yes." Sam now felt convinced that by obtaining a master's degree, he would return to the Central Valley better equipped to help his community. When he was ready to start writing his statement of purpose, the librarian introduced him, via e-mail, to a colleague at another university so he could benefit from having two information professionals look at his drafts. Sam received the insightful feedback he needed and submitted his application.

Teamwork is essential to ensuring that the library school candidate will always have someone to turn to for help and receive encouragement in an extremely stressful process. Sam was not only accepted to the university he wanted to go to, but he was also awarded a fellowship. The librarian still keeps in touch with him from time to time. He is very busy with his studies and happy that he chose to become a librarian. Sam always closes his e-mail with a huge thanks to the librarians who got him started in library and information science.

Example Two: Beatrice Found Her Calling

Beatrice had been working in a library for over 15 years as a library assistant. She saw her job as a temporary thing and would make a change as soon as she finished her master's degree in electronic commerce. Beatrice had also worked in a library during most of her undergraduate student years in business administration. However, everything changed when a reference and instruction librarian at her place of employment, an academic library, met her and saw librarian potential in her. Beatrice was so comfortable with library work that she not only managed electronic serials and reference but also did troubleshooting for the information technology department.

Although at one point when she had first started working there, the university librarian had proposed the idea of library school to Beatrice, she had never considered it as a possible career option for herself. Beatrice was an extremely busy person; she was studying for a master's degree, had a job in the library, and also worked in her family's business. Her decision to pursue a master's in electronic commerce was aimed at helping the family business expand. If she dared, in the near future she would go into business for herself. But once she finished the master's, she did not feel the way she thought she would, so she continued to work at the library.

The librarian's strategy with Beatrice was to tap into her feelings regarding business and how to apply them to information studies. During the time the librarian had known Beatrice, she noticed how good Beatrice was with computer troubleshooting and the library's business resources, as well as monographic and serials cataloguing. The librarian slowly involved her in more professional library activities and, after about a year, asked Beatrice if she had ever considered going to library school. She said she had thought about it but had not realized before how much she enjoyed working in a library setting. Beatrice wanted to work in a library as an information technologist or a business librarian. She realized that she wanted to try this new career, and if it ended up not being what she wanted, she could always start her own business as a consultant for small businesses within the Mexican community of Southern California.

The librarian continued to encourage Beatrice. A few months later, Beatrice shared that she needed help with her library school statement. The librarian gladly helped her with the process and also wrote a letter of recommendation to the information studies program. Over the next two years, the librarian continued her commitment to Beatrice and wrote several letters of recommendation for scholarship opportunities. Thus far, this proactive mentoring relationship had included presenting twice as a team at library conferences.

A professional relationship was successfully built between Beatrice and the librarian. It grew out of continual support and earned trust. Beatrice felt comfortable with the librarian and was candid throughout the entire process, sharing the fact that before she had met her she had never found what librarians did to be very exciting. The librarian took this very special opportunity to explain to Beatrice that there are many types of information specialists in the field. Academic librarianship is just one of the areas, with boundless possibilities for learning and development. In the end, librarianship is as exciting as what *you* make of it. Beatrice is about to graduate with her master's in library science and is truly excited about starting to work as a librarian, either in a business or academic setting. Sometimes the desire to become a librarian is dormant or unclear, and it is a recruiter's job to awaken and nourish this desire!

Example Three: Terry against All Odds

Terry was a full-time librarian at an academic library who felt she had reached her potential after three years because she was not encouraged by her supervisors to engage in any new projects. Terry contacted a research librarian who had known her since she was a graduate student in information studies. This librarian had even hired Terry as one of her graduate assistants at a research library at a university in California. Terry had been excited about working as a professional, but before graduating with a double master's, she had the opportunity to participate in a graduate education abroad program in a Spanish-speaking country. She loved the experience and the challenge of studying Spanish grammar formally; for the first time, Terry appreciated and valued her bilingualism.

While working for the research librarian, whenever Terry completed her assigned library duties, they would have conversations about getting a PhD. Was she too old to start one? What would her topic be? She knew she had the support of her family, which really mattered to her. But was it worth it to enter a PhD program in library and information sciences? The research librarian always told her yes, as long as she was passionate about earning a doctorate, because it involved commitment and sustained hard work for a few years. Right after library school, Terry took a job as an academic librarian to consider in what direction to take her research.

They kept in touch through the following three years. The conversations regarding a PhD never ceased, and the research librarian never stopped encouraging her. When it came to time for Terry to apply for the PhD program, she took the opportunity during a library conference that they both attended to seek the opinions of a group of librarians. All through this discussion, academic and research librarians challenged her to defend why she wanted a PhD. Other librarians also shared their thoughts. Needless to say, Terry received many different opinions (both negative and positive) on why she should or should not apply to a PhD program. Most of the librarians she sought counsel from considered her age a problem. Some of the librarians, while encouraging her, made sure they mentioned that she should prepare for ageism, among many other -isms. One very bold librarian suggested that Terry consider coloring her hair. Another librarian very kindly told her that she would probably be accepted to a program, but there was no guarantee she would finish it.

A few months later, Terry came to the research librarian and had a heart-to-heart conversation about applying to a PhD program. The librarian asked her to be honest with herself; it had been three years after all. Terry needed to ask herself if anything was stopping her from applying to a doctorate program. During their conversation, Terry acknowledged that in addition to knowing that she was an older candidate, many of the issues raised in their previous discussions had already been in the back of her mind. She was especially grateful for the extensive conversation they had that day; with no time limit, she was able to sort out all of her thoughts and doubts.

The talk challenged her to think about why she really wanted a PhD and what her dissertation topic would be. It was the first time she had challenged herself to consider whether she indeed wanted the degree. Weeks later, she e-mailed a preliminary draft of her personal statement to the research librarian. She had a lot of work to do to get the application ready, which was daunting at first. By the end of the process, however, she knew she wanted a PhD, so she would go through the applications and see if it was meant to be. Terry applied to a number of programs, and when she was accepted to one, it came with a fellowship. She is currently enjoying the challenges of the program and has accepted the fact that even if she only gets to teach for 12 to 15 years, she will work very hard during those years to serve as a role model for those needing reassurance that it is *never* too late to achieve the top level in the field.

Summary of Examples

All of these examples show us how proactive mentoring is an ongoing and engaged process. It is never limited to a one-time meeting or pep talk with a potential future librarian at a career fair or conference. The best proactive mentoring is done over a few meaningful years. Genuine encounters always help support mentees throughout the process of understanding what librarianship is: a career where we will help others, just as our mentor/s helped us before we became librarians.

Conclusion

At the end of our review, we concluded that the main reason for the slow increase of Hispanic Americans in the library and information science field is due partly to a pipeline problem. Not enough Hispanics are entering four-year colleges, and many of them may choose to go to community colleges or HSI colleges to acquire a degree that would lead them into the workforce as soon as possible (Bordes & Arredondo, 2005; Chapa & De La Rosa, 2006). Therefore, they may not consider a master's degree in library science as a choice, either because of economic reasons or because they were never made aware of such a career option. Yet although there is much to be done to reach our goal of increasing the number of Hispanic students in our field, we have the strategies to achieve it during this century. Today, we not only have the support of national library and information science professional organizations but also of many universities attempting to bring more diversity to their student bodies and staff. Most importantly, many dedicated information specialists are committed to finding ways to close the diversity gap in our field. The ranks of Hispanic American information professionals are slowly but steadily increasing through the hard work of many of our colleagues.

We need to take advantage of the opportunities provided in the 21st century and proactively recruit. Refocusing our aims and expanding our pool of recruits and recruitment efforts can only increase our chances of success. Through a multilayered approach, we can concentrate our outreach efforts on nontraditional venues such as high schools; community colleges, including HSI colleges; and universities. Information specialists now have more knowledge and tools to attract, recruit, and retain Hispanic students in the field. But we must not lose sight of the non-Hispanics who also want to serve Spanish-speaking immigrant communities. We need to be inclusive if we are to provide first-rate service to this growing sector of the population.

Proactive mentoring is a difficult mission. It requires a librarian's commitment to take time out of a busy schedule not only to recruit but also to mentor for several years. It is an ongoing process. Nonetheless, as evidenced in the preceding examples, there are Hispanic American students who are willing to enter our field. What we need are more librarians willing to reach out to them. The time and effort are most certainly worth it if we can change potential students' minds and help them perceive the joys of our career choice.

As Hispanic American information specialists, we practice proactive mentoring on a daily basis. To date, we have recruited eight people, mostly Hispanics, but also others from varied racial and ethnic backgrounds. We show them that we wholeheartedly enjoy being librarians. It is how we repay our debt to our own mentors, whose encouragement and example inspired, recruited, and mentored us into information studies. We would not be here but for their kind words and excellent work ethic.[21] They showed us the way, and to continue their work, we recruit others to the information studies field.

The goal is to bring into our field dedicated, caring, and proactive individuals who will increase diversity, which is greatly needed in a society still polarized by racism and xenophobia. We can only hope that the reader will also help to diversify the field by applying the tools provided in this article.

Notes

1. For this chapter, we are using Hispanic American instead of Latino. Both terms are interchangeable and usually refer to the descendants of Spanish-speaking people from Latin American and the Caribbean. We do make a distinction between Hispanic and recently arrived immigrants from those countries since their needs (for language and library services) are very different from Hispanic Americans that are U.S. citizens and have lived in the United States for several generations.

2. Data from the U.S. Census Bureau, 2005–2009 American Community Survey, Hispanic or Latino Origin at http://factfinder.census.gov/servlet/DTTable?_bm=y&-geo_id=01000US&-ds_name=ACS_2009_5YR_G00_&-redoLog=false&-mt_name=ACS_2009_5YR_G2000_B03001. Accessed January 24, 2011.

3. Unfortunately, the final data on Hispanic Americans in the United States from the decennial census of 2010 was not available by the time this essay was submitted for publication. But early indications seem to point to an increase in the Hispanic American population. For the latest numbers visit, the U.S. Census website: http://www.census.gov/.

4. Data from Labor Force Statistics from the Current Population Survey, table, "Employed persons by detailed occupation, sex, race, and Hispanic or Latino ethnicity, 2009" at http://www.bls.gov/cps/cpsaat11.pdf. Accessed December 30, 2010.

5. Data from Table II-3-a-2 Summary, Comparative breakdown by Ethnic Origin of LS Degrees Awarded and U.S. Bureau of Census Estimates 2008, Wallace and Naidoo, ALISE: Statistical Report 2009, 12.

6. For the full list of goals of the RBMS Diversity Action Plan, see http://rbm.acrl.org/content/4/2/74.extract.

7. The Knowledge River is a program at the University of Arizona that focuses on library and information issues from the needs and perspectives of Hispanics and Native Americans. Knowledge River participants graduate with an MA in Information Resources and Library Science. http://sirls.arizona.edu/KR/. Accessed December 30, 2010.

8. University of California, Los Angeles (UCLA)'s Department of Information Studies—Diversity http://is.gseis.ucla.edu/about/explore_diversity.htm. Accessed February 21, 2011.

9. University of Tennessee Libraries Diversity librarian residency program http://www.lib.utk.edu/diversity/activities/residency/. Accessed February 21, 2011.

10. Data from U.S. Department of Education, National Center for Education Statistics. (2010). The Condition of Education 2010 (NCES 2010–028), Table A-19–2, http://nces.ed.gov/programs/coe/2010/section3/table-sde-1.asp. Accessed January 24, 2011.

11. See Table 6: Primary Language among Latinos, p. 8 at http://pewhispanic.org/files/reports/22.pdf

12. From the Hispanic Association of Colleges & University website: "Today, HACU represents nearly 450 colleges and universities committed to Hispanic higher education success in the United States, Puerto Rico, Latin America, Spain, and Portugal. Although our member institutions in the U.S. represent less than 10 percent of all higher education institutions nationwide, together they are home to more than two-thirds of all Hispanic college students." http://www.hacu.net/hacu/HACU_101_EN.asp?SnID=196242059. Accessed February 23, 2011.

13. For an excellent report to understand Hispanic enrollment choices, see the Pew Hispanic Center Factsheet 2004, Hispanic College Enrollment: Less Intensive and Less Heavily Subsidized, http://pewhispanic.org/files/factsheets/7.1.pdf. Accessed January 24, 2011.

14. Due to the financial and budgetary crisis that began in 2008, many school librarians' positions have been eliminated in many areas of the country, and very few school librarians are left to serve the needs of big school districts. Public librarians can step in and give support to their local schools (K–12) to fill the gap and still reach out to students.

15. Reese and Hawkins mentioned this club in their 1999 book *Stop Talking, Start Doing!: Attracting People of Color to the Library Profession*, 66.

16. Paula Clemmons, Personal Communication, July 23, 2007.

17. Laura Bush 21st Century Librarian Program, http://www.imls.gov/applicants/grants/21centurylibrarian.shtm. Accessed February 21, 2011.

18. The Urban Libraries Council is "an association of public libraries in metropolitan areas and the corporations that serve them. Believing that thriving public libraries are a result of collaborative leadership, the trustees, library directors, and corporate officers of member institutions work together to address shared issues, grasp new opportunities, and conduct research that improves professional practice." http://www.urbanlibraries.org/. Accessed May 14, 2009.
19. Janine Goodale, Personal Communication, September 20, 2007.
20. Alma C. Ortega attended the first Joint Conference of Librarians of Color in Dallas, Texas, in October 2006 and was present at the awards ceremony where the speaker made the call to all librarians.
21. Alma C. Ortega was recruited by a Catholic librarian, while Marisol Ramos was recruited by a Northern Irish archives professor to the field of information studies.

References

Bordes, Veronica and Patricia Arredondo. "Mentoring and 1st-Year Latina/o College Students." *Journal of Hispanic Higher Education* 4, no. 2 (April 1, 2005): 114–133.

Brezosky, Lynn. "Cataloging a librarian shortage / Border communities find it hard to compete with corporations for expertise." *Houston Chronicle*. August 19. Section B, Page 3, 2 STAR Edition, 2007.

Chapa, Jorge and Belinda De La Rosa. "The Problematic Pipeline." *Journal of Hispanic Higher Education* 5, no. 3 (July 1, 2006): 203–221.

Dewey, Barbara and Jillian Keally. "Recruiting for Diversity: Strategies for Twenty-First Century Research Librarianship." *Library Hi Tech* 26, no. 4 (2008): 622.

Echavarria, Tami. "Recruiting Latinos to Librarianship." In *Latino Librarianship: A Handbook for Professionals*, edited by Salvador Güereña, 18–27. Jefferson, NJ: McFarland & Co., 1990.

Espinal, Isabel. "Wanted: Latino Librarians; Bilingual Latino Librarians are Few and Far between, a Reality that Turns Away Patrons and Bodes Ill for the Spanish-Language Book Market." *Críticas* (September 1, 2003): 19.

Grady, Jenifer Lyn. "Minority Recruitment in Schools of Information and Library Science: The Methods Used and the Reasons Students Choose Particular Schools." MLS, University of North Carolina at Chapel Hill, 1993.

Grob, Julie. "RBMS, Special Collections, and the Challenge of Diversity: The Road to the Diversity Action Plan." *RBMS: A Journal of Rare Books, Manuscripts, and Cultural Heritage* 4, no. 2 (Fall 2003): 74–107, accessed February 21, 2011, http://rbm.acrl.org/content/4/2/74.full.pdf

Güereña, Salvador, ed. *Latino Librarianship: A Handbook for Professionals*. Jefferson, NC: McFarland & Co., 1990.

Kim, Kyung-Sun. "Recruiting and Retaining Students of Color for LIS Schools: Perspectives from Librarians of Color (Preliminary Report)." Kyung-Sun Kim: Diversity Research. 2007, accessed February 21, 2011, http://slisweb.lis.wisc.edu/%7Ekskim/diversity_preliminary_findings.html

Kim, Kyung-Sun and Sei-Ching Joanna Sin. "Recruiting and Retaining Students of Color in LIS Programs: Perspectives of Library and Information Professionals." *Journal of Education for Library and Information Science* 47, no. 2 (Spring, 2006): 81–95.

Love, E. "Generation Next: Recruiting Minority Students to Librarianship." *Reference Services Review* 38, no. 3 (2010): 482–492.

Lutz, Amy. "Barriers to High-School Completion among Immigrant and Later-Generation Latinos in the USA: Language, Ethnicity and Socioeconomic Status." *Ethnicities* 7, no. 3 (September 1, 2007): 323–342.

Portes, Alejandro and Richard Schauffler. "Language and the Second Generation: Bilingualism Yesterday and Today." *International Migration Review* 28, no. 4, Special Issue: The New Second Generation (Winter, 1994): 640–661.

Reese, Gregory L. and Ernestine L. Hawkins. *Stop Talking, Start Doing!: Attracting People of Color to the Library Profession*. Chicago: American Library Association, 1999.

Santos, Silvia J. and Elena T. Reigadas. "Latinos in Higher Education: An Evaluation of a University Faculty Mentoring Program." *Journal of Hispanic Higher Education* 1, no. 1 (January 1, 2002): 40–50.

Suro, Roberto and Jeffrey S. Passel. *The Rise of the Second Generation: Changing Patterns in Hispanic Population Growth*. Washington, DC: Pew Hispanic Center Study, 2003.

Valverde, Michelle R. and Roy C. Rodriguez. "Increasing Mexican American Doctoral Degrees: The Role of Institutions of Higher Education." *Journal of Hispanic Higher Education* 1, no. 1 (January 2002): 51–58.

Veltman, Calvin J. "The Status of the Spanish Language in the United States at the Beginning of the 21st Century." *IMR: International Migration Review* 24, no. 1 (Spring, 1990): 108–123.

Wallace, Danny P. and Jefrey Naidoo, eds. *ALISE: Library and Information Science Education Statistical Report 2009*. Chicago: Association for Library and Information Science Education, 2010.

Winston, Mark D. and Kimberly Walstad. "Recruitment and Diversity: A Research Study of Bilingualism and Library Services." *Library & Information Science Research* 28, no. 3 (2006): 390–406.

Chapter 9

Leadership in Libraries: Latino Leadership in Libraries

Luis Herrera

The role of libraries is evolving, due in part to the changing demographic landscape of America and the global technology revolution. Libraries are seeking to remain relevant and to foster a sense of place and community. Librarians are seeking better approaches to support education and to empower users through information services and technology. Libraries are also challenged to attract the generations of youth that are redefining social networking and information-seeking behaviors. In an educational setting, the school or college library can play a critical role in the success of students if librarians participate fully as academic partners in this goal. For libraries to thrive through rapid societal change, bold and visionary leadership will be needed to lead change and to sustain this vision of libraries. In particular, the constant demographic change has given rise to multicultural communities where this new leadership is essential, and because the most significant demographic changes in the United States is the growth in Latino- and Spanish-speaking populations. Latinos can make a difference in helping create a new vision for libraries. They can demonstrate leadership at all levels and aspects of the library. Latinos can provide expertise in direct service design and delivery, through language and cultural competencies, and in unique leadership skills that bring an added value to librarianship.

A Legacy of Leaders

In ALA's *Diversity Counts* report, the number of Latino librarians is placed at 2,200 or roughly 2 percent of the total (American Library Association Office of Research and Statistics, 2007). While the sheer number has grown over the last two decades, the percentage has not increased relative to the growth in the Latino population in the United States. On the positive side, Latino librarians have contributed significantly to American librarianship in the last quarter century, due in part to trailblazers who championed the cause of services to the Spanish speaking. Today, we can boast Latino leadership on the executive board of the American Library Association: a Latina who headed it as its executive director and two Latinos who served as presidents of ALA divisions. Other Latinos served and continue to hold prominent positions as directors of major public libraries as well as deans at university libraries. Numerous Latinos have also been elected to the governing board of the ALA. In 2010, the first Latina to serve as president of ALA ushered an even greater sense of change, accomplishment, and contribution. This is a departure from the 1960s through the 1980s, when few Latinos held positions of influence and power. Advocacy for basic aspects of services to the Spanish speaking such as Spanish language collection development, outreach services, and recruitment of bilingual/bicultural librarians were ongoing political struggles. Several Latino leaders whose vision created hope and shaped the future led this change.

One of the most influential librarians who helped usher the era of services to Latinos was Arnulfo D. Trejo, professor emeritus at the University of Arizona Graduate School of Library Science (now School of Information Resources and Library Science).

He championed the need for more bilingual bicultural librarians and founded REFORMA. Founded in Dallas in 1971, REFORMA continues to evolve and thrive as the leading advocacy association for services to Latinos through a legislative agenda, recruitment strategies, and scholarship opportunities. Trejo went on to establish the Graduate Library Institute for Spanish Speaking Americans (GLISA), which produced the single largest number of bilingual/bicultural librarians during the 1970s and '80s. Trejo encouraged social change through libraries and librarian activists and will long be remembered as a pioneer, change agent, and charismatic leader. As Sal Guereña, another GLISA graduate and former student wrote: "Of all the people who have contributed to Hispanic librarianship in this country, there is probably no one who has made a greater impact on advancing this cause than Dr. Arnulfo D. Trejo. He was . . . a visionary, but most importantly, a man who put his words into action con todo el corazón" (Yamashita, 2002). One of the key ideas that Trejo espoused was the importance of completing the "circle of commitment" by helping others after receiving help. In an interview with his wife, Ninfa Trejo, she noted that his vision was the gift of looking into the future for possibilities but also having a keen sense of people's potential and recognizing who could carry his vision of libraries into the future. His leadership strength also lay in understanding his limitations and successes, yet never resting on his laurel but always looking into the next project or venture (Trejo, 2008). Trejo lived by this lesson, and in 2001, ALA recognized his lasting contribution to libraries and librarianship by awarding him an honorary membership.

Another trailblazer during the formative stages of Latino Librarianship was Elizabeth Martinez. Elizabeth began her career at the County of Los Angeles Public Library (LAPL) and served as regional administrator. She went on to serve as director of the Orange County Public Library (OCPL) and the Los Angeles Public Library. After her tenure at LAPL, Martinez was appointed as executive director of the American Library Association. In her capacity as CEO of the world's largest library association, she spearheaded ALA 2000, one of the most significant change initiatives undertaken by the ALA. To Martinez, the challenges were exciting and significant. She defines her career as one of activism librarianship. "I became the leader of efforts of librarians to serve the Chicano community—grant projects, recruitment of librarians, collections, and programs—the voice" (Martinez, 2007). Martinez also exudes confidence in defining and understanding her role as a leader and target. In this regard, she recognized that to succeed she needed to be the "best possible at my work so that I could not be marginalized by technicalities." These leadership traits—activism and passion, confidence and competencies were essential in developing her leadership acumen. Most recently, Martinez has come full circle and returned to lead the Salinas Public Library.

Cesar Caballero, dean of libraries at California State University, San Bernardino (CSUSB) also helped transform Latino librarianship through his advocacy and leadership. He was instrumental in leading a movement that changed the power structure of the El Paso Public Library board in the 1970s at a time when no Hispanics served on the board and when the need for services to a significant segment of the population was met with indifference.

He was the first Latino elected to the library's governing board, which ultimately led to a more inclusive and responsive system. Caballero was also the first Latino elected to the executive board of the American Library Association. According to Caballero, the major obstacle that the limited number of Latinos leaders faced during that time was a conservative and entrenched status quo that was reluctant or unwilling to accept change. Caballero goes on to say that Latinos lacked experience and knowledge in dealing with the established systems. Other barriers noted were institutional racism, personal struggles, and family and other Latinos who did not fully understand or support what they were trying to accomplish. Caballero emphasizes the need for Latinos to establish a path of leadership through vision that he describes as a trajectory of knowing where you are going and what you want to be (Caballero, 2008).

Leading through Cultural Competencies

The values, culture, and history that define the Latino experience bring a unique set of attributes to library organizations. Staffs that possess Spanish language skills enhance the ability to communicate effectively and solicit input on specific information needs. Cultural awareness and sensitivity positively impacts policies that eliminate barriers to service. This expertise creates a cultural bridge that produces relevant programs and services and allows librarians to evaluate the impact of programs and services more effectively because of the ability to relate to community needs and expectations. This bridge may also extend to other communities of color that have similar information needs. Cultural competencies allow for a more open and receptive partnership with service providers because of the connection to language and cultural values. This trust is an important element in developing an ongoing relationship with the community served. It provides an advantage for community building and partnerships with social service agencies and community-based organizations that share a similar mission to enhance services and opportunities for the Latino community. Language skills and cultural awareness provide libraries with a competitive edge in designing programs and services to effectively reach out to Latino communities. Cultural competencies also extend to skills in collection development by understanding information needs, reading interests, and how to connect Latinos to reading. Spanish language ability and cultural awareness is an added dimension to effective marketing and promotion of library services and in designing and implementing effective outreach strategies. Whether providing direct service to children and families such as bilingual story time or literacy, presenting programs in Spanish, or selecting relevant books and databases that meet the needs of Latino users, Latinos can exert expertise and understanding of their community. In libraries, these skills allow us to empathize with a constituency that is often not effectively served by libraries. Latino leaders have an opportunity, if not responsibility, to articulate the Latino perspective in designing services that respond to their needs.

The Challenges of Leading: Image, Identity, and Culture

In her article *Diversity and Leadership: The Color of Leadership*, Camila Alire identifies a list of leadership qualities, traits, and skills compiled from experience, discussions, and observations of library leaders of color and other leaders (Alire, 2001). I modified the list to a total of 28 leadership skills to include the following:

adaptable, advocate, ambitious, change agent, creative, collaborator, communicator, courageous, decisive, delegator, flexible, humanistic, humorous, innovator, inspirational, mentor, motivator, networker, optimist, political, respectful, risk taker, role model, self-confident, team builder, tolerant, trustworthy, visionary

A select list of Latino librarians were invited to respond to the following leadership questions:

1. From the leadership skills listed, select seven that you possess.
2. Of those seven leadership skills possessed, please specify your top three.
3. Of your seven skills selected, do you attribute any of these traits, skills, and qualities to your ethnic/cultural background?
4. In your experience and career in libraries, list the top three to four challenges you faced as a Latino/Latina leader.
5. From the list below, check five areas of skills-building advice that you would give to future Latino/Latina librarians aspiring to be leaders in their respective library organizations? (Skills-building list: communication skills, change management, building networks, persuasive skills, mentoring, political acumen, Spanish language skills, cultural competencies, conflict management, management, supervisor skills).
6. Any additional comments or observations on Latino leadership?

The respondents ranged from library directors to librarians with varied experience and involvement in leadership positions either in their respective libraries or as association leaders. When asked to list the most significant challenges facing Latino librarians, their responses centered on image, identity, and culture. These concepts determine how Latinos are viewed and accepted within the library organization and have a significant impact on self-worth, confidence, and success. Latino respondents noted that library organizations had limited awareness of Latino culture. As a result, certain assumptions and stereotypes about the role of Latino librarians often give way to unrealistic expectations. Respondents noted that they are often pegged as resident experts on all things Latino, and assumptions are made about their ability to speak Spanish fluently.

They become the go to person on far-ranging aspects of Latino culture, but misconceptions lead to generalizations and false expectations. Latino librarians are often tapped for duties and responsibilities solely because of these assumptions. The danger lies in that Latino librarians are often seen as one dimensional instead of allowing for opportunities to demonstrate skills and talent in a variety of areas. This has the potential to marginalize Latinos in library organizations and stunt career opportunities and mobility. Latino librarians shared a sense of frustration in feeling trapped and typecast to duties related to their ethnicity and not their expertise. Another pattern that emerged from respondents was organizational indifference, isolation, and lack of cultural awareness. Latinos bemoan the feeling of isolation in library organizations where they may be the only Latino or Latina. As Latinos, we bring our identity to the job, and both legitimization and a sense of belonging is important to our self-worth. Latino librarians often feel added pressure to prove their worth and competence. Having to prove oneself or believing that they were hired because of their ethnic identity and not their ability may stifle potential and growth. Respondents cited internal politics and service equity as legitimate concerns; and while overt racism was not cited by respondents, the lack of acceptance and cultural insensitivity translated to perceived institutional racism.

Because of the cultural disconnect, Latino librarians often find a disconnect with the larger organizational culture. In organization dynamics, groups may devalue someone by ignoring him or rendering him invisible. This is a form of marginalization that diminishes confidence and self-worth (Heifetz, 2002). Labels and assumptions, limited expectations, and lack of cultural awareness inhibit professional growth and leadership development. The end result is a failure to capture additional potential and contribution to the organization. A forward-thinking library organization will create a culture of engagement and allow for other voices within the organization to validate other cultures and perspectives and create a responsive and community-centric library.

Dimensions of Leadership

Is there such a thing as Latino leadership? Do Latinos possess values that make for unique leadership traits? If so, how do we define this leadership style, and what are the implications for Latino leadership in libraries? Sixty percent of respondents to the survey believe that Latinos bring a different set of values and characteristics to leadership. Participants in the survey were asked to select 7 skills they possessed from the list of 28. The results of the survey revealed common characteristics among the respondents. The top seven characteristics possessed by Latinos leaders were (1) advocacy, (2) collaboration, (3) communication, (4) humanism, (5) risk taking, (6) respect, and (7) team building. These seven leadership characteristics were clustered into three dimensions that further define Latino library leaders as *collaborators, communicators, and culture keepers.*

Latinos as Collaborators

Latinos place a high value on collaboration and working together toward a common goal. They function well in group settings where the strengths and talents of the individual contribute to collective decision making and problem solving. Group benefit and collective success is important. The team approach implies that leaders must possess skills to facilitate group dynamics, delegate effectively, and understand project management. Leaders articulate the goals and vision for the team and pursue results by recognizing and building on individual team member strengths to produce results. Networking is another significant strength for Latino leaders, and while networking is also important in mainstream culture, Latino networking implies a more informal approach than the traditional professional networks. For Latinos, networks are less structured, based on the oral tradition where informal conversations, friendships, and loyalty play a key role in relationship building. These relationships are long lasting, extend beyond career, and evolve into lifelong friendships. The reliance on networks has positive implications for work in libraries. Latinos draw on these networks for resource sharing, political support, and recognition of the talents and strengths of individual members of their network. Developing a network is paramount to success. As mentioned previously, most Latino networks are informal—family, friends, and colleagues. These networks provide an important resource for career support such as mentoring, help in navigating institutions, and identifying other resources. REFORMA is an example of an organization that provides both the formal and informal network structures critical for success. Since its inception more than 30 years ago, REFORMA has served as a training ground for future Latino leaders. Through involvement in committees, fellowship through celebrations, and a sharing of a common vision to improve services to the Spanish-speaking community, REFORMA has provided a platform for leadership development. For more information, contact REFORMA's website at reforma.org.

Latinos as Communicators

The notion of Latino leaders as communicators emphasizes three key characteristics: advocacy, interaction, and activism. Advocacy in Latino librarianship emphasizes a service model that demonstrates a close connection to issues that affect the Latino community. Dynamic library leaders promote a vision of libraries as places of engagement and empowerment. Librarian activists see the library as a leading government institution that can impact all aspects of Latino empowerment—politics, economics, power, and opportunity. In this sense, library services are defined in a broader community context where a high value is placed on relevant issues such as reading and literacy, language development, and information access. High importance is placed on promoting services through community outreach and interaction with service providers. In this role, libraries serve as information clearinghouses on vital public policy issues such as immigration, health, education, housing, and employment. Latinos see libraries as gateways for immigrants, a strong value on culture, language and diversity, and a direct connection with educational opportunities.

Thus, promoting the resources that libraries have to offer as tools for engagement and empowerment becomes a passionate commitment for the Latino library leader. Latino leaders will need to forge stronger alliances with political stakeholders such as elected officials, educators, business, and non profits to convey how libraries can help address the myriad of needs in the Latino community. To advocate effectively, Latino leaders will need to better articulate how libraries change lives and help build stronger communities.

Latinos as Culture Keepers

One of the more interesting and unifying dimensions of Latino leaders is their pride in culture. Cultural identity through history, language, music, dance, and food forges a unifying bond that defines the Latino experience. This experience brings an added dimension and aptitude set to our leadership styles. The notion of culture keeper represents three dimensions for leadership—documenting history, creating cultural relevance, and nurturing our core values. The Latino experience affords the ability to navigate in a multicultural world. Latino leadership represents an opportunity to apply these cultural values to make libraries relevant. Libraries have failed in their core mission of validating and documenting histories of people of color. The perspectives, visions, and aspirations of diverse people are often missing in collections and archives of libraries. Latino librarians have the responsibility and opportunity to document, preserve, and promote the history and culture of the Latino/American experience. But this can happen only if greater emphasis is placed to train bilingual/bicultural librarians to develop expertise as archivist and preservationists. Creating cultural relevance also means that libraries must represent and reflect the Latino experience through collections, programs, and exhibits. To accomplish this, leadership will require a greater commitment to enhanced support staffing, funding, and resources to make libraries relevant to Latinos. Library organizations can also benefit from core values inherent in Latino culture. Based on the responses from Latino leaders, these values include trust, respect, and humanism. Moreover, the high value placed on the concept of family, relationships, and a focus on people add a significant leadership dimension. Latino values bring a humanistic approach to the organizational culture that is essential to healthy and productive work environments. Leaders will need to seek full engagement from staff and community in program development and a collaborative approach to service delivery, collection development, and outreach.

A Philosophy of Latino Leadership

As collaborators, communicators, and culture keepers, Latinos are in a position to lead library organizations in a unique and different way. Our cultural experiences and values create a philosophy of leadership that can be defined as communal, personal, and purposeful. Latino leadership in libraries extends beyond self through a journey of discovery defined by passion and vision.

Leadership Beyond Self—Latino leadership can be defined as collective leadership. It extends beyond the individual and focuses on group success. Success is not self-centered but rather relies on teamwork, collaboration, and relationships.

The extended network of friends, colleagues, family, and community confer leadership rather than the individual assuming leader status. A *We* instead of an *I* mindset is the cornerstone of leadership. In defining leadership for a multicultural age, Juan Bordas describes the concept of We as an important value in the tribe, community, and familia. It is a "collectivist orientation that centers on the common good rather than the individual" (Bordas, 2007). The collectivism philosophy places attention on group welfare, unity, and harmony. In library organizations, this implies that leaders are sensitive to what others want, think, and need and puts a premium on two values that Latinos deem significant—humanism and respect.

The concept of family is also a widely held value in Latino culture, and values associated with the family such as respect, sharing, and nurturing are imbued in the Latino way of life. These character traits are taught and are carried into the work setting to provide close working relationships and an understanding of group dynamics and teamwork. The family values transfer as an asset in working with diverse age, cultural, and linguistic groups. This leadership model is also community centric. Community is seen as an extended family—services need to be family centric and community based. Shared power and collective decision making is rooted in a strong commitment to the concept of family. In organizational culture, this shared leadership model has the potential for collective ownership of decisions, a voice in the design of services, and an expectation that the services will benefit the community. A connection to community through a legacy of service is also inherent in leadership beyond self, and giving back to family and community is deemed a social responsibility. This strong commitment to service and community mirrors Greenleaf's philosophy of servant leadership that embraces the notion of giving back and core values of social responsibility, equity, justice, and moral responsibility (Lawrence, 2004). Similarly, Bordas discusses the importance of respect as *personalismo* or the ability to engender respect from others because of your reputation and character. Earned respect is thus a powerful concept in Latino leadership as it is earned and conferred through garnering credibility and trust. A blending of both the individual identity that is part of the American culture and collective leadership is essential in order to thrive in a changing library environment.

Leadership as a Journey—Latino leadership evolves through experience, self-awareness, and self-development. Leadership is collective wisdom acquired over time. In the formative years, Latino leadership requires a deliberate approach to career development that emphasizes core values and competencies gained through experience and practice. This evolution in leadership also involves a journey in self awareness through a commitment to lifelong learning. Our education extends beyond library school, and personal growth involves seeking a deeper meaning of our role and contribution to community. As such, the Latino cultural identity becomes a significant aspect of our work and service philosophy. Latino values and seeking to put them to practice are key to Latino leadership. Leadership is rooted in a service philosophy centered on community and a balance between individual achievement and collective success. Royatzis describes three key elements of a resonant leader—mindfulness, hope, and compassion (McKee, 2005). These are important concepts for Latino leaders as they embrace characteristics of Latino values.

The journey involves an awareness of one's past and history as a people. Historical perspectives help Latinos understand the present and create a stronger future. It helps validate our values and gain understanding of the barriers and obstacles that have confronted Latinos and other people of color. Perhaps this understanding helps form the basis for an appreciation of libraries as institutions that symbolize equity and access.

Latino leaders thus share a core philosophical framework as champions of the underdog with an obligation to represent the views of those who may be disenfranchised. The journey also helps refine core values and their meaning and application in our work mission. These values also establish an ethical framework where respect, integrity and honesty, and personal relationship are at the heart of our work and family life. The journey nurtures confidence in leadership and comes full circle when our personal growth leads to a sense of purpose and service to community.

Leadership with Passion and Purpose—Our Latino culture and experience evoke passion, emotion, and conviction. These traits translate to a style of leadership where the heart and soul are at the core of how we lead. But having "corazon" begins with a sense of purpose and vision. Defining your vision means having a clear understanding of what you want to accomplish and how you can influence the service mission of the library. Clarity of vision means that you find where your passion lies and what gives meaning to your work. It answers the question of how you can make a difference, how you can impact change, and how you can put into practice the core values you espouse. The underpinning of your vision and purpose rests on having a strong cultural identity. Latinos can combine cultural identity, passion, and expertise to derive an added dimension of leadership and puts into practice the values that define who we are as a people. A strong spirit, soul, and passion are at the heart of Latino leadership. The self-awareness requires gaining and identifying your strengths, finding your passion, and having a balance of work and home life. Leaders love to lead, but they must have the passion and commitment to know where they want to go. Leadership development derives from the evolution of our personal goals, values, and abilities.

Preparing to Lead

Leaders evolve. Through experience, emerging leaders can gain confidence and strong leadership skills that will serve them through the duration of their career. This formative skill development phase should parallel a journey of self-awareness and a progression of professional development. The changing model of leadership calls for collective leadership instead of the old view of the central authority figure. This new model provides an opportunity for Latinos to excel in leadership roles. Shared power, engagement and ownership of issues, and a collective approach to problem solving will offer Latinos opportunities where skills are natural. As the next generation of Latinos enter the profession, it will be important to think strategically about career paths that develop a diverse skills and knowledge portfolio. It begins by establishing a strong foundation in librarianship—that is, the basic tenets and principles that will establish a philosophical and technical framework to last throughout a career. Thus, cultural, communication, managerial, and network skills will provide a diverse leadership portfolio for Latinos to develop.

Cultural competencies provide Latino librarians with a competitive edge. These added skills include Spanish language ability, expertise in culturally relevant collection development, community partnering skills, and knowledge in planning and evaluating culturally relevant services and programs. Skill building in archival preservation, culturally relevant historical collection development, also offers opportunities for Latino leadership in libraries.

Management competencies call for expertise in planning and evaluation, organizational development, change management, team building, and group dynamics. Additionally, excellent communication skills, including ones in public relations and marketing can enhance opportunities for effective leadership. These skills facilitate community engagement and active participation in community life.

Networking acumen means active participation in professional development and activism in associations that develop leadership capabilities. REFORMA and other ethnic caucuses provide excellent venues for collaboration and addressing issues impacting librarians of color. These leadership skills also extend to gaining skills in community organizing and promote your identity by being active in civic and organizational life.

Advocacy and communication are essential leadership development skills necessary to thrive in 21st century librarianship. Foremost is political advocacy that will be crucial in telling a compelling story of the importance of libraries for the Latino community. Strength in people skills to develop political partners and connections and the ability to create a network of people and resources are vital leadership qualities. Library organizations that will thrive in the next decades are those that will embrace change and integrate services that are relevant to communities of color. Dynamic libraries support new styles of leadership, empower leadership at all levels of the organization, and challenge long-standing assumptions of traditional librarianship. Leadership development initiatives that focus on Latino values such as humanism and collaboration,

Latino leadership in libraries is poised to have greater impact in the future. Demographic change, globalization, and shifts in political power make an imperative case for Latinos to play a leading role in ushering an era of change and relevance for libraries of the future. In providing words of advice to future leaders, Elizabeth Martinez offered the following insight: "be brave, and follow the path paved by our ancestors to respect life."

References

Alire, Camila A. "Diversity and Leadership: The Color of Leadership." *Journal of Library Administration*, 2001: 95–109.

American Library Association Office of Research and Statistics. *Diversity Counts*. Chicago: American Library Association, January 2007.

Bordas, Juana. *Salsa, Soul and Spirit: Leadership for a Multicultural Age*. San Francisco: Berrett-Koehler Publishers, Inc., 2007.

Caballero, Cesar, interview by Luis Herrera (April 24, 2008).

Heifetz, Martin Linsky and A. Ronald *Leadership on the Line: Staying Alive Through the Dangers of Leading*. Boston: Harvard Business School Publishing, 2002.

Lawrence, Larry C. and Michele Spears. *Practicing Servant-Leadership: Succeeding Through Trust, Bravery, and Forgiveness*. San Francisco: Jossey-Bass, 2004.

Martinez, Elizabeth, interview by Luis Herrera (November 5, 2007).

McKee, Richard and Annie Boyatzis. *Resonant Leadership: Renewing Yourself and Connecting with Others Through Mindfulness, Hope and Compassion*. Boston: Harvard Business School, 2005.

Trejo, Ninfa, interview by Luis Herrera (May 31, 2008).

Yamashita, Brianna. "Criticas." *Arnulfo D. Trejo, Founder of REFORMA Dies*, September/October 2002: p. 7.

Chapter 10

Digital Resources: Developing Chicano/a Latino/a Digital Resources

Alexander Hauschild

As we examine Chicano/a Latino/a digital resources available today, we can only be proud of how far we have come. The historical significance of the materials available, the visual impact, the intellectual value, and the easy accessibility are impressive. The number of users accessing our materials dwarfs the traffic we have experienced in the past. Among popular culture, Chicano/Latino ideas have permeated the society. Many ideas have become mainstream, as was the case in Robert Rodriguez's recent film *Machete*, featuring a plot riddled with familiar Chicano themes. The Pew Hispanic Center reports that two-thirds of Latino (65%) and black (66%) adults went online in 2010, while more than three-fourths (77%) of white adults did so (Fox & Livingston, 2009). According to projections of the *eMarketer*, which has been cited consistently for its insight into the habits of the Hispanic population online, there were 18.8 million Hispanic Internet users in the United States in 2007, and the number of users was expected to reach 20.9 million in 2010. Instead, Hispanic users online outpaced the growth of total U.S. Internet users by 50 percent. *eMarketer* has since revised its initial estimates to 24.4 million Hispanic Internet users in the United States by 2011, or 11.6 percent of the total U.S. user base (Williamson, 2010).

Having moved beyond the minimum necessity of making people aware of the history through our resources, we are beginning to understand that unique materials carry their own imperative. They must be digitally disseminated if they are to thrive in the digital information age. Indeed, without digital dissemination, these materials may cease to exist in an intellectual sense. Once we take it for granted that materials must be digitized, and that the most important and significant discoveries within the materials can be made through easy query, we have to ask ourselves: how do we guide users to discoveries that they don't even know they want?

Interpretation of Online Cultural Heritage Materials

The digital information age represented a turning point in how we disseminate information but also how that information is interpreted when interacting with it. Digital dissemination affects how scholarly material is redistributed and synthesized by its users according to *their* needs, habits, and expectations: not ours. As we master the methods for digitizing and disseminating our resources, we have learned that the technical and pragmatic methodology for developing Chicano/a Latino/a digital resources is not inconsistent with the best methods and standards applied to digital development of other cultural heritage material. Proper metadata, descriptive terminology, and accurate digital image preservation are mandatory for all digital resources. These standards have all been laid down in guides such as *The NINCH guide to good practice in the digital representation and management of cultural heritage materials*, but Chicano/a Latino/a digital resources differ from other types of resources. Their method of creation carried an implied directive because they were generated from a particular philosophy. If we accept and embrace this philosophy, developing Chicano/a Latino/a resources can't be an ivory tower procedure. It can't be done in isolation, aloof and disconnected from the world it attempts to reveal. The process of developing Chicano/a Latino/a resources should involve us in the interweaving cultural and social movements: movements rooted in activism.

The structure of an online collection should reflect the methods that this particular community of people used to grow their movement. In a sense, since the creators of the collections used liberation methodology to enrich, enliven, and validate their own historical significance, we need to reflect this process in our collections. If we want to guide users through the learning experience in an organic way, we begin by being cognizant of how digital materials are sometimes confused and amalgamated remotely by the user. Chicano/Latino users access materials differently than average users. They access music and online culture more often than average users. Consumer research firm Scarborough Research finds that Hispanic users are 21 percent more likely to download digital content then the average user (Scarborough, 2008). Downloadable content most often includes music video and images. Knowing this, we can begin to design more heavy multimedia resources. The continual and ever-present preoccupation with what the user will want, what that user thinks he wants, what the user doesn't know he wants, what the user can actually use, and how that information will be interpreted dictates our design.

Again, because of our position as advocates for the materials and our understanding of the user community's needs, habits, predilections, and experience, librarians and archivists are uniquely qualified to develop a unified strategy for the advancement of Chicano/a Latino/a digital resources. We are capable of providing much more than accurate search and retrieval systems. We can actively research and relate digital resources outside of our local holdings so that we can connect the dots for users in a credible, intellectually superior way. We cannot wait and hope that a user's search will discover our intricately tagged material and will then magically understand its relationship to the larger Chicano/Latino experience. We have to do it for them: we have to retake our role as leaders and guide them.

Digitizing Chicano cultural heritage materials causes a collective reexperiencing of artifacts, many of which have not seen the light of day since their creation. Because we live in a time when the Chicano/a Latino/a identity—the collective cultural self-understanding—is constantly under assault, this reexperiencing needs to be guided and protected by experts. The forces of external prejudice, internal cultural "gentrification," and mass-market redefinition all create pressures that distort and blur the lived reality of the Chicano/a Latino/a experience. These competing pressures create their own intrinsic counterimperative for the collection developer. This imperative dictates the creation of an information system that provides fair and equal access to this information, while resisting the corrosive influence of players who would diminish the Chicano/a Latino/a experience. The balance struck between these competing and unique variables is a never-ending obstacle course, but as with all digital resource development, as long as we focus on the user's perspective, we can predict his or her interpretation.

The solution seems simple; we must expand our authority within our resources. We have to take more proactive control of how users discover links and narratives inside the collections. We must provide them with guided educational leadership, through intuitive and often invisible flow built into our interfaces. In addition, and this is critical, we must provide obvious and constant pointers to related and interlinked collection resources, especially when they exist outside of our depository. But this solution requires us to do much more then collect, archive, list, and disseminate. We have to become agents of change, designing curriculum specific to the materials, providing scholarship that informs and influences future scholarship and so on.

This added value closes the loop between users and educators, expanding the interest in scholarship, and creating new networks of users and resource providers. This broadening of the basic function of accessibility and online distribution opens the door to a more interactive community. In the past, this kind of "hands on" approach to digital scholarship was sometimes avoided. Collection developers considered it a secondary and superlative responsibility and most often were unaware how to proceed. Even our largest repositories neglected opportunities to tie into external resources. For example, the Library of Congress's Hispano Music and Culture section contains The Juan B. Rael Collection. Within this collection, they provide the following links to related collections and exhibits: Buckaroos in Paradise, 1945–1982; California Gold: Folk Music from the Thirties, Historic American Sheet Music, 1850–1920; The South Texas Border, 1900–1920; Voices from the Dust Bowl, 1940–1941; a glossary of Spanish terms; a map of the region; and some ethnography. However, each of these related resources exists within the Library of Congress. If the collection developers had taken it upon themselves to kick-start researchers and the time to find related materials outside of the Library of Congress, they would have opened up their users to the multitude of Chicano Latino resources. And if those external resource providers had paid attention to the same principle of interlinking communities, guiding users to other resources outside of their repository, they would have established the nodes of a vast and growing network of online Chicano Latino context. This idea of establishing nodes of access is important in and of itself, but in the case of Chicano Latino collections, we would have simulated the methodology of the original Chicano Latino communities by interlinking proactive scholarly advocates.

Who better than librarians and archivists to guide the user to specific discoveries? Librarians, archivists, and collection developers have unique skills and knowledge sets that make them the most obvious advocates for user discovery. In an era when your phone will suggest which word you actually meant to spell, why do we as collection holders hesitate to suggest which resources a user might want to find? A more proactive stance about modifying and guiding user queries unquestionably adds to the quality of research. Now that we have a better picture of how online collections thrive amidst the noise of misinformation, if we relax our role as gatekeepers of information and pursue our role as leaders, we create what can be called "value-added research reference."

Value-Added Research Reference

What is a digital library? Even a full 15 years into what can be rightfully called the digital information age, we tend to define the digital library according to what we need it to do rather than its subject materials. In the online *Report of the Santa Fe Planning Workshop on Distributed Knowledge Work Environments: Digital Libraries*, Paul Duguid defined the digital library as "an environment to bring together collections, services, and people in support of the full life cycle of creation, dissemination, use, and preservation of data, information and knowledge" (Duguid & Atkins, 1997). The same expansive collective definition can be applied to the development of Chicano/a Latino/a digital resources *wherever* they are created. Not just our local resources for which we have received a mandate to distribute. But what if we changed our definition? What if we focused less on the function of digital libraries, took for granted that the digital environment is the environment that information exists within, and focused instead on relating our materials to the contexts that make them important in the first place?

As developers, we should emphasize the idea that our collections are part of a universe of ideas, scholarship, and theory. It is the entire environment, or what we would call the scope of online digital resources, that defines the evolving "meta" library of Chicano/a Latino/a resources. It is the relationship of materials to other materials that defines their value. Developing Chicano/a Latino/a digital resources necessitates envisioning local resources as part of a larger contextualized network of resources, *as if each collection is but a single node in the net.* While it is equally imperative that we publish our local institution's unique information to the digital arena as quickly as possible, it is not enough for us to disseminate the contents as if they are valuable in isolation. We must make active networking, with external digital resources, an integral part of the development process. If we do not do this, we lose the opportunity to link the community of scholars and users into the modern arena of social communication.

For Chicano/a Latino/a subjects, the philosophical rationale behind this imperative is obvious. Latino/a Chicano/a history, cultural heritage, and scholarship derive from a social movement. Because of this origin point, they cannot be isolated from their inspiration, from other elements of the movement from which they were derived. They cannot be separated from the ideal, from *la gente*. Within the Chicano/Latino movement, there is a simple concept. If you do not understand where you are from, you cannot know where you are going. The same concept drives Chicano/Latino digital content development. If the user does not understand where they (the materials and artists) come from, they cannot understand why they are important. Every developed resource constitutes but a single brick in the larger cultural heritage digital library that evolves when other resources are linked to their related resources by the developers.

To further elaborate, when faced with the challenge of presenting Chicano/a Latino/a materials to users, the digital collection developer faces the same challenges that art gallery and museum curators have faced when presenting Chicano/a Latino/a art in a decontextualized setting. Placing Chicano/a Latino/a art in an art museum or gallery as an artistic movement devoid of political or social activism deprives the viewer of crucial context. Alicia Gaspar de Alba (1997) when writing about the CARA exhibition, maintained that the principal issue at the heart of the conflicts that CARA encountered and engendered in the mainstream art world was the insider/outsider polemic, or the decontextualizing of works from their native source, the general public. Distribution of Chicano/a Latino/a resources through digital means runs the similar risk of devaluing the materials by removing them from the context of the social movement that they are a part of. Throughout the process of dissemination, from access to description, we run the risk of ignoring a primary tenet of the Chicano/a Latino/a experience in general: the communication of ideas to the original user community as a *whole*. Because the artists, authors, musicians, and filmmakers of the Chicano Latino community are and were dedicated to reaching a mass audience through mainstream methods, we must honor that process. In the words of Charles Almaraz, "Let us make an art that is not for ourselves, not for museums, not for posterity, and certainly not for art's sake, but for mankind" (Goldman, 1984, p. 84).

It is in our best interest to learn more about the people and organizations that use our digital collections, but it is not enough for individual institutions and collection managers to learn about their own subject-specific audiences. For instance, a collection of Chicano/a Latino/a resource material focusing on or including prominently the Mexican immigrant experience is not complete if it does not also cite resources on both the Cuban American and the Guatemalan immigrant's experience. In the same vein, we have to ask ourselves: is any contemporary Chicano/a Latino/a digital resource featuring topics of immigration complete if it excludes reference links to the Homeland Security Digital Library site?

As developers of Chicano/a Latino/a digital resources, we will expend significant effort on the creation of metadata, trying to provide accurate retrieval to our users in specific subject matter. By creating these descriptive tags and pointers, it is our hope that we will help to guide our users to the retrievals they need. But how much effort will we expend to guide users *away* from our own resources to external relevant sources? In an interactive information age, it is not part of our mandate to cut through the noise. If we do not, we tacitly abandon our user community to Google and the other search engines guiding Latino users to relevant information.

What we are striving for is the interlinking, living communication of Chicano/a Latino/a historical resources—forming a network that becomes the digital library that, in turn, becomes a part of the contemporary lexicon that informs our users' perspective. Our individual institutions are only nodes in that network, and it is up to us as development agents to guide our users to the wider network. Until we make that final step of consistently cross-referencing our resources with others, we are only providing partial knowledge access to our user community. Clifford Lynch

defined as a digital library, a group of online collections or digital repositories that understand the users' new relationship with information in
the digital age (Lynch, 2002).

People who are working together on common interests find each other
only if they are guided to their commonalities, yet the institutions that
are providing access to their digital resources are still using an old para-
digm. They are viewing their collections as discrete elements, as whole
and complete entities when really they are parts of the puzzle that must
be interlocked before the community can really access the full scope of
Chicano/a Latino/a digital resources. When trained, credible educators
make these connections for them, new communities will be created, and
users will synthesize multiple sources on their own, obtaining complete
and more accurate answers to their questions. In the following section, we
examine collection development following these ideas.

The California Ethnic and Multicultural Archives (CEMA)

The California Ethnic and Multicultural Archives (CEMA) became a participant cohort when they became, as Ybarra-Fausto called it, "the producers of visual education . . . as visual educators with the important task
of refining and transmitting through plastic expression the ideology of a
community striving for self-determination" (Ybarra-Fausto, 1986). Due
to the strong visual nature of materials housed in CEMA, the collection
manager was in a better position than most to take advantage of the rise
in Internet technologies. When the Internet took off as a consumer service
in the mid-to-late 1990s, the development of virtual space provided the
perfect congruence of function and form for the archives. CEMA became
part of the spectrum of content providers: from museums, universities,
cultural heritage institutions, to government agencies offering compelling noncommercial content to users during the first waves of consumer
migration to the Internet.

What distinguished CEMA's attempt to create wider community access was the combination of interpretive tools that accompanied their
objects into the digital arena. The collection featured a user-centered design that took into account the purpose and audience for the raw materials and how they were collected in the first place. In other words, CEMA's
digital collection became structured content that facilitated the beginning of communication with the target group. It may be that CEMA had
an advantage over traditional library collections because its cultural heritage materials have a more obvious and well-constructed community to
focus on. And it might be that the combined materials related directly to
educational communication. It might also be due to visual objects being

easily interpretable in a digital environment, but for these and other reasons, CEMA emerged with a digital collection well suited to the needs of its target audience. By providing interlaced structures of similar materials often referring to one another, CEMA created a metaresource that allowed users to access cultural heritage materials and direct them to the context in which the materials were created. When this occurred, the materials value became greater then the sum of its parts. As Lynch explains: "the aggregation of materials in a digital library can be greater than the sum of its parts" (Lynch, 2002). Lynch quantified his statement at the time with an example from the Perseus Project at Tufts University: "What happens is through computation plus the contribution of additional intellectual effort by the designers and curators of the digital library, you begin growing a corpus that is more then the sum of its parts that evolves over time and becomes richer and richer (Lynch, 2002).

What Do We Do Next? Who Is Doing it Right?

Now imagine what the CEMA collection will do as it cross-references itself at many levels, within digital objects, with other digital Chicano/a Latino/a resources? Imagine any of the discrete Chicano/a Latino/a digital resources providing not only a lexicon of their local collections but guided research-level cross-referencing to related resources. It is such a simple idea to expand our descriptive efforts into the realm of guided research, and there is really no better way to shape the conversation of the user community. Because of, and even in spite of, the new accessibility that the digital age provides, we need to expand our mission into guided learning. We need to lead our community to the connections they need to make in order to advance the efficacy of all Chicano/a Latino/a digital resources at the same time. Providing credible, research-level guidance from collection managers and developers themselves is the next essential phase in developing Chicano/a Latino/a digital resources. That guided, value-added research reference is the way we can create real community interaction in both the provider and user spheres of the community.

Providing the Vital Pathfinders

Washington State University provides an excellent example of educational potential and community building. The Washington State University site entitled *Focusing on the Latino/a West the Multicultural West Chicano/Latina and Borderlands Sites* is not a digital collection in its own right but rather a portal or pathfinder to a multitude of Chicano/a Latino/a digital resources. This amalgamation of resources provides a model for how institutions can easily provide guided educational direction for scholarship and features some of the most exceptional Chicano/a Latino/a resources available online. Arranged into a simple flat list or pathfinder, divided by the categories historical sites and documents, arts, letters and culture, professional associations, and archives and centers, a wide swath of the scope of Chicano/a Latino/a digital resources is provided. As we explore and negotiate the sites listed, we notice again and again how unusual this simple interconnection between resources really is. When we follow the links, we see that very few of the sites that are linked to, link back to this pathfinder. The vast majorities of Chicano/a Latino/a digital resources online do not connect users to related collections and thus do not communicate directly to related but unknown user groups.

Communication, the essence of interactivity in the information age, and the cornerstone of providing true educational potential, is shut off. Some communities already have established networks (teachers, scholars, tour guides, staff, professional organizations, fan sites, blogs, e-mail lists), and we need to access these networks to engage in a collaborative networking process. If we do not, we will have little chance of providing meaningful services to our general audiences or those users that fall outside of the familiar ones (those who speak languages other than English, for example). Users who are passionate about a hobby, users who are engaged in formal continuing education, a scholar, or a student user working on a school assignment may all use the same digital object or collection in different ways. But with guidance from the digital resource developers, librarians, and archivists who constitute the caretakers of these resources, we can vastly improve the quality of community interaction on both sides of the educational equation. Often we as caretakers forget that our work provides us the opportunity to understand more about the needs of our user communities than they understand about themselves. We can effectively gather interconnected digital resources in our design interfaces that will create information relationships that our user community might never make. This flexibility is important to sustaining the vitality of digital collections for the future and in providing true accessibility.

Conclusion

We have come a long way toward providing true freedom of access to our user communities, but the creation of a truly definitive Chicano/a Latino/a digital library is only beginning. By focusing on the digitization and preservation of our unique resources, we have introduced thousands of people to parts of their history that they might never have known existed without us. But we can do more and should do more. Re tooling part of our skill set for the future should be such a simple thing. Where we used to point and direct our users to the stacks in our libraries, now we must, albeit electronically, stand behind them and suggest additional reading. We are uniquely situated as subject specialists and research-level scholars to provide higher level cross-referencing to related online sources. We should care as much about where our users go when they leave our collections as we do about getting them to our resources in the first place. If we can close the gaps and begin to provide true active educational stewardship on the web as well as in our local institutions, we can reinvent the reference librarian for the information age.

References

Fox, Susannah and Gretchen Livingston. 2009. *Latinos online, 2006–2008: Narrowing the gap.* Pew Internet & American Life Project and Pew Hispanic Center, Washington, DC. http://pewhispanic.org/files/reports/119.pdf

Gaspar de Alba, Alicia. 1998. *Chicano art inside/outside the master's house: Cultural politics and the CARA exhibition.* Austin: University of Texas Press.

Goldman, Shifra M. 1984. *Chicano art history: A book of selected readings.* Jacinto Quirarte, ed. San Antonio: Research Center for the Arts and Humanities, University of Texas at San Antonio.

Humanities Advanced Technology and Information Institute, University of Glasgow, and National Initiative for a Networked Cultural Heritage. 2002. *The NINCH guide to good practice in the digital representation and management of cultural heritage materials.* Washington, DC: National Initiative for a Networked Cultural Heritage. http://www.nyu.edu/its/humanities/ninchguide/

Lopez, Mark Hugo and Gretchen Livingston. 2010. *How young Latinos communicate with friends in the digital age.* Pew Hispanic Center, Washington, DC. http://pewhispanic.org/files/reports/124.pdf

Lynch, Clifford. 2002. *Digital collections, digital libraries and the digitization of cultural heritage information.* First Monday. 7. no. 5. http://www.uic.edu/htbin/cgiwrap/bin/ojs/index.php/fm/article/view/949/870

Meléndez, Edwin 2007. "About." *Centro de Estudios Puertorriqueños: [online].* New York: El Centro. http://www.centropr.org/about.html

Rael, Juan Bautista. 1998. *Hispano music & culture of the Northern Rio Grande: The Juan B. Rael Collection.* Washington, DC: Library of Congress. http://memory.loc.gov/ammem/rghtml/rghome.html

Santa Fe Planning Workshop on Distributed Knowledge Work Environments, Paul Duguid, and Daniel E. Atkins. 1997. *Report of the Santa Fe planning workshop on distributed knowledge work environments:*

Digital libraries. March 9–11, 1997. Ann Arbor, MI. (304 West Hall, 550 E. University 48109-1092): School of Information, University of Michigan.

Scarborough Research Corporation. 2008. *The power of the Hispanic consumer online.* New York: Scarborough Research Corp. http://www.scarborough.com

Williamson, Debra Aho as reported by eMarketer. 2010. *Hispanic Americans online: A fragmented population.* New York: eMarketer, Inc. http://www.emarketer.com/

Ybarra-Fausto, Tomas. 1986. "Introduction in Lockpez, Inverna." *Chicano expressions: A new view in American art.* New York: Intar Latin American Gallery.

Chapter 11

Conference Presentations

HISTORICAL PERSPECTIVES ON THE RECRUITMENT OF LATINOS TO LIBRARY SERVICE: THE COMMITTEE TO RECRUIT MEXICAN AMERICAN LIBRARIANS—A LEGACY FOR LATINO LIBRARIANSHIP

John L. Ayala

The central purpose of this paper is to give a historical background on the recruitment of Latino/Spanish speaking into library service, and co-incidentally academic library service, and to give you some perspective of what happened in the distant past, recently, and what may be possible for the future in this realm of diversity and recruitment in the 21st century for our profession. How do we know where want to go if we don't know where we have been? I believe that some of the points I will share with you today are applicable for today and the future. It also illuminates what a small dedicated cadre of professionals can do to shape the future of library service.

A Personal Commitment to the Committee to Recruit Mexican American Librarians

The Committee to Recruit Mexican American Librarians (CRMAL) was a committee of librarians established by Dave Barron of the Los Angeles Public Library, who was a human resource manager for the system; and Elizabeth Martinez, the first Mexican American librarian hired by the County of Los Angeles Public Library.

The impetus for the Committee to Recruit Mexican American Librarians came from a suit filed against Los Angeles Public Library because of their lack of services and staffing for Mexican Americans. Dave Barron needed to recruit Mexican American librarians to address the problem exposed by the suit. He spoke to Elizabeth Martinez in 1969. The outgrowth of this conversation was the Committee to Recruit Mexican American Librarians whose members were comprised from Los Angeles Public Library—Dave Barron, Jose Taylor, and others; and County of Los Angeles Public Library—Elizabeth Martinez, Harriet Covey, Carole Witten, and so on.

My direct *encuentro*, or encounter, with the Committee to Recruit Mexican American Librarians was very personal. In 1969–1970, I was completing my senior year of undergraduate work at California State University, Long Beach (CSULB). My education had been interrupted by the U.S. government, which necessitated my joining the United States Air Force and being sent on a paid vacation and tour of Pleiku, Central Highlands, Republic of Vietnam.

When I returned to finish my senior year at CSULB, things had changed on campus. There was a new student organization for Mexican American students, UMAS (United Mexican American Students), which eventually became MEChA (Movimiento Estudiantil Chicano de Aztlan) or the Chicano Student Movement of the Southwest or the historical Aztlan of the Aztecs of Mexico.

In the fall of 1969, MEChA had a gathering place on campus: a trailer/club room, where members congregated during the school day. One morning after finishing my classes for the day, I returned to the trailer and found some young Chicanas and Chicanos berating a middle-age Anglo in a business suit. The gentleman had come to recruit us into library service. The students were excoriating this well-intentioned gentleman about the lack of services and relevancy of libraries to Chicanos in general. I heard the conversation as I walked into the trailer. Since I knew most of the members in the MEChA trailer at the time, I spoke up and stated that I worked in the public library as a bookmobile driver and that I believed libraries were relevant to assisting Mexican Americans in all of life's areas. These libraries included the realm of education and college ones, and Mexican American librarians were essential for services to our underserved people and as another "pathway" to achieve the American dream of success with the wealth of information that libraries offered. The tone of the conversation changed for the positive, and a conversation ensued that discussed the value of libraries to our Latino community. When the students left to go to classes, I stayed on to visit with our guest.

This was a fortuitous *encuentro* for both of us. I'm sorry I don't remember the gentleman's name. We sat and talked for quite a while. He introduced himself as a member of CRMAL. He spoke of Harriet Covey, who

I knew as my branch librarian in Long Beach, and as the key person who recruited me into library service and assisted me in my employment in Long Beach Public Library as a bookmobile driver. He also spoke of Elizabeth Martinez as a member of CRMAL. He took my name to share with the committee.

The other part of this fortuitous *encuentro* led to CRMAL assisting me in obtaining a U.S. Department of Education fellowship to Immaculate Heart College's (IHC) Master of Library Science program. At that time, there were three library schools in Los Angeles. The University of Southern California (USC) and the University of California, Los Angeles (UCLA) offered me packages of aid, but with encouragement from CRMAL, Immaculate Heart College offered me the best aid package.

I subsequently met Elizabeth Martinez while in library school. She immediately recruited me to become a member of CRMAL. My life as a student changed very swiftly. In 1971 I graduated from library school at IHC. I became the chairperson of CRMAL in 1972 and served until 1973 (Martinez, 1971).

As an active professional committee, CRMAL had many activities, tasks, projects, and issues that it dealt with in its approximate five years of existence. I am including a memo sent from Elizabeth Martinez, the chairwoman of CRMAL; and committee members, dated September 3, 1971 (Martinez, 1971). It will serve as an example of the types of efforts put forth by the committee and Elizabeth Martinez. The text of the message is as follows:

Nationwide Recognition

Our efforts to recruit Chicanos into the profession have earned us substantial help and recognition plus a reputation of commitment to the cause.

For instance:

7/22: Mr. Jose Vasquez from the Mexican American Council on Education (MACE) in Chicago visited seeking our help in starting a Chicano Library Association within ALA with their organization acting as a vanguard due to their being near the ALA offices. He was referred to us by Miss Peggy Barber, director office for recruitment, ALA. A letter endorsing such a move was sent to ALA from the Congress of Mexican American Unity. MACE will contact us as plans crystallize.

8/2–3: Mr. Armando Orellana, director of the Center for the Spanish Speaking in Milwaukee arrived to interview any local person of Latin descent interested in a 2two-year fellowship at the University of Wisconsin in Milwaukee leading to an MLS. Dr. Laurence Sherrill, director, School of Library & Information Science had contacted us two weeks prior to

Mr. Orellana's visit. We arranged for an interview on Channel 34 with my name and phone number given as the source for more information. A substantial number of phone calls and letters were received.

8/6: Mr. Arthur Kerwin, director, Library Training Program at the State University of New York in Albany called seeking Chicano applicants for a three-year program leading to an MLS. The program paid for transportation to Albany, full fellowships for the junior and senior year leading to a BA degree, and a third year for the MLS. We got subsequent calls about this same program from Miss Peggy Barber and Jose Vasquez in Chicago and Miss Frances Lujan, Model Cities Library in Albuquerque. (Such are the rewards of attending ALA.)

We submitted seven names of which two decided they could not go to New York. To date two local Chicanas have been accepted and left Sept. 2. A third applicant is still being considered.

Our files of names of future applicants to library schools are expanding. We need everyone's cooperation. As you hear of any Chicanos interested in becoming librarians, please send me their names, addresses, phone numbers, and year in school. This will facilitate matters when we hear of scholarships available. Thanks.

Publicity

Carole Witten and John Ayala have been working on TV coverage for us. We've been accepted for "La Siesta Is Over" sometime within the next three weeks.

U.S. Office of Education Proposal

Harriet Covey, Mrs. Doris Banks, and I have been working on a proposal for an Institute-In-Training grant through Cal State Fullerton. It was submitted July 12; an addenda submitted on August 11. If granted it would provide one year fellowships for an MLS for 20 Chicanos. Though caught in President Nixon's freeze, we are still hopeful that it will be allocated. It would be the first such Institute-In-Training program for Chicanos in the Southwest. For more information contact me at (213) 728-2817.

College Recruitment, Fall '71

Materials for campus recruitment visits are available from both Jose Taylor and EMS. October and November are usually the best time. If you would like to participate, please indicate this to me and let me know the college you prefer.

Next Meeting

I hope to call a meeting in October. Anyone have a suggestion for a date?

CLA Annual Convention: San Francisco, December 1971

Who is planning to attend CLA this year?

We need ideas and a plan. We must let everyone know that there is a need for real commitment supported with money and/or fellowships for the recruitment of minorities by library schools, etc.

Struggle

Just a brief review of this memo gives the reader some idea of the variety of activities and efforts the committee was involved in. There are the nationwide contacts with various community organizations, MLS graduate programs in different parts of the nation, and networking with students interested in receiving scholarships and fellowships to graduate programs. There are members working on getting publicity for the "cause." Other members are working on a grant proposal to provide fellowships for library school at California State University Fullerton, library school. Plans are being worked on for fall recruitment visits to colleges. The committee members are looking forward to attending the California Library Association Conference and pushing efforts for obtaining funding to continue recruitment of minorities to library school. I believe the last word of the memo "Struggle" illustrates the attitude of Elizabeth Martinez and the committee members she was working with in this effort. It was a "struggle" working against professional and societal attitudes that did not place a value on having Chicanos or Latinos in library service. The Latino community was not valued or served adequately by libraries. What the committee did was break new ground for librarianship.

The committee produced a recruitment brochure in 1973. The recruitment brochure was titled "*Bibliotecarios: Para La Raza*" with the inner portion of the tri-fold document subtitled "*Bibliotecarios: Trabajando Por Nuestra Raza y Cultura.*" The significant text in the interior portion of the brochure reads as follows: The people of La Raza attending college today are facing tremendous challenges as numerous career and professional opportunities become available to them. One such area of challenge is in the field of professional librarianship; a career which is an important and basic right to read.

Libraries throughout the United States are awakening to the need for Spanish Speaking librarians to bridge the gap which separates them from various Spanish speaking ethnic groups: Chicanos, Puerto Ricans, Latinos, and Cubans. These librarians have a major role to play in the operation of public, special, school, and academic libraries. Their experiences, cultural heritage, and language are needed in libraries that serve Spanish speaking people as well as the general public. Because of their ethnic rapport they are better able to inform community people of the services the library can provide.

Today libraries are expanding their collections of books and materials to reflect the true culture and history of bilingual, bicultural ethnic groups in the United States. Professional librarians are searching for books and selecting materials to place in community, agency, and school libraries and are building practical and scholarly collections which will be hallmarks of that heritage.

Unfortunately, there are only a very few librarians from the various Spanish speaking ethnic groups to serve the special needs of La Raza. Graduate library schools are now inviting qualified applicants to apply for enrollment. Scholarships, fellowships, and other sources of financial aid are available. The opportunities are here. Spanish speaking students have a challenge to make libraries meaningful to La Raza.

The inner portion of the brochure also highlighted pictures of young Latino Librarians listing their current employment and dispensing words of praise and wisdom about the career they had chosen. Here are some examples: Daniel Duran, outreach librarian, Richmond, CA Public Library: "If the Chicano/Latino community is not coming to the library, we must find ways of taking the library into the community."

Nelly Fernandez, Union City, CA Public Library: "Our libraries should reflect our communities: they should be bilingual and bicultural."

John Ayala, librarian (Director Pacific Coast Campus Library) Long Beach City College, California: "There is much work to be done and we need more Chicano Librarians to do that work for La Raza."

CRMAL also produced a bibliography in 1972 titled "*Chicanismo*" that was sold at conferences and other events to raise funds for their recruitment effort. The introductory page reads as follows: This compilation of Chicano materials has been selected by the Committee to Recruit Mexican Librarians to fill the need for a representative collection in libraries everywhere. We have concentrated exclusively on materials in English and on the Chicano, not Mexico or the Mexican. In addition to lists of adult and children's books, periodicals, films, and a list of Chicano publishers, we have included some sources for Spanish language materials in California.

The Committee to Recruit Mexican Librarians is comprised of librarians from the Los Angeles County and the Los Angeles City library systems who are actively engaged in recruiting for the library profession. Current statistics indicate that there are approximately 14 million Spanish-surnamed in the United States and far too few librarians from this minority.

There is a tag line at the bottom of the introductory page that reads: Printed with Federal Library Services and Construction Act Funds. There were also unsuccessful attempts to enlist the University of Southern California Graduate School of Library Science. In a memo sent to members of CRMAL dated May 18, 1972, from Elizabeth Martinez (Martinez, 1972) she discusses a proposal sent to USC: "April 17, we submitted our proposal for a Minorities Recruitment Project at USC to the School of Library Science. A meeting was held May 9 with Dean Boaz, Miss Katherine Laich, Roberto Haro, Jose Taylor, and myself (Elizabeth Martinez). Dean Boaz outlined the conditions under which a program they participate in must operate. Since there are provisions in the proposal unacceptable to Dean Boaz, we must rewrite the proposal.

Anyone interested in rewriting the proposal is asked to contact me at 728-2817. I would appreciate any and all help." The program was never implemented because of Dean Boaz's opposition to involving USC Library School in this type of minority recruitment effort. In the same memo it chronicled the successful effort of helping a young Chicana win a scholarship to library school. It reads as follows:

Miss Lilia Maria Vasquez, Winner of ALA Scholarship

With help from our Committee, Lilia applied for and received the ALA Scholarship for $2,500. She will attend USC. Lilia has also been invited to attend the ALA convention in Chicago to receive her scholarship and be honored by the Executive Board.

The previous examples cover some of the efforts of the committee in achieving their ultimate goal of recruiting Mexican Americans into library service and having them become librarians. The next example will depict a success and serve as an example for other Latino librarian programs that would follow.

CRMAL's greatest achievement in recruiting is as follows: In 1971, members of CRMAL, Harriet Covey; Elizabeth Martinez; and Doris Banks, dean of the Library School, California State University Fullerton, submitted a grant proposal to the U.S. Office of Education as an Institute-In-Training Grant. The proposal was caught in President Nixon's budget freeze in 1971 and subsequently denied. Dean Bank's persistence paid off and in 1972 CSUF School of Library Science received the federal grant that would be a groundbreaking and historical achievement for recruiting Latinos to library service.

The grant provided for 15 scholarships of $2,400 (plus $600.00 per dependent). The year of graduate study for 15 Mexican American students would lead to a Masters in Library Science with a specialty in School Library Media. Dr. Patrick Sanchez was employed to direct the program which came to be known, by the participants, as the Mexican American Library Science Program at CSUF. The program began in September of 1972 and ended in spring of 1975.

Several lessons were learned from this program that were passed on to subsequent programs of recruitment and education for Latinos. The primary lesson learned was that we had to tailor the program to Latino students who were intent on serving Latinos/Spanish speaking. They, the students, were not interested in the traditional curriculum of library school. Secondarily they wanted to see Latinos teaching some of their classes. They wanted Librarian role models so we gave them role models. If memory serves me correctly, the Latino librarians who taught in the program were myself, Jose Taylor, and Elizabeth Martinez. We taught various courses and lectured on special topics related to our expertise as working librarians.

We also learned another valuable lesson in that there should always be two interviewers per candidate for the program. Two interviewers can discern more than one interviewer. I would be inclined to turn down a candidate because of what I perceived as a lack of commitment to the profession or a lack of enthusiasm. I was persuaded more than once that a candidate was worthy of the program even though I was not impressed by the candidate for whatever reason. And as it happened the students who I did not find impressive did graduate from the program and found employment. My role with the program was as an advisor, lecturer, and instructor.

Several of the distinguished graduates of the CSUF program include Robert Trujillo, head of Special Collections, Stanford University; Carmen Martinez, director of the Public Library for the City of Oakland, California; and Antonio Arroyo, director of the Desert Vista Community College Library, Pima Community College District, Tucson, Arizona. The CSUF program graduated 45 Mexican American Librarians during its three-year duration.

The CSUF program was the precursor to the University of Arizona's Graduate Library Institute for Spanish Speaking Americans. In early 1974 Jose Taylor, newsletter editor for REFORMA and a future president of REFORMA (he worked for LAPL); Dr. Arnulfo Trejo, founding president of REFORMA (professor of library science at University of Arizona); and myself a subsequent VP-president elect of REFORMA (director of the Pacific Coast Campus Library of Long Beach Community College) were returning from a library conference and waiting in an airport. Jose and I were advisors, instructors, and lecturers in the CSUF program, and we had previously agreed to speak to and encourage Dr. Trejo to submit a grant proposal to United States Office of Education for an Institute-In-Training grant. While waiting for our respective flights we explained the efficacy of beginning a program at the University of Arizona MLS graduate program. Dr. Trejo worked diligently to get the U. of Arizona's cooperation. The proposal was submitted and was successfully funded. The program (Graduate Library Institute for Spanish Speaking Americans) began in 1976. The program's duration was 1976 to 1980 and graduated 59 Latino librarians. My role in this program was as an "advisor" and lecturer.

Distinguished graduates of the GLISSA program include Margo Gutierrez, Mexican American and Latino Studies librarian, University of Texas at Austin; Martin Gomez, executive director of the Urban Libraries Council (currently Library Director for the city of Los Angeles); Luis Herrera, director of the San Francisco Public Library; Salvador Guerena, director California Ethnic and Multicultural Archives, Donald Davidson Library of the University of California Santa Barbara. Guerena is also a distinguished author of several monographs dealing with Latino Library issues.

The '80s and '90s, for the most part, were not significant times for recruitment of Latinos into library service. In 1997, here's a familiar name, while Elizabeth Martinez was the executive director of the American Library Association, the Spectrum Initiative began. The stated purpose of the program was to recruit and award scholarships to Latinos, African Americans, Asians, Native Americans, Native Hawaiians/other Pacific Islanders for graduate programs in library and information science. It celebrated its 10th anniversary at the ALA Annual Conference in Washington, DC, in June 2007. Its success is due, in large part, to the mentoring, networking, and environment for professional development. I do not have a definitive number regarding Latino graduates of this program but I do know that there have been hundreds of minority librarians graduated from this program (ALA website, 2007).

The most recent major effort for Latino recruitment is the "Knowledge River" program at the University of Arizona, founded in 2001, which focuses on Latino and Native American librarianship. Dr. Patricia Tarin, a protégé of Elizabeth Martinez, directs the program. I don't have current statistics. I do know that the program has been very successful (Knowledge River website, 2007).

My chapter had several purposes. I wanted to highlight historical efforts to recruit Latinos to library service and MLS programs. CRMAL was the precursor to subsequent efforts and has left a legacy that can never be repeated. I don't want CRMAL's efforts to be forgotten. I continue to believe that some if not all the lessons we learned as members of CRMAL are applicable today and in the future for recruitment into our profession. The concepts continue live in the aforementioned scholarship programs.

CRMAL was also a precursor to REFORMA (National Association to Promote Library and Information Services to Latinos and the Spanish Speaking) and we know the influence that REFORMA has as an affiliated organization of ALA. Let's not forget REFORMA awards scholarships for qualified MLIS candidates at the national level and the local chapters of Bibliotecas Para La Gente (San Francisco Bay Area), Los Angeles and Orange County award local scholarships. I know that the scholarships are not limited to Latinos but that you must be willing to work in Latino or Spanish speaking service areas.

Recently the Joint Conference of Librarians of Color had a successful conference in Dallas, Texas (Oct. 11–15, 2006). One of the stated purposes was to raise money for minority scholarships. The conference was put together through the cooperation of the five ethnic caucuses of American Library Association: REFORMA (The National Association to Promote Library and Information Services to Latinos and the Spanish Speaking), the Black Caucus of ALA, Asian Pacific Americans Library Association, Chinese American Librarians Association, and American Indian Library Association. I do know that national REFORMA will invest some of the profits from the conference into its scholarship fund.

I do understand that my experience may be unique in that I studied to be a bilingual reference librarian in a public library setting, and I was recruited to become an academic librarian which led to my career as a community college library director for 34 years in three community colleges. I believe that I was in the right place at the right time and was able to avail myself of the opportunities to serve Chicanos, Latinos, and other minorities in making librarianship a much more colorful profession and make library service more committed to serving people of color.

My hope is that important lessons have been learned and that you will have drawn from my sharing of my experience with CRMAL some valuable lessons, information, and encouragement to assist in recruiting even more Latinos and minorities into librarianship so that our profession will be more reflective of the society in which we live. Gracias!

References

American Library Association. "Spectrum-New Voices, New Visions!" www.ala.org/a/a/diversity/spectrum/spectrum.htm Retrieved April 17, 2007.

Committee to Recruit Mexican American Librarians. Minutes and Documents 1971, 1972, 1973.

Espinal, Isabel. (October 1, 2003). "Wanted: Latino Librarians," *Criticas* 3, no. 5.

Martinez, Elizabeth. Committee to Recruit Mexican American Librarians (CRMAL Memo 1971).

Salvador Güereña

The long history of our nation's ethnic groups is rich and culturally diverse, but Latinas(os) are still poorly represented in the archives of our major institutions. To this day, with some notable exceptions, the documentary record of the Latina/o cultural presence has largely been ignored by collecting institutions. Understanding the cultural history of our Latino population involves a reconstruction of the past that is predicated on a gathering of the evidence as we piece together what, at best, has been documented spasmodically. This article is a call to action by first defining what is cultural heritage and why it is important. It makes a case for making hard choices and for having a vision for the future. Closing the gaps in historical neglect is a central issue, while the solutions offer a preservation of cultural legacy through the forging of partnerships, perseverance, and by playing a role in helping to close the digital divide.

What Is Cultural Heritage, and Why Is it Important?

Unesco's *Living Cultures* defines culture as the flow of meanings that people create, blend, and exchange . . . [that] "enables us to build cultural legacies and live with their memory. It permits us to recognize our bonds with kin, with community, with nation state, and with the whole of humanity. It helps us to live out a thoughtful existence."[1] The physical evidences of this cultural heritage document our cultural life and are found in myriad of texts, objects, images, performances, and the built environment that surrounds us.

Our societies recognize these cultural evidences by collecting, preserving, and educating about these through museums, libraries, and archives. We are challenged to preserve the collective memories of our Latino communities in all their richness and diversity because the producers of our cultural heritage have always been at risk, often only a heartbeat away from permanent loss. Those defined as most at risk are our elders who have hidden in their hearts their family stories and historical narratives, and it is our community-based organizations, venerable, yet operating on shoestring budgets on the brink of penury. These are the ones that

Presented at Memoria, Vozy Patrimonio, the First Conference on Latino/Hispanic Film, Print, and Sound Archives, August 15–17, 2003, UCLA play a critical role in the cultural life of our communities. As archivists, we lack the luxury of time to wait because people do grow old and die and memories fade. Writer Gordon Dalbey states: "the problem with this broken world lies not in our imagination, that we cannot anticipate the future—from solar-powered cars to marriage vows—but in our memory. Our problem is that we cannot confess the authentic past. Without our knowing our roots, knowing what we're made of and how we've been designed to function; not knowing where we came from, we can't know where we're going."[2]

Greater meaning and purpose in life follows that point of self-discovery and yields a deep sense of pride about one's cultural heritage. People from all ethnic backgrounds can overcome racial misunderstanding through acquiring knowledge, information, and an appreciation about other racial and ethnic groups and their struggles and experiences. This is defined as cultural literacy, which leads us to gain a greater understanding of each other as we live and work together; it leads us to develop a shared vision of our future.

Making a Commitment Requires Making Hard Choices

Institutions must make some hard choices if they wish to commit to developing a sustainable Latino archival collections initiative. Often this involves reordering some priorities and redesignating funding and space allocations to ensure that adequate staffing, materials, space, and services are deployed to support such archives over a long-range period.

Historically it was the norm for institutions to skew their commitments and choices toward the white cultural and social elite. With a few notable exceptions, the history of Latino archives in general had been a history of uneven priorities and shoestring programs that were subject to the changing whims of whoever happened to be in charge. Potential Latino donors were understandably reticent upon being solicited by archival repositories, and it is quite understandable why they would seek assurances that their donated collections would not be destined to the netherworld of unprocessed collections.

Outside grants are always a good option, and there are various funding agencies that will support well-conceived, well-planned, and worthy projects. A sustainable Latino archives program will not rely on such grants for the bulk of the work needing to get done. The aim should be to develop the existing infrastructure and then complement it with grants. This process will add strength to grant proposals and make them more competitive. One of the greatest concerns of Latinos writers, artists, and performing arts groups vis-à-vis archival institutions has been their ability and willingness to make a long-range commitment. Institutions must also be patient and persistent. It might take a decade of pursuit to attract a major archival collection. Potential donors have had a good reason to pause, given the lack of permanence of some Chicano/Latino studies programs and Chicano/Latino library programs.

A Vision for the Future That Can Translate into a Collections Plan

There must always be a vision for the future and one that is consonant with the mission statement of your home institution. There should be a well-thought-out strategic plan that is flexible to welcome new opportunities and a collection policy that has a coherent, well-defined focus that will guide your acquisitions: one that sets out your purpose and the scope of your acquisitions.

Many repositories lacked primary sources in this field and were ill prepared to meet the growing demands of scholarship. East Coast universities were filled with the papers of the white male elite, but very few institutions were collecting the papers of the leading edge of the Chicano/Latino community in literature, in the arts, and in the political arena. In California, the population of Chicanos/Latinos is growing at an unprecedented rate. Chicano studies research, scholarship, and teaching are growing exponentially. Archival programs that were created on several of the University of California campuses and at Stanford University were followed suit by several California State University (CSU) campuses, such as the CSU, Northridge Oviatt Library's Hispanic Serving Institutions Archival collections. These Latino programs have become well positioned to serve the academic needs of Latino research. Some programs have a long history, such as the Arizona State University Library's Chicano Research Collection, founded in 1970 in response to the emerging needs of Chicano faculty and students. The interdisciplinary nature of much of the contemporary research is drawing increasing attention to the interrelatedness between the social sciences and the humanities, and this requires a broader spectrum of scope and intensities.

Collections development is the crux of any library and archives program. Selection and acquisitions requires that choices be made because of that other critical role, being a good steward of someone else's treasures that are entrusted to us. While the preservation role is paramount, so also is providing access to these. Therefore, if we purport to assume responsibility for the cultural heritage materials that are our "*memoria*" (memory) and our "*patrimonio*" (cultural heritage), then our actions should be driven by principles, guidelines, and policies that help us to fulfill our charge. The principles are the philosophy and mission of your home institution;

the guidelines delineate the parameters, and the policies form the mechanism that enables us to implement these. There is an interdependent relationship between these three.

While there is time to act, what should we be made to understand about the difficulties, and how can we overcome those so that our collections may become more representative of the increasingly multicultural society around us? There is a context to acquisition strategies that have worked and not worked. There is a lens of cultural bias that tends to filter our collections decisions. Everyone of us is influenced by that bias, and as collectors we need to work against that.

Closing the Gaps Left by Historical Neglect

Frank Burke, in *Research and the Manuscript Tradition*, points out that to understand history requires that we try to reconstruct the past, to map the road to it, and that to have a clear path to scholarship we must first gather the evidence.[3] Indeed, at best, what we know about the past is documented in fits and spurts, through snapshots in time, and based on a variety of media. This is the grist of historical research that requires as many of these as possible to cobble together someone's life or an event. Moreover, ethnic studies scholars are in the business of reevaluating research paradigms only to form new ones that provide us all with valuable and new insights. Access to the primary sources becomes paramount. Unfortunately there is a pressing need to close the huge gaps in the historical record on cultural minorities, in general, and about Latinos, specifically, because the collection development work is still an uneven patchwork; and opportunities do come but just as often, they also go, never to be seen again. Never mind that 100 years of history may pass, and these will by then disappear, but within our own lifetime we will experience great loss. Whenever someone dies, if no provisions had been made for the safeguarding of their old letters and documents, oftentimes those are as good as gone.

Going to the Community and Building Relationships

Most of the same difficulties we have in documenting Latino culture and society involve factors that contribute to the relatively low use of libraries by Latinos. Many people simply don't know yet about the usefulness of libraries, and they lack the skills needed to access and exploit library resources effectively. Therefore, it is important for libraries and archives to go out into their Latino communities, develop visibility, build relationships with community leaders, and involve them whenever possible in the planning process. Once they understand the usefulness and benefits to them, they can become donors as well as users of personal papers and organizational records. They can become the eyes and ears in the community: valuable sources of referrals to potential donors.

The University of Texas at Austin is one of the earliest repositories that reached out to the Latino community. Through the pioneering outreach work of such Latino scholars as Carlos E. Castañeda and George Sanchez, many important archival and manuscript sources were identified and subsequently preserved. Castaneda in 1927 was made librarian of the Genaro Garcia collection at the University of Texas and is considered to be one of the earliest Chicano historians.[4]

There are many contemporary success stories involving community outreach that involve Special Collections exhibits. One such example is attributed to Texas A&M University in College Station, Texas. Miguel Juarez, assistant professor and curator of Hispanic/Latino Studies Collections Studies at the Cushing Memorial Library and Archives, curated the exhibit "¡Siempre! Hispanics at Texas A&M Celebrating 180 Years." This exhibit addressed a long-neglected facet of local Latino history. The curator made extensive visits into the community and conducted oral history interviews with community leaders, drawing them into the project. Business and community leaders not only donated additional materials but also contributed essays that enriched the educational value of the project. The essays were published simultaneously in the exhibit catalog and on the exhibit website.[5] This award-winning 2006 exhibit made an encore in 2009, entitled "¡Siempre! Otra Vez," cosponsored by the College Station Heritage Programs, Amigos del Valle de Brazos, and Brazos County Historical Commission. According to Anne Boykin, College Station Heritage Programs coordinator, "The Hispanic history in Brazos County is very rich, yet very elusive. This exhibit will be a perfect opportunity to acquaint our community with the many contributions that have been made by local Hispanic families."[6]

In building the California Ethnic and Multicultural Archives (CEMA) at the University of California, Santa Barbara, it took years for the archivist to travel up and down the state of California, driving through rural farmlands to meet with Cesar Chavez at the United Farm Workers compound in La Paz; to the back country of San Juan Bautista, to meet with Luis Valdez and his Teatro Campesino, to East Los Angeles, San Diego, and Sacramento to talk to artists' collectives about the need to preserve their work. However, the fieldwork began to pay off with some superb collections donated as gifts to the university, in theater, literature, and visual arts, including all the major Chicano/Latino centers of cultural production in California. These were centers that were strategically located in the neighborhoods where they had long been the catalysts for arts-based community making in San Diego, Los Angeles, San Francisco, and Sacramento. The visual documents and historical texts that were acquired, including many thousands of silkscreen prints and posters; tens of thousands of slides and photographs; printed files; artifacts; and ephemera showed how these artists and those *centros*, the artist collectives, functioned to build community and how they stimulated political action and made an impact on social and cultural consciousness.

CEMA aggressively pursued these important cultural producers at a time when many institutions were giving scant attention to such groups and individuals. It was not until much later that their artwork, their plays, their novels, and their poetry would be respected and sought after by archival institutions. The Smithsonian Archives of American Art, for example, eventually recognized these as part of the canon of American culture and founded a western regional office housed at the Huntington Library in San Marino, California, to pursue the personal collections of individual Chicano and Latino artists.

Committing to Rescuing Latino Cultural History

Today there is a greater value placed on ethnic, cultural, and family roots. Archivists must be sensitive to the fact that they are asking people to part with something that defines who they are; it's what connects them to their known past; and these are much more than historical records: these are also family artifacts. But they must also be convinced that it is in their best interest to have the archivists care for them; it is not in their best interest for these to be stored in garages, basements, and attics where they may deteriorate and suffer loss. Stories abound of Latino cultural materials forever lost or nearly lost to broken water and sewer pipes, fires, and good-intentioned people who planned to return borrowed photographs or slides.

Preserving a Cultural Legacy means Forming Partnerships

Among the criticisms of institutions like ours are the negative perceptions in the Latino community of the "ivory tower" mentality at colleges and universities, and over the increasingly theoretical focus in Chicano and Latino studies. That is one of the reasons why forming partnerships with community groups is so important; in fact, years ago, the California State Library founded its own grant program "Partnerships for Change" to challenge libraries to break out of their traditional insular mode and begin working with community groups and community-based organizations to develop adaptive and innovative services to meet their needs.

Bridging the Gap in the Digital Divide

The digital divide is a term that's been used to describe the gulf between those who have access to computers and Internet content and those who don't. While low income and immigrant groups are increasingly accessing the Internet, the amount of culturally relevant information to such groups is still far and few between. Wendy Lazarus, cofounder of the Santa Monica based Children's Partnership expressed the same concerns as have those of us involved in addressing cultural diversity and digital collections. She states: "Though many underserved communities are gaining access to the Internet, many are not benefitting fully because of barriers related to content. Four of the most important barriers are: lack of local information, literacy barriers, language barriers, and lack of cultural diversity." She makes the point that there are 50 million people on the outside of the content gap.[7]

Our goal should be to keep up with the times and find new ways to provide useful and unique content on the World Wide Web drawn from our Latino special collections. And this content could include sound, images, and video as well as text in both English and Spanish, so that these cultural materials do not remain relegated to the shelves of special collections departments but can be made more visible, user friendly, and accessible to all—from wherever people connect to the Internet, be it from school, home, office, or public library.

Clearly, library and archive programs have to change to effectively play out their role as digital information providers to the Latino community. It won't be easy to manage the increasing amount of information that is born digital, but at the same time, many institutions are creating digital surrogates from their special collections. A recent survey of the Association of Research Libraries showed that 91 percent of responders were either already or planning to digitize special collections materials or were already doing so. Within the context of our Latino archives, it all goes back to our need not only to breath new life into Latino cultural resources, but as stewards of these materials, as the demand increases for these rare and fragile artifacts, we can do a better job at protecting the originals by making available their surrogates for displays and for access over the Internet.

Conclusion

The present state of American archives and manuscripts is a problematic one when viewed within the Latino context. A major effort will be required to offset the presently skewed representation of American culture as reflected in many of this country's libraries and archival institutions. There is a need for at least a modicum of consortial development of Latino archives and manuscript collections among those institutions that are either presently building or planning to acquire such materials. There is a published Code of Ethics for Archivists. We must respect already existing archival arrangements between donors and their repositories. A healthy spirit of competition is bound to stimulate special collections departments to begin acquiring Latino-related documents. But there is also a need for greater interinstitutional dialogue that can lead to cooperative and coordinated ventures.

Many Latino archives and manuscripts are contemporary in nature. There are many living writers, playwrights, poets, artists, and other cultural leaders. Many institutions purchase the manuscripts of living writers. Are they willing and able to make a lifelong commitment to those writers, or will they do so only until they run out of funds and space? Analogous to that is the scenario involving archives of contemporary organizations. This calls for making a long-term commitment to regularly augment and process future-generated materials. Often, such organizations need to have working copies made and may need an archivist's assistance and advice with their records management. This becomes more complex when taking into account the plethora of record types that are associated with folk traditions, theater, music, and art. Other complications involve literary property rights, access policies, and legal issues. There also is the matter of the growing volume of organizational records that will be augmented over time.

There will be many challenges ahead for committed and persistent archivists, as well as exciting prospects and opportunities for preserving the historical memory of our Latino culture and society. There will be positive outcomes for those who apply themselves in a principled and diligent manner, are willing to educate themselves to the task at hand, and will keep their fingers on the pulse of the Latino community.

Notes

1. Elisa Lanzi, "What is Cultural Heritage Information and Why is it Important?," in *Introduction to Vocabularies: Enhancing Access to Cultural Heritage Information* (Los Angeles: Getty Research Institute, 1998), 3.
2. Gordon Dalbey, *Sons of the Father: Healing the Father-Wound in Men Today* (Wheaton, IL: Tyndale House, 1996), 1.
3. Frank Burke, "The Recovery of Reality," in *Research and the Manuscript Tradition* (Lanham, MD: Scarecrow Press, 1999), 18.
4. Salvador Güereña, "Archives and Manuscripts: Historical Antecedents to Contemporary Chicano Collections," *Collection Building* 8, no. 4 (1988): 3–11.
5. Miguel Juarez, interview by Salvador Güereña, November 20, 2008.

6. Anne Boykin, "Brazos County Hispanic Culture Exhibit Opening in October," http://www.cstx.gov/index.aspx?recordid=5027&page=3089 (accessed May 6, 2010).
7. Wendy Lazarus and Francisco Mora, *Online Content for Low-income and Underserved Americans: The Digital Divide's New Frontier, a Strategic Audit of Activities and Opportunities* (Santa Monica, CA: The Children's Partnership, 2000), 17.

PRESERVATION OF LGBT HISTORY: THE ONE ARCHIVE

Yolanda Retter Vargas

This article is about Latina lesbian history and LGBT (lesbian, gay, bisexual, transgender) archives. The task of preserving the records of LGBT history and culture is not easy. LGBT people's history is under-recorded and under-preserved, and too often it has been destroyed. In many cases, we cannot even be sure if people were LGBT because too many LGBT people were (and are) afraid to publicly claim their identity.

Who is a lesbian (in this case a Latina lesbian) can be debated ad nauseam. While heterosexual women do not have to prove that they consorted with a man nor officially proclaim that they are heterosexual, lesbians are required to say that they were intimate with a woman and/or proclaim a lesbian identity before they will be classified as such in historical texts and in many archives and collections. While I am willing to spend some time debating who is a bona fide member of Lesbian Nation, I am more concerned about collecting, preserving, and making visible the history of Latina lesbians.

At present, Latina lesbian history is underrepresented in both LGBT and non-LGBT archives and collections. This is part of a general pattern. The history of lesbians of color is generally hidden between the lines of heterosexual, male, and white history. Although lesbians of color have been consistently present in all facets of quotidian life and in social movements, it was not until the late 1970s that they began to organize "out" groups, present their viewpoints at conferences, edit anthologies, and reclaim and preserve their history.

Their history is not easy to find because in many cases, lesbians were and are afraid to come out; because collecting it, only recently became part of the LGBT agenda; and because Latina lesbians are triply invisible as women, people of color, and lesbians. In some cases our presence is underplayed in non-LGBT archives and collections, perhaps out of fear of alienating homophobic donors and supporters. In the LGBT community, efforts to collect and manage materials related to lesbians of color are sometimes met with interference and resistance from people not of color, who feel that they are the owners of LGBT archives and arbiters of what and who represents our history. Our Latina lesbian history has generally been collected by default, as when a Latina lesbian individual or group donates materials to an archive or in one case because a Latina working in an archive decides to actively collect it.

While neglecting people of color in general and lesbians to some extent, LGBT people have nevertheless been collecting and preserving their history for over 75 years. The first known LGBT archive was founded in Germany by Magnus Hirschfeld at the Berlin Institute of Sexual Research in 1919. The institute was destroyed by the Nazis in 1933.

The preservation of LGBT history is part of LGBT activism. By that I mean that it is one proactive approach taken on behalf of a despised and marginalized group. In the case of archives, proactive means collecting, preserving, and making our history visible. For those who are not familiar with LGBT history in the United States, I would like to provide a brief introduction, one that also demonstrates the significant gaps in U.S. Latina lesbian history. One of the earliest documented records of a Latina/o LGBT person in the United States is the story of Elvira Mugarrieta, daughter of a 19th-century Mexican diplomat stationed in San Francisco. Babe Bean Garland (as Elvira was known) dressed in male attire, passed as a man, worked as a journalist in the Philippines during the Spanish-American War, and later worked with homeless men in San Francisco where Garland died in 1936. Garland did not state she was a lesbian and did not spend much time with women. Today she might identify as transgender.

The first known gay group met briefly in Chicago in 1924 and published several issues of a newsletter *Friendship and Freedom*. The all-male group broke up after the wife of one of the members reported them to the police. The first known lesbian newsletter (*Vice Versa*) was published in 1947–1948 by a white woman who used the name "Lisa Ben" (as in lesbian). Lisa worked in Burbank, California, at a movie studio, and her boss told her to always look busy. This was before mimeograph machines and photocopiers, so Lisa typed two copies of each newsletter using 5 carbons, for a total of 12 copies per issue. She is still alive and thinks that her newsletter was no big deal.

The first lasting activist LGBT groups in the United States formed in California in the 1950s during the McCarthy era. They were Mattachine, ONE, and DOB (Daughters of Bilitis).

Mattachine and DOB also had chapters in other cities. These groups worked on behalf of homosexual rights at a time when U.S. society was almost unilaterally homophobic. DOB was founded by eight women, including two lesbians of color, one of whom was Chicana. In the 1960s, Ada Bello, a *Cubana*, joined DOB in Philadelphia. She edited the chapter newsletter and later was editor of the Homosexual Action League (HAL) newsletter. HAL was a co-gender organization with a strong lesbian presence and blatantly proclaimed itself to be a gay activist group rather than a (less threatening) gay social group.

In the midst of the turbulent 1960s, a watershed event for LGBT people took place. On a hot summer night in June of 1969, when police raided The Stonewall, a gay bar in New York City, patrons fought back. This was the first homosexual uprising/riot in the United States. Sylvia Rivera, a drag queen and later a transgender activist of Puerto Rican and Venezuelan descent, was an active participant that night.

After the uprising, LGBT people all over the United States formed Gay Liberation groups, and there was a dramatic change in how LGBT people saw themselves and in how they worked to change how others saw them. However, few lesbians or people of color joined these groups. There were approximately three Latinas in Lesbian Feminists, an early Los Angeles activist group (ca. 1971). In 1974, a small group of Latina lesbians briefly met in Los Angeles under the name Latin American Lesbians. Salsa Soul Sisters, which formed in New York City in 1974, had several Latina members before it became an African American lesbian group that exists to this day as African Ancestral Lesbians United for Societal Change. As LGBT groups proliferated, so did LGBT publications. One of these, *The Lesbian Tide*, is arguably the newspaper of record for the lesbian feminist decade (the 1970s). Although *The Lesbian Tide* printed little about lesbians of color, its publisher was Jeanne Córdova, a lesbian of Mexican and Irish descent.

Unfortunately, many of the LGBT records generated between the 1950s and the early 1970s were not preserved, and many events were not recorded. This was due in some cases to fear on the part of participants, while in other cases, we did not realize that our activism was historical and worthy of preservation. It was also a time when video cameras were expensive so while there are photos, little film footage exists.

We are fortunate that a few people like gay activist Jim Kepner realized years before Stonewall that LGBT people were invisible, had no public role models, and no history to be proud of. In 1942, Kepner began buying the few available gay and lesbian books and studied police reports and obituaries in newspapers and learned to read between the lines. His collection, at first stored in his living room, grew exponentially and eventually became the International Gay and Lesbian Archive. In the mid-1990s, his archive merged with ONE Incorporated to become the ONE Institute and Archives in Los Angeles.

The ONE is affiliated with the University of Southern California (USC) Library but is owned as a nonprofit organization by the LGBT community. It is housed in a USC building that, ironically enough, used to be a fraternity house. ONE is the largest gay archive in the world. When I say gay, I mean gay male. The largest lesbian archive is the Lesbian Herstory Archive in New York City, which began in activist Joan Nestle's kitchen in the early 1970s. Los Angeles is also home to another lesbian collection, the June Mazer Archive located in West Hollywood. These are only 3 of the more than 120 estimated LGBT archives and collections in the United States and the world.

Like most LGBT archives and collections, the ONE collection contains both primary and secondary sources. This is because for so long we had so little material that anything remotely related to LGBT issues was collected. There is also some fear that someday a backlash in mainstream U.S. culture might cause public institutions to deaccession LGBT materials. ONE's holdings include approximately 6,000 journal titles (representing more than 25 languages), over 19,000 books going back to the 19th century, 13,000 subject files, hundreds of pamphlets, and more than 3,000 videos. Artifacts include political buttons, tee shirts, lobby cards, and original art. There are thousands of photographs of both LGBT-identified people and many whom we can only guess about. This guessing game (about whether or not the subject of an image is a member of a specific community) is a constant challenge for those preserving and/or researching LGBT history.

As with other underfunded, community-owned archives and collections, many of the archival collections at ONE are unprocessed. The difference in funding available at/to academic institutions compared to most community-owned LGBT archives and collections is considerable. This gives rise to the question: should one donate one's LGBT materials to a community archive that has a special interest in preserving the materials but few funds; or to an educational institution that may not have a special interest in processing the materials and making them visible, but has the resources to at least preserve them and is likely to have longevity?

While LGBT archives have managed to save thousands of LGBT items, most co-gender archives lack a substantial amount of material on people of color and lesbians, and all archives, (including those that are lesbian focused) lack material by/about lesbians of color. Materials on bisexual, transgender, and intersex people are also scarce in any archive. The historical lack of lesbian visibility at ONE was one reason that in the mid-990s, a group of lesbian activists suggested that ONE establish a separate lesbian collection. The existence of such a collection at ONE (the LLC) is a reflection of an ongoing political/ideological debate within the LGBT community. Some community members feel that separate collections are a type of ghettoizing, while others consider separate collections to be a form of strategic essentialism and resistant action on the part of lesbians who have for years dealt with sexism and invisibility in male-dominated organizations and projects.

The conflicts over gender and ethnicity within the LGBT communities can be seen in the content of LGBT publications. Much of that content between the 1950s and 1980s focused on white-dominated organizations, groups, people, and events. While male publications published little on lesbian issues, white women overcame that invisibility by producing many lesbian-specific publications. They, in turn, gave little coverage to lesbians of color. Until the 1980s there were few LGBT people of color publications and groups, and this adds to their invisibility in the historical LGBT record.

One of the challenges in gathering material on lesbian and people of color is a lack of trust. Many women and people of color do not trust white and/or male-dominated LGBT archives. This suspicion is similar to that which community groups sometimes feel toward academic archives. Under those circumstances and in an effort to save and preserve lesbian materials, I have at times gone against traditional archival practices. For example, I have accepted materials on loan rather than as gifts. The rationale for this is that in most cases, if we stay in touch and keep the faith, the loan will become a gift. To the argument that an archive cannot afford to process materials that it may be asked to give up later, I say that we can afford to create a brief description or guide to the collection. A brief record is useful to researchers and does not tax our limited resources. At times, those who lend will offer to pay for the guide. Nontraditional situations demand nontraditional responses to ensure the preservation of valuable and scarce materials. The archival practices literature reflects little thinking on why and how collections representing the history and culture of marginalized people must at times be treated differently than other archives.

So what information specific to Latina lesbians do LGBT and non-LGBT archives and collections have? Several years ago, ALA gave me a grant to inventory lesbian materials in West Coast archives and collections. At each stop, I asked about lesbians-of-color materials but found very little. Since that time, I have continued to actively look for sources of Latina lesbian history. I divide these sources into five types: overt, subtle, hidden, destroyed, and unrecorded.

"Overt" is that material where the subject identifies as lesbian. An example is the collection of writings by Juana Maria Paz, a welfare activist and mother, who lived on women's land including several lesbian-of-color land projects in the 1970s and 1980s. This material is housed at the Lesbian Herstory Archives (LHA) in New York City. The LHA also has materials donated by writer and activist Mariana Romo-Carmona, dating back to the early 1980s. This includes materials related to Las Buenas Amigas, a New York group that Mariana helped form in 1986. The Lesbian Legacy Collection at ONE includes several files and a collection of photographs of Lesbianas Unidas, a group that was active in Los Angeles between 1984 and the 1990s.

"Subtle" material is that where one infers through bits of evidence that the woman most likely was lesbian. People like Barbara Jordan fall into the former category. This category also includes instances where the person may have been out of the closet, but an archive hesitates to underscore her lesbian identity. Writer and Professor Sheila Ortiz Taylor falls into the latter category. Her papers are housed at the University of California, Santa Barbara (UCSB). Formerly they were described without reference to her lesbian identity except for the brief statement: "The Oxford Companion to Women's Writing in the United States called [her novel] Faultline 'the first Chicana lesbian Novel.'" Since then, the archivist, upon consulting with the donor, brought her to the "overt" category.

"Hidden" is material that includes the contributions and/or papers of lesbians who were part of a non-lesbian group and/or organization. The organizational records of feminist and women's organizations often contain material by and about lesbians, including Latina ones. However, most descriptions and finding aids do not reflect this presence. Should the person creating the finding aid mention this issue, and how often do they know? How do we ensure that this part of Latina lesbian history is made visible, and what of cases where the Latina lesbian does not want to be "outed"?

"Destroyed" is material that the subject herself and/or families and friends disposed of in order to avoid embarrassing the subject's memory or themselves. "Unrecorded" means that the woman was a lesbian but did not create a personal record that helps us identify her as lesbian. Unlike those women in the "subtle" category, there is little information on the woman. This is a category that due to homophobia may only be important to LGBT people. Unlike other groups, where people are recognizable or remembered as members of a specific community, LGBT people have lost a tremendous amount of their history simply because LGBT (and non-LGBT) people were afraid.

Some Latina lesbian history is difficult to identify because while the woman did not hide her lesbian identity, she did not necessarily focus on lesbianism in her life and work. Stanford University, for example, houses the papers of photographer Laura Aguilar. Her first photo series, which was funded by Connexxus Womens Center/Centro de Mujeres (a West Hollywood lesbian/women's organization) in the late 1980s, was a series on Latina lesbians. Aguilar's subsequent work focuses on cultural and personal themes that are not lesbian specific. The description of the Aguilar collection does, however, include clear references to her lesbian identity.

While much has been lost, lesbians are now saving and collecting Latina lesbian materials. In New York, Juanita Diaz Cotto (aka Ramos), the editor of *Compañeras: Latina Lesbians*, has a collection of lesbian materials from both the United States and Latin America. The June Mazer Archives has several files on Latina lesbians as well as papers donated by writer Terry de la Peña. In Arizona, Yolanda Leyva holds a collection of oral history interviews with Latina lesbians. The Lesbian Herstory Archives in New York has several files on Latina lesbians as well as the aforementioned materials of Paz and Romo Carmona.

As a Latina lesbian activist, I want to ensure that material about lesbians and people of color is collected and made accessible at the ONE and other LGBT and non-LGBT archives. Access to this material can be enhanced via the Internet as in the Lesbian History Project website, which includes a section on lesbians of color. Databases are another access point. A major LGBT database published by EBSCO will soon be available. Its main source of retrospective content is the ONE Archives. As the consultant for people of color content, I search through anthologies, short-run journals, ephemera, dissertations, and videos and books with photographs, identifying Latina lesbian material that seldom appeared in earlier periodicals and monographs.

Some of this material will become part of the LGBT database, and all of it will become part of the Latin@ History and Archives Project. This project will collect written materials (even if they are copies of originals), collect and conduct oral histories, and place information on a website. An important component is a database that will contain locations of primary and secondary materials and also citations and references from articles, books, oral histories, and so on. Perhaps that information can be integrated into the Chicano Database, which at this time retrieves fewer than 100 items under the terms "gay" or "lesbian."

Oral histories are an important method of gathering the history of marginalized groups. In the late 1990s, LLEGO (The National Latina/o Lesbian, Gay, Bisexual, and Transgender Organization) gave Lesbianas Unidas a grant to videotape Latina lesbians and sponsor a community forum on oral history. The Lesbian Legacy Collection at ONE served as the technical consultant. Approximately 10 women were interviewed, and copies of the videos were placed at the LLC. Other LLC Latina lesbian interviews include those done by Alice Hom and Yolanda Retter for their respective dissertations. There are also audiotapes and videos made by University of California, Los Angeles students for a class on Latina lesbians taught in 2001. One obstacle we have found when seeking to interview Latina lesbian elders is that some who are old enough to remember the bad old days are reluctant to be interviewed. One exception is Nancy Valverde, who remembers being harassed and arrested by Los Angeles police during the 1950s for "masquerading" (not wearing the legally required three pieces of female clothing).

A large amount of material is still held in Latina lesbian homes, be it the papers of prominent Latina writers or the *lesbiana* next door. As awareness of the historical importance of the material increases, more Latina lesbian history will make its way to LGBT and non-LGBT collections and archives. The larger challenge is to uncover materials about Latina lesbians who are no longer alive, who lived before the LGBT movement, and who did not publicly identify as lesbian. Hopefully new generations of Latina lesbian scholars will help fill in some of the blanks.

In closing, I would like to make a few suggestions: If you are an archivist and you have received (or in the future receive) LGBT materials (be they overt or covert), please create descriptions and finding aids that reflect the LGBT content of the collection. I invite those of you who are interested in participating in the project of uncovering, collecting, and preserving our Latina lesbian heritage, to contact ONE to discuss issues of preservation, visibility, and finding aids as well as policies and procedures for managing collections that represent the history and culture of marginalized groups.

REARTICULATING THE DIGITAL DIVIDE FOR THE LATINO COMMUNITY

Romelia Salinas

The digital divide is an important issue that merits attention and discussion. In recent years, the issue of the digital divide has received less attention by researchers, policy makers, and the media. The ubiquitous presence of information technologies such as computers, cell phones, and wireless networks within our society may have created the illusion of a diminishing or disappearing digital divide. However, for the Latino community, the digital divide continues and grows. As information professionals, it is imperative that we refocus attention to this social dilemma and work toward addressing it.

The intent of this article is to report on the current status of Latinos and the digital divide and to introduce a broader and multidimensional conceptualization of the divide for consideration.

First, the following observations are made about the social context in which information professionals work.

- *Living in a networked world*: We are living in an era known as the "information age" or the "networked world." An age ushered in by the pervasive availability and use of information and communication technologies (ICTs). These tools have freed individuals from time and spatial constraints and have changed the way people communicate, learn, work, and play.

- *Libraries becoming more digital*: The Internet and other technologies have also changed libraries. This shift is evident in the constant increase in subscriptions to electronic databases and online journals and in services such as electronic reserves and online reference.
- *Increase and diversity of Latino population*: In addition, there has been not only an increase in the Latino population in the United States, but it is becoming more diverse. People come for many different countries, with unique cultural customs, histories, and languages.
- *Low household access to the Internet for Latinos*: At the same time, Latinos continue to lose ground in terms of household access to the Internet.

This diagram (see Figure 11.1) charts data from the various *Falling Through the Net* reports since 1997 (ntia.doc.gov/reports/anol/index .html). As is illustrated, there has been an increase in the access gap between whites and Latinos. In 1997 there was only a 13-point difference; whereas in 2003, the gap had widened to 28 points so Latinos lost ground over the years, even though rates have increased not at the same pace compared to other ethnic groups.

The most current statistics available on this issue are California based. Californians generally have high rates of computer and Internet use. However, according to a recent study released in 2008 by the Public Policy Institute of California, Latinos in California lag far behind other groups. Only 48 percent of Latinos reported using the Internet whereas other groups were found to have close to 80% percent use rates. A close examination of the use rates reveal that they have not increased since 2000 for

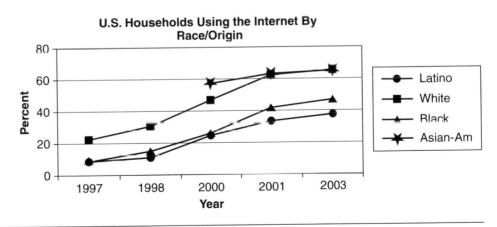

FIGURE 11.1

Source: Public Policy Institute of California, June 2008

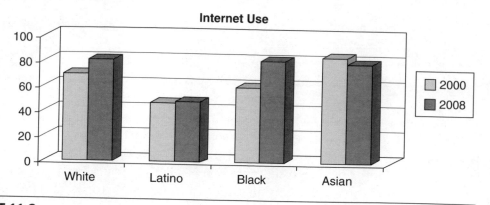

Internet Use

FIGURE 11.2

Source: Public Policy Institute of California, June 2008

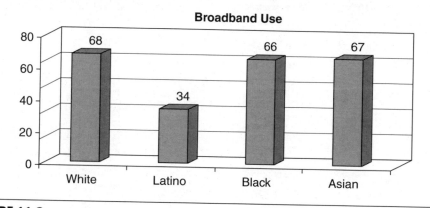

Broadband Use

FIGURE 11.3

Source: Public Policy Institute of California, June 2008

Latinos, whereas increases for other groups are evident. Figure 11.2 illustrates these findings.

In terms of broadband use (see Figure 11.3), that same report showed the lowest rates of use with 34 percent for Latinos. Broadband access is crucial for accessing many of what we would call Web 2.0 technologies or second generation Internet applications. These more interactive, multi-media applications require faster connections for maximum benefit.

So far this article has addressed Latinos as a general group. But even within the group there are certain sectors that are at greater risk of experiencing the digital divide. The following statistics are from a 2007 report conducted by the Pew Hispanic Center and the Pew Internet Project.

- *Home computer ownership rate for youth*: Native-born youth (ages 5–25) in the United States who are white, African American, or other boast a home computer ownership rate of 77 percent, whereas 58 percent of Latino native born and 36 percent of Latino immigrant youth have home computers. So clearly, Latino immigrant youth are excluded from the benefits provided by owning a computer. The disparity is the greatest for young immigrants.

- *Internet use by language*: Seventy-eight percent of Latinos who are English dominant and 76 percent of bilingual Latinos use the Internet, compared with 32 percent of Spanish-dominant Hispanic adults. These statistics identify the Spanish-speaking Latinos as less likely to use the Internet. It should also be noted that the disparity can be due to a lack of relevant content for this particular subsection of the Latino community.
- *Internet use by educational attainment*: Eighty-nine percent of Latinos who have a college degree, 70 percent of Latinos who completed high school, and 31 percent of Latinos who did not complete high school go online. Again, these statistics indicate that Latinos who did not graduate from high school have less access to the Internet. This is a grave issue considering that the Latino community has one of the highest high school dropout rates in the nation.

Up to this point, this article has discussed the digital divide in terms of the technology and whether people have access to it or not. What I would like to do now is provide a much broader conceptualization of the digital divide. In my research, I conducted an extensive literature review to determine how the digital divide has been conceived. At the end of this effort, I was able to group the various barriers to accessing digital information into four categories:

- *Connectivity Barriers*: These are related to the technological apparatus required to access and use the digital information such as computers, software, and connections. This is the most prevalent way the digital divide is measured in the literature; consequently, the dominant understanding of the digital divide has been one about access to the physical technology. However, there are more than connectivity barriers to the digital divide.
- *Literacy Barriers*: The second types of barriers are those related to literacy. This includes computer and information literacy. Basic computer/technology is essential, but to be able to do more demanding information seeking requires higher levels of information literacy. These various forms of barriers have been referred to as second-level digital divides. So it is important to know not only who uses the Internet, but also to distinguish varying levels of online skills among individuals. For users who lack the skills to manipulate the computer and make sense of the information, physical access alone will not be beneficial. Hence variation in literacy does create disparity among users.
- *Content Barriers*: The third type of barrier has to do with the available content. The reality is that digital content to meet the needs

of certain populations may not exist or may not be available in a language or at a level that the user needs. The Children's Partnership produced a key report illuminating this issue, entitled *Online Content for Low-income and Underserved Americans: the Digital Divide's New Frontier* (childrenspartnership.org). They challenged the belief that everything exists on the web. Their report found that content of interest to low-income communities was limited or unavailable. Users who are nonmainstream, low literate, or speakers of languages other than English are most affected.

- *Psycho-Social Barriers*: The last way the digital divide has been framed within the literature is as a psychological and social issue. Some users find it psychologically uncomfortable to use computers or to navigate the complexities of the Web. Hence, these users will avoid using the web or will have a more frustrating experience. This is not unlike the concept of library anxiety that has been well documented in the LIS literature. While other studies have found that users with access to human support networks are more likely to successfully access and use the Internet. Those who lack such support networks get stuck if they encounter a technical or literacy problem. They don't have anyone to turn to for assistance in the problem-solving process. Clearly, there is a psychological and social element to the digital divide that also needs to be considered as libraries seek remedies to this social dilemma.

I conclude by stating that the digital divide is more than not owning a computer or not having access to the Internet. It a complex phenomenon that shifts as information communication technology permeates our information-seeking behaviors. As librarians it is important to have a more holistic understanding of the digital divide, so that we can implement programs and initiatives to address the multiple dimensions of the digital divide. It is only by broadening our definition of the divide that we can truly bridge that divide for the Latino and similar communities.

Chapter 12

The Role of the Library Associations

SALALM, THE SEMINAR ON THE ACQUISITION OF LATIN AMERICAN LIBRARY MATERIALS: THE EVOLUTION OF AN AREA STUDIES LIBRARIANSHIP ORGANIZATION

Ana María Cobos and Philip S. McCleod

The Seminar on the Acquisition of Latin American Library Materials (SALALM) celebrated its 53rd annual meeting in New Orleans, Louisiana, May 30–June 3, 2008. What started as a one-time meeting about the acquisition of Latin American materials evolved into a central forum to consider all types of issues that impact Latin American librarianship. The organization's constitution states that SALALM's purpose is:

> To promote the improvement of library services in support of study and research activities in Latin American and inter-American Affairs; to provide an association for study programs in which scholars, librarians and others interested in book and library resources relating to Latin American and inter-American studies can discuss problems, and carry out programs of common interest; and to promote cooperative efforts to achieve better library services as a means of encouraging and advancing international understanding of the Western Hemisphere.[1]

This essay examines SALALM's history and the changes the group experienced during the past 50 years. The first half recounts SALALM's first 25 years, including its foundation and early history, incorporation and subsequent development, major activities, and early collaborations with other organizations. The second half of the essay describes SALALM's growth and organizational development over the last 25 years including collaboration with groups that share a similar interest and its various activities to reach out to colleagues in Latin America and promote library development in the region.

Background

The post–World War II era witnessed the United States' emergence as a major global power. Within the ivy covered walls of American academia, a new generation of scholars perceived a general lack of knowledge about the developing world and harbored concerns about the status of foreign area studies inside the university. For libraries, this raised issues centering on the question of how to collect foreign language materials needed to support research in these emerging fields. Against this backdrop, a group of librarians and Latin American specialists decided to take concrete action.

First SALALM

A Seminar on the Acquisition of Latin American Library Materials convened at Chinsegut Hill, an estate belonging to the University of Florida located in Brooksville, Florida, on June 14–15, 1956. This assembly was principally organized by the tireless efforts of Marietta Daniels Shepard, the head of the Organization of American States' Library Development Program. The seminar sought to address three central problems of Latin American library material acquisition: "How to know what has been or is being issued; how to get what is needed for the particular library; and how to process and preserve the material acquired."[2] Thirty-two participants represented major research universities, United States government and international libraries, and private and public libraries, as well as an international book dealer.[3] The first seminar consisted of five sessions that considered 16 working papers dealing with material selection, book purchase and exchange, nonbook materials, periodicals, and government documents.[4] A final session allowed for a summary of the discussions and the adoption of resolutions for further action. One resolution called for the seminar to become an annual meeting.

Later Events

Because the seminar was intended as a one-time event, there was no forethought about the need for a formal governing mechanism.[5] Early SALALMs adopted a very basic organizational structure. Marietta Daniels

Shepard of the Organization of American States (OAS) was selected as SALALM's first permanent secretary, a position she occupied until 1973. Additionally, an organizing committee was selected to assist in the planning of the annual meeting and other administrative functions, but, in reality, Marietta took it upon herself to create the agendas and run the meetings.

In this early period, SALALM had no members in the traditional sense, and there were no membership dues during the organization's first 12 years. Payment of the conference registration fee was paid by the attendee's institution and is the closest approximation of membership at the time.[6] SALALM participants received a copy of the *Final Report and Working Papers* and an invitation to attend the next seminar. The annual meetings proved to be self-supporting, even producing a profit that meeting attendees would normally vote to share with the institution hosting that year's meeting and the OAS.[7] Attendance at SALALM's annual meeting grew dramatically during the 1960s. The number of participants increased from 47 at the 6th SALALM in 1961 to 121 at the 12th SALALM in 1967.[8] As attendance grew, the new participants no longer exclusively represented the prestigious research universities with large Latin American collections.

Incorporation

By the late 1960s it became apparent that the group needed a more formal structure to administer and coordinate all SALALM activities. This infrastructure would also provide a more stable financial basis than the pay-as-you go annual meeting. In 1967, SALALM decided to incorporate. At the 13th SALALM (1968) in Lawrence, Kansas, the membership adopted a constitution, bylaws, and approved articles of incorporation.[9]

The constitution provided for an executive committee of four officers: president, vice president, executive secretary, and treasurer who have the responsibility to take urgent administrative measures, in addition to their defined duties.[10] The constitution also provided for a larger executive board whose duty is to administer the affairs of the organization. The executive board consists of the four members of the executive committee and other elected and ex-officio officers.[11]

The bylaws provided for dues and created three types of membership: personal, institutional, and special. Personal membership is divided into four categories: regular, student, honorary, and emeritus.[12] The bylaws also distinguish between dues-paying members and participants in the annual meeting.[13] Membership figures for SALALM became available in 1968–1969. For the first time, the seminar had 201 members of which 143 were personal members, and 58 were institutional ones.[14]

The bylaws also created a formal basis for the organization's committee structure. A set of *Basic Documents* was adopted in 1968 that outlined committee responsibilities and procedures.[15] SALALM has two types of committees executive board committees whose job is to maintain the organization, and the substantive committees (including the subcommittees) that have achieved many of the organization's most notable accomplishments.[16] SALALM's committees have been an important part of the organization since its founding in 1956. Much of SALALM's work has been conducted through its committees. The number of committees has varied over time depending on the needs and interests of the membership. A hallmark of SALALM is the high degree of involvement of its members in the organization's activities. One study showed that for 1977–1978, almost 40 percent of SALALM's membership held committee appointments.[17]

Changing Times

The formal incorporation and continued growth of SALALM increased significantly the secretariat's workload by the early 1970s. Long-time SALALM executive secretary Marietta Daniels Shepard's primary job duty was to direct the OAS's library development program, and it proved increasingly difficult for her to balance all of her responsibilities. The day had arrived when SALALM would have to consider moving the secretariat from the OAS.[18]

After a great deal of discussion, SALALM's executive board mailed out over 400 letters to different institutions seeking proposals to host the secretariat in 1973.[19] The executive board accepted a proposal from the University of Massachusetts Amherst, to host the secretariat for a period of three to five years. The University of Massachusetts offer included a half-time work release of SALALM's new executive secretary, Pauline Collins; the provision of clerical support, offices; and storage space. SALALM paid for the move of the secretariat and cover its recurring postage, telephone, and printing costs. After a three-year stay in Amherst, the secretariat moved to the University of Texas at Austin in 1976.[20] SALALM marked another significant milestone in the late 1960s and early 1970s when the organization sought to expand its international presence and began to hold its annual meetings outside of the continental United States on a regular basis. SALALM 14 (1969) met in San Juan, Puerto Rico; SALALM 15 (1970) was held in Toronto, Canada; and Puebla, Mexico, played host to SALALM 16 (1971). Other meetings held outside the United States include SALALM 18 (1973) in Port-of-Spain, Trinidad and Tobago; SALALM 20 (1975) in Bogotá, Colombia; and SALALM 23 (1978) in London, England. SALALM's unofficial policy became to hold one annual meeting outside of the United States every two to three years.[21]

SALALM in the 1970s

SALALM continued to grow over the decade. In 1970–1971, SALALM had 163 personal members and 91 institutional ones. By the end of the decade (1979–1980), the organization had 270 personal members and 121 institutional ones.[22] Many new members came from institutions that had smaller Latin American collections or focused on undergraduate teaching.[23] The interests of the organization moved beyond the acquisition of Latin American materials to include such matters as reference, bibliographic instruction, the training of librarians, technology, vendor relations, interlibrary cooperation, library operations, services to the Spanish-speaking community in the United States, and Latin American Studies.[24] These trends continue to the present day and are still evolving to address the needs of programs that focus on the rapidly expanding Latino populations in the United States.

SALALM's Annual Meeting

The annual meeting is the most obvious manifestation of SALALM's activities. SALALM 2 (1957) through 9 (1964) concentrated almost exclusively on geographically focused themes, acquisitions issues related to a particular nation or group of countries. The themes of later annual meetings, SALALMs 11 through 20, considered not only acquisitions issues but also developing collections of different sizes; collection of science, technical and legal materials; and the education of area specialists. The themes of the annual meeting became even broader when SALALM 20 (1975) in Bogotá considered "New Writers of Latin America," and SALALM 23 (1978) in London dealt with Latin American Studies in Europe.[25]

The annual meeting gradually increased in length from two days in 1956 to five days by 1976.[26] The organization of the conference program was and continues to be the responsibility of SALALM's president.[27] The conference schedule includes committee meetings, meetings of interest groups, reports on the activities of collaborating organizations, an opening session and keynote address, sessions where formal papers are presented, workshops, and a business meeting at the conclusion.

Publications

Publications are another very important activity of SALALM. The most important publication was initially called the *Final Report and Working Papers*. One edited volume appeared after each SALALM meeting. The organization of the volumes included an introduction by the executive secretary, a summary of all of the sessions, the conference program, resolutions adopted at the meeting, a register of participants, a list of SALALM committees, and the body of each working paper. Starting with the 20th volume, the *Final Report* adopted the theme of the conference as its title, and the subtitle is the number of the annual SALALM proceeding. These volumes contain the conference program, a summary of each session, annual reports, and the text of the working papers.[28]

SALALM started publishing its *Bibliography Series* in 1969.[29] The series was later renamed the *Bibliography & Reference Series*.[30] An editorial board oversees the publications program and makes recommendations about specific ones.[31] Examples of some of the publications that have appeared in this series include the *Basic List of Latin American Materials in Spanish, Portuguese, and French*; *A Directory of Vendors of Latin American Library Materials*; several lists of serial publications available for exchange; and the *Bibliography of Latin American and Caribbean Bibliographies*.[32]

For its first decade and a half, SALALM lacked a formal means to update its members outside of its annual meetings. The first SALALM newsletter appeared in January 1973 as a more regular source of information for the membership. The newsletter began as a semiannual publication but soon became a quarterly. Now the newsletter is issued six times per year. The newsletter includes messages from the president, news from the secretariat, news about significant acquisitions, member and institutional news, information about book vendors, conferences and book fairs, and related subjects.[33]

SALALM and Other Organizations

Since its inception in 1956, SALALM has enjoyed and actively pursued formal and informal collaborations with other organizations. SALALM's initial association with the Organization of American States proved beneficial for the first 17 years of its existence. The OAS provided a permanent home for the organization between the annual meetings. Marietta Daniels Shepard, as SALALM's executive secretary, with financial support from the OAS, developed the seminar's agenda with that year's host organization, assigned authorship of working papers, invited conference participants, and sent out the working papers prior to the meetings. After the seminar, Daniels Shepard distributed the resolutions adopted at the meeting and edited and distributed the *Final Report and Working Papers*.[34]

SALALM pursued several other notable collaborations with different organizations during its first 25 years: to help obtain Latin American imprints, the Latin American Collaborative Acquisitions Program (LACAP); to preserve endangered and bulky research materials, the Latin American Microforms Project (LAMP); and to provide better bibliographic access to periodical literature, the *Hispanic American Periodicals Index* (HAPI). SALALM also has enjoyed more informal relations with groups that have similar interests such as the Hispanic Division of the Library of Congress (LC) and the Latin American Studies Association (LASA).

LACAP

Since the first SALALM, there had been discussion of forming a collaborative program to acquire Latin American books and other imprints. William Kurth of the Library of Congress undertook a three-month trip in 1958 to explore publishing and the acquisition of materials from Chile, Paraguay, Peru, Bolivia, Colombia, and Venezuela. He reported his findings at the Fourth SALALM (1959) and stated his belief that it would be necessary to have a "cooperative acquisitions representative" in the region to secure needed publications.[35]

The Latin American Cooperative Acquisitions Program (LACAP) began in 1960 under the informal agreement of the University of Texas at Austin, the New York Public Library, and the private firm of Stechert-Hafner. Dr. Nettie Lee Benson of the University of Texas at Austin made an initial trip for LACAP to Ecuador, Peru, Chile, and Bolivia with instructions to purchase multiple copies of most significant Latin American publications. The major problem Benson encountered was finding multiple copies of every title. She would later report to the Fifth SALALM (1960) that the majority of books were distributed by authors, not the publishers. Moreover, even the major Latin American publishers did not have complete records of all imprints. Dr. Benson made two further acquisitions trips in 1961 and 1962. The firm of Stechert-Hafner engaged a full-time purchasing agent in 1962 to travel throughout Latin America to maintain personal contact with vendors to ensure that book dealers in the various nations supplied a continual flow of books.[36]

LACAP had difficulties acquiring materials from certain regions, especially Brazil and the Caribbean; and certain types of materials, such as government documents and university press publications. Nevertheless, LACAP annually acquired some 4,000 titles over its 12-year history and established foundational collections of Latin Americana in many North American libraries.[37] In 1969, the Stechert-Hafner firm was acquired by Crowell, Collier and MacMillan. LACAP did not prosper under its new management. The program's high overhead and increasing rate of duplication made it progressively less attractive to both owners and clients. With the resignation of Stechert-Hafner's president in 1971, LACAP's demise was assured, and the arrangement terminated two years later.[38] Still, LACAP had made Latin American book dealers aware of the potential of the North American academic library market and that they could offer books at a lower price and still make a profit.[39]

With the end of LACAP, SALALM 18 stepped into the breech inviting many Latin American book dealers to its annual meeting. SALALM 18 included several panels dealing with the book trade.[40] By 1975, book dealers accounted for 6 percent of SALALM members, and this increased to over 10 percent of the membership by 1981.[41] To this day, SALALM continues to provide a major forum where Latin American book dealers and librarians can meet to forge personal relationships, discuss the needs of the profession as a whole, and ensure that individual libraries receive the publications they require.

LAMP

The Latin American Microform Project (LAMP) was the product of SALALM's special concern for the medium as a way to make Latin American publications more accessible to researchers.[42] Since its earliest days, several SALALM member institutions undertook large microfilm projects. In 1964, the first *Microfilms Project Newsletter* appeared, reporting on microfilming programs that were in the planning stages, in progress, or completed.[43] Reports on microfilm projects became an agenda item at SALALM's annual conference.

In 1973, SALALM formed an advisory committee to the Center for Research Libraries that served as the genesis for the creation of LAMP.[44] Founded in 1975, this voluntary program is funded by an annual fee from member libraries and administered by the Center for Research Libraries.[45] LAMP conducts microfilming projects of unique Latin American materials. Although not specifically a SALALM project, most of the members of LAMP's executive board are SALALM members. A LAMP membership meeting is conducted during the annual SALALM meeting to report on the status of active microfilming projects and to consider new undertakings.

HAPI

The *Hispanic American Periodical Index* (HAPI) is another example of SALALM's cooperation with other organizations. HAPI was founded at Arizona State University in 1970 and later moved to the UCLA Latin American Center. HAPI began as a printed "Annual index of citations to academic journals with Latin American content." Since 1996, HAPI has been available via the Internet. The HAPI website was recently redesigned, and SALALM members provided valuable feedback throughout the process.[46] While HAPI is not a SALALM project per se, it relies heavily on SALALM members as volunteer indexers. The director and staff of HAPI provide an annual report and training for the volunteer indexers during the SALALM conference.[47]

Library of Congress

The Library of Congress is an example of a long-term informal relationship that influenced SALALM's development throughout its history. The foundation of the Hispanic Division of the Library of Congress pre-dates that of SALALM by 20 years, and members of the Library of Congress staff played important roles in the establishment of the organization. Dr. Howard Cline, director of LC's Hispanic Division in 1956, encouraged SALALM to become an annual meeting, proposed the regional and country specific focus of the early SALALM conferences, and promoted examination of the issue of cooperative acquisitions. LC also provided SALALM with a list of recommended Latin American book vendors after the termination of LACAP in 1973. Members of the Library of Congress staff attend SALALM's annual conference, often providing updates on LC's activities; publications; its collections; and most notably, the *Handbook of Latin American Studies*. Some LC staff members have been elected president of the organization.[48]

LASA

The support of Latin American studies has always been a major focus of SALALM. The Latin American Studies Association (LASA) was founded in 1966. SALALM has had a more casual working relationship with LASA over the years than with other groups.[49] Many SALALM members attend LASA meetings on a regular basis, and the greatest interaction between the two organizations occurs in LASA's Committee on Scholarly Resources. Traditionally, SALALM members have chaired this committee, and some Scholarly Resource Committee projects have been discussed at SALALM meetings.[50] One example of a long-standing collaborative project is the *Bibliography of Sexuality Studies in Latin America*.[51]

Other Organizations

SALALM made efforts to maintain contact with ALA and REFORMA. The early SALALM annual meetings were often held at times and locations that facilitated members' attendance at the American Library Association's annual summer conference. For years, the SALALM executive board would conduct a meeting at ALA's midwinter meeting. As a result of recent efforts to collaborate more closely with ALA, SALALM became an affiliate with them in 2007. With respect to REFORMA, Dr. Arnulfo Trejo was actively involved with SALALM in its early years.[52] This would eventually form the basis for further connections between the two organizations.

SALALM, 1980s to the Present

By the late 1970s and early 1980s, SALALM had become a mature organization that had no other area of study could rival, in great part due to Marietta Daniels Shepard's extraordinary dedication and that of her many colleagues who also believed in Latin America, librarianship, cooperation, and communication.[53] As the years passed, SALALM continued its development as a professional group through its annual conferences and numerous research and organizational activities.

By the early 1980s, the association had successfully achieved its primary mission of establishing strong Latin American research collections, primarily in North American and European academic libraries, to support Latin American Studies teaching and research. These collections, and the bibliographic compilations and research aids, are exemplary achievements in terms of national and international collaboration.[54] The need to maintain and develop these rich collections is an ongoing concern, but the urgency to create new collections to support Latin American Studies programs had passed by the 1980s.

By the early 1980s, in response to its own achievements, membership interests, and changing needs of the Latin American Studies research community SALALM's leadership began to steer the organization in other directions. We can categorize SALALM's development during the last 25 years into four types: (1) organizational growth and development, including expansion of its own publications; (2) membership development and outreach; (3) technology; (4) and growth of collaboration with organizations that share a similar interest.

Organizational Growth

As noted earlier, SALALM developed substantially as a professional organization during its first 25 years. By the 1970s, SALALM had incorporated and grown from an initial one-time meeting of fewer than 50 Latin Americanists in 1956 to a membership of almost 400.[55] SALALM's strong leadership nurtured its organizational infrastructure so that by the 1980s, it was a very solid and secure organization whose members had made lasting contributions to Latin American bibliography.

A very important achievement of the organization during this period concerns its financial stability. Initially, the seminars managed to recoup the cost of the conferences, and a few meetings made a small profit that would be folded into the costs of the subsequent seminar. For many years, the institution that hosted the secretariat provided support in terms of staff, space, and other in-kind contributions. As the organization's needs became more extensive, fewer institutions were able to provide such support, and it became evident that SALALM had to provide for some or all of the needs of its secretariat. Through the dedicated stewardship of the Finance Committee, SALALM established an endowment and developed investment plans that have allowed the organization to support several critically important activities, including its ability to assume a greater proportion of the cost of running the secretariat.

These foundational achievements made it possible for SALALM to focus on its other mission: that of supporting library development and librarianship in Latin America through various organizational and individual efforts. Among the initiatives made possible by the organization's solid financial footing are its Enlace/Outreach program and the endowment established for the Marietta Daniels Shepard Scholarship at the University of Texas at Austin. These programs are discussed below.

SALALM's publications developed along with the organization to maintain communication among its members and share its knowledge and expertise with the Latin American Studies community and other researchers. Starting in the mid-1980s, SALALM publications took on a more professional look as the editorial board developed strict publication guidelines. SALALM publications are distributed to institutional members, and they are available for sale from the secretariat. In addition, since 1992, SALALM documents have been deposited in one location in each Latin American country.[56]

An example of how the organization adapts to changing needs of the research community is the affiliated group, Iberian Studies in SALALM (ISiS). Created in 2005, ISiS's mission "is to provide a forum within SALALM for identifying, collecting, organizing, providing access to and preserving information resources from and about the Iberian Peninsula in support of education and research." This interest group reflects the job description of many Latin American Studies bibliographers who also have collection responsibilities for Spain and Portugal. The ISiS website provides a wealth of resources and reports on membership activities. For example, SALALM members' reports of their activities at the international book fair, LIBER 2006, are posted at the site.[57]

Most recently, during the 2007 conference in Albuquerque, New Mexico, a new ad hoc group called Academic Latina/o Zone of Activism and Research (ALZAR) organized itself, "To channel efforts to serve a wide range of collection development and other information needs in response to the growing presence of Latina/os in the United States and the development of U.S. Latino Studies programs." This newest affiliate group's "Goal is to provide a link (virtual and real) to resources addressing Latina/o issues in the academic setting." The group reflects the need for resources to support the growth of Latino/a studies at the undergraduate and research levels in the United States and beyond. This is another example of a group of librarians within SALALM collaborating to respond to evolving needs of the library community. About 50 to 75 academic and public librarians and other professionals attended this first meeting in Albuquerque. The ALZAR website became a reality in the summer of 2007.[58]

Membership and Outreach

SALALM's membership numbers are in the hundreds rather than the thousands. The 2007 membership stands at 373, with 264 personal and 109 institutional members.[59] Although its membership may not seem large when compared with the membership of ALA, REFORMA, or other library associations, SALALM's extremely high level of active member participation in its committees, conferences, and other activities is the envy of other librarian organizations. SALALM's membership represents a wide variety of librarians and other professionals ranging from those who work in large research institutions like UCLA, University of Texas at Austin, Columbia, Harvard, and New York Public Library to numerous undergraduate colleges and universities, a significant number of book dealers and publishers, and more than 80 personal and institutional members from countries other than the United States.[60]

For the 1991 San Diego conference, SALALM's executive secretary prepared a study of the organization's membership through 1990.[61] This analysis showed that the membership had not only grown significantly over time to a total of 464—with 316 personal members and 148 institutional members by 1990, but also that SALALM's membership had changed from the initial group that was constituted mostly of academics and administrators to one that is made up almost entirely of working librarians and book dealers.[62] Still, though the membership had grown to be almost 18 times its original size, it had stabilized and mirrored the "graying" of the library profession at large as well as the "graying of the foreign language and area studies community."[63] Further, the study showed that newer members often represented smaller institutions that support undergraduate teaching. These newer members frequently held positions that assumed collection development responsibilities for Latin American Studies among one or more additional collection duties including ethnic, multicultural, and cultural studies.

As the original members of SALALM began to retire, the organization made the decision to recognize its founding members and others who had made significant contributions to the organization by establishing an honorary membership status in 1968.[64] Twenty-five SALALM members have been recognized with this status through 2008. All honorary members have played a vital role in SALALM's early years and beyond.[65]

Another example of the organization's maturity and financial stability is the creation of the José Toribio Medina Award in 1981. SALALM created this award to recognize outstanding contributions by SALALM members in the area of bibliography. The recipient of the award receives a certificate plus an honorarium of $250. Thirty-three SALALM members have been recognized with this award through 2008. Among those listed are the editors and authors of standard Latin American Studies reference works such as the *Handbook of Latin American Studies*, the *Hispanic American Periodicals Index*, the *Encyclopedia of Latin American History and Culture*, among other significant contributions.[66]

Beginning in the late 1980s, in response to the stabilization of the membership, the membership committee and other leaders started to explore options of reaching out to other professionals both within and beyond North America and Europe to publicize the organization's work and its many benefits. The membership committee developed brochures in English, Spanish, and Portuguese, and then sent these to library schools and other organizations in an effort to identify new members. In addition, a new members' orientation is offered at the annual conference and brief introductions are posted in the SALALM listserv (LALA-L) and published in the newsletter to welcome new members and encourage their active participation. In 2005, the membership committee established the New Member Travel Fund whose purpose is to increase both membership and outreach.[67] To aid with its mission, the membership committee also has a prominent place on the SALALM website.

In 1986, SALALM created a travel grant program, called Enlace/Outreach, as one part of its efforts to expand outreach to colleagues in Latin America. The goal of the Enlace/Outreach Committee "Is to foster professional contacts between U.S. and Latin American and Caribbean librarians and other professionals who work in library settings."[68] Enlace grants provide financial assistance to offset most of the costs associated with conference participation. Funding for the grants is provided in part by SALALM, by member contributions, but primarily by the very successful Enlace raffles held during the annual conference. The call for applications (in English, Spanish, and Portuguese) is posted on the SALALM website, sent to numerous listservs (in the United States, Latin America, and beyond) and is published in the SALALM newsletter in the fall to disseminate information about the availability of the travel grants program.

Since 1986, Enlace has supported the participation of Latin American colleagues at the annual conference where they must take an active role in the conference program. In that first year, three colleagues, one from Mexico and two from Argentina, were invited to present papers at the Berlin conference. Within a few years, this experimental program was institutionalized so that by the 2008 conference, SALALM had hosted a total of 70 Latin American colleagues as conference participants.[69] Eleven past and five current Enlace "becarios" (travel grant recipients) attended the 2006 conference in Santo Domingo, Dominican Republic.[70] Another indication of the program's success is that several Enlace "becarios" have become active members of the association. The contributions of Enlace "becarios" provide valuable perspectives about Latin American resources and the needs of the profession in Latin America and the Caribbean.

A further reflection of its commitment to the development of librarianship and the library profession in Latin America, and its own financial strength, is SALALM's approval of an effort to support library development in Latin America in 1985 through the creation of the Marietta Daniels Shepard (MDS) Endowed Scholarship at the School of Information of the University of Texas at Austin.[71] To date, at least 10 students from Argentina, Brazil, Guatemala, Mexico, Peru, and Uruguay have received support from the MDS scholarship to complete a master's, post-master's, or doctoral degree. At least two of these scholarship recipients are or have been active SALALM members.[72]

Another example of SALALM's efforts to share its knowledge and expertise with colleagues from Latin America and also learn about Latin American resources, programs, and services, is the grant that SALALM received in 1992 from the Fideicomiso para la Cultura México-Estados Unidos. SALALM hosted five librarians from Mexico who spent two to three months in libraries in California, Arizona, and New Mexico. At their host institution, these Mexican colleagues had opportunities to learn about academic librarianship through active participation in a variety of projects and share their knowledge and expertise with their counterparts. Three of these Mexican librarians maintain current professional and personal relationships with SALALM colleagues in the host libraries.

In 1991, SALALM 36 was held in San Diego; and Luis Herrera, then deputy director of the San Diego Public Library, was invited to present a paper at the conference. In his presentation, he challenged SALALM to forge partnerships with other organizations such as REFORMA, whose membership is constituted almost entirely by public librarians, to share its knowledge and expertise about acquiring Spanish language materials to serve the rapidly growing Latina/o populations served by public librarians.[73]

Although SALALM's primary mission has been that of creating and supporting Latin American collections and research, individual members of the organization have been interested in addressing the information needs of the Latino populations in the United States. In the 1970s, SALALM approved the Joint Committee on Library Materials for the Spanish and Portuguese Speaking in the United States. In 1974, this committee held a postconference workshop on materials for children and young adults.[74] Several SALALM members are also members of REFORMA, and in 2002, a group of concerned SALALM members organized a preconference in Tempe, Arizona, whose goal was to reach out to the public library and undergraduate community. The preconference program focused on collecting Spanish language materials. Approximately 50 undergraduate and public librarians attended the one-day program. Among the librarians who attended this preconference program was Susana Hinojosa, then president of REFORMA and librarian at UC Berkeley. This was the first time that Ms. Hinojosa had attended a SALALM conference. Ms. Hinojosa and other librarians who attended the preconference program became members of SALALM.

Another example of efforts to reach out to the members of organizations with similar interests is the cross-posting of announcements that appear in LALA-L, the SALALM listserv; to REFORMANET, the REFORMA listserv; and vice versa. These cross-postings are an effective way of increasing the visibility of both organizations among each other's memberships. The postings are not only informational but also serve to answer reference questions and to announce new resources, publications, conferences, and so on.

One more example of SALALM's maturity, financial means, and outreach commitment is that the Finance Committee approved in 2000 the Presidential Travel Fellowship to support the president's conference program while also reaching out to potential new members.[75] The purpose of the fellowship is to encourage active conference participation by new members to the organization from the United States or other countries, who have "programmatic responsibility for Latin American Studies."[76]

Most SALALM members are also active members of ALA. Individual SALALM members try their best to promote the organization at the ALA midwinter meeting and annual conference and through its committees, but the two organizations have not forged strong ties. One successful example, however, of how the organizations are developing ties is that SALALM has actively promoted attendance at the Feria Internacional del Libro (FIL), the international book fair in Guadalajara, Mexico, through ALA's "free pass" program. In Guadalajara, SALALM, REFORMA, ALA members, and other library professionals have opportunities to promote their organizations among those attending FIL. SALALM members are actively involved in the new members' orientation for both academic and public librarians. At the 2007 ALA Conference, SALALM hosted its first booth, and those in attendance report that the experience was a resounding success. Several new members signed up to join SALALM, and information about the organization was provided to library schools.[77] The secretariat sent SALALM posters and brochures to 135 library schools.[78]

Technology

SALALM has embraced technological developments, and these are evident in its successful collaborations with HAPI and HLAS as these publications automated their processes and eventually became web resources. In 1991, LALA-L, the SALALM listserv was launched.[79] Throughout its 16-year history, LALA-L has become an invaluable communication tool for the membership. LALA-L is an excellent means of consulting colleagues with reference questions, publicize new resources, announce conferences, and the like.

SALALM's first website was launched in 1996 by Cornell University Library where it remained until summer 2007.[80] In summer 2007, the redesigned SALALM website, hosted by the SUNY Binghamton Library, was launched. The SALALM website has current and historical information about the organization, its publications, links to book dealers and book fairs, along with a rich variety of other resources such as bibliographic instruction tools and e-resources.[81]

Expansion of Collaboration

In the 1970s and 1980s, collaboration with HAPI and the HLAS became more institutionalized as these publications established official representation within SALALM through committees or interest groups. In the 1990s, SALALM members provided invaluable support (volunteer indexers) for HAPI and HLAS as these standard Latin American Studies tools automate the compilation and editorial process and eventually become fully searchable web resources.

In 2006, an ad hoc group collaborated with the Choice/Bowker *Resources for College Libraries* database. The ad hoc group identified and annotated basic electronic resources suitable for this undergraduate database.[82] This project provides SALALM with an opportunity to share its wealth of knowledge and expertise and thereby enhance its visibility among the greater library profession.

Other examples of collaboration are SALALM's affiliated groups: CALAFIA, LANE, LASER, MOLLAS, and LARRP.[83] These affiliates are of different types, although they were all created and developed through SALALM professional and personal relationships. The first four affiliates are regional collection development groups (in California, the North- and Southeast, and the Midwest) that meet regionally to make joint collection development decisions. CALAFIA, the California Cooperative Latin American Collection Development Group, is a consortium of California academic libraries (public and private), and among their achievements is an agreement to divide up collection of materials from the northern and southern Mexican states; LASER, the Latin American Studies Southeast Regional libraries, compiled a list of newspaper holdings; LANE, the Latin America Northeast libraries consortium, compiled a list of archival collections that had a Latin American literary content, among other valuable contributions.

LARRP, the Latin American Research Resources Project, is an example of cooperative collection development at the national level whose membership is almost entirely constituted by members of SALALM. LARRP is an affiliate group that is administered by the Center for Research Libraries in collaboration with the Association of Research Libraries and the Association of American Universities.[84] LARRP participants agree to devote a portion of their budgets to collecting country-specific materials for a region or specialized topic. Fifty libraries participate in LARRP, and its annual membership meeting is held during the SALALM conference.

LARRP's two main digital initiatives are the Latin American Periodicals Tables of Contents (LAPTOC)[85] and the Latin American Open Archives Portal (LAOAP).[86] Both projects are hosted by the Latin American Network Information Center (LANIC).[87] While LANIC's primary connection to SALALM has been through LARRP, since its founding in 1992, LANIC has participated actively in SALALM's annual conferences. SALALM members are frequent contributors to LANIC at many levels, such as conducting training workshops at conferences in the United States and Latin America, contributing resources for the LANIC directory, and facilitating contacts with Latin American publishers and librarians.[88]

Additional examples of collaboration from the 1980s and 1990s are that SALALM held two joint conferences, one with LASA in 1982 in Washington, DC; and the other with the Association of Caribbean University, Research and Institutional Libraries (ACURIL) in Miami in 1987. In addition, the January 1990 issue of the SALALM newsletter was a joint issue with REFORMA.[89]

Examples of more recent collaborations that reflect the need for resources to support growing Latina/o populations in the United States are the *America Reads Spanish* (ARS) electronic newsletter that is now posted to the SALALM and REFORMA listservs. ARS is a joint publication of the Spanish Institute for Foreign Trade and the Spanish Association of Publishers' Guild. This same group recently published the *Essential Guide to Spanish Reading*. Many SALALM members contributed to this publication.[90]

Conclusion

SALALM's strength belies its relatively small membership base and the significant contributions it has made through its 50-year history. As the organization continues to grow and develop in response to the needs of the Latin American and Latino/a Studies undergraduate programs and research communities and the fast-growing Latino populations that live in the United States, SALALM is very well positioned to participate in developing the necessary resources to meet these interesting challenges.

Notes

We are grateful for the information and suggestions provided by our colleagues, Carol Avila, David Block, Hortensia Calvo, Jane Garner, Adán Griego, Ruby Gutierrez, Sean Knowlton, Molly Molloy, Kent Norsworthy, Iliana Sonntag, and Gayle Williams.

1. SALALM. "Constitution, art. 2, sec. 1." http://www.salalm.org/about/constitution.html (accessed December 19, 2010).
2. Jackson, 240.
3. Wisdom, 119.
4. Jackson, 240.
5. Ibid., 243.
6. Jane Garner, e-mail message to A. M. Cobos. September 16, 2007 (8:36 P.M.).
7. Ibid., 250–253.
8. Ibid., 256–257.
9. Ibid.
10. SALALM. "Constitution, art. 4, sec. 1." http://www.salalm.org/about/constitution.html (accessed December 19, 2010).
11. Ibid., art. 5, sec. 1.
12. SALALM. "Bylaws, art. 1, sec. 1." http://www.salalm.org/about/constitution.html (accessed December 19, 2010).
13. Jackson, 251.
14. Hodgman, 219.
15. Jackson, 248–249.
16. Hazen 1986, 754.
17. Jackson, 249.
18. Ibid., 245–246.
19. Wisdom, 145.
20. Jackson, 247.
21. Ibid., 257–258.
22. Hodgman, 219.
23. Jackson, 259.
24. Jane Garner, e-mail message to A. M. Cobos on September 16, 2007, indicates that in 1971 a Joint Committee on Library Materials for the Spanish and Portuguese Speaking in the United States was approved but in 1979 was disbanded due to inactivity.
25. Ibid., 256–258.
26. Ibid.
27. Hazen 1986, 753.
28. Jackson, 268.
29. Ibid., 270.
30. Hazen 1986, 755.
31. Jackson, 270.
32. SALALM. "Current Publications: Bibliography and Reference Series." http://www.salalm.org/publications/bibliography.html (accessed December 19, 2010).

33. Jackson, 269–270.

34. Jackson, 243, 271.

35. Wisdom, 121–122.

36. Ibid., 123–125.

37. Savary, 224–226.

38. Ibid., 226–229 and Wisdom, 137–143.

39. Savary, 227, 230.

40. Wisdom, 147.

41. Hodgman, 217.

42. Center for Research Libraries. LAMP. http://www.crl.edu/area-studies/lamp (accessed December 19, 2010).

43. Wisdom, 127.

44. Ibid., 148–149.

45. Hazen 1986, 755 and Deal, 22–27.

46. HAPI Online. "History of HAPI as an Institution." http://hapi.ucla.edu/web/free/aboutus.php (accessed December 19, 2010) and Ruby Gutierrez, e-mail message to A. M. Cobos, September 12, 2007.

47. HAPI Online and Hazen 1986, 755.

48. Wisdom, 119, 147.

49. Jackson, 271.

50. Wisdom, 128.

51. Adán Griego, e-mail message to A. M. Cobos, September 13, 2007. Bibliography website is http://www-sul.stanford.edu/depts/hasrg/latinam/balder.html (accessed September 15, 2007).

52. Wisdom, 129.

53. Grover, 39.

54. Morse, 173.

55. Hodgman, 219.

56. SALALM. "Code of Executive Board Decisions, Decision #81." http://www.salalm.org/about/code.html (accessed December 19, 2010).

57. ISiS. Iberian Studies in SALALM. http://library.brown.edu/gateway/ISiS/index.php (accessed December 19, 2010).

58. ALZAR. Academic Latina/o Zone of Activism and Research. http://www.salalm.org/alzar/index.html (accessed December 19, 2010).

59. SALALM Secretariat, e-mail message to A. M. Cobos, August 27, 2007.

60. Ibid.

61. Hodgman, 215–223.

62. Ibid., 215.

63. Greenwood, 3.

64. Jane Garner, e-mail message to A. M. Cobos. September 16, 2007.

65. SALALM. "Honorary Membership." http://www.salalm.org/honors/honorarymembership.html (accessed December 19, 2010).

66. SALALM. "José Toribio Medina Award." http://www.salalm.org/honors/toribiomedina.html (accessed December 19, 2010).

67. Jane Garner, e-mail message to A. M. Cobos. September 16, 2007.

68. SALALM Enlace Travel Awards. http://www.salalm.org/conference/enlace.html (accessed December 19, 2010).

69. SALALM. "Past Enlace Fellows." http://salalm.org/conference/becarios .html (accessed December 19, 2010).
70. Adán Griego, e-mail message to A.M. Cobos, September 13, 2007.
71. SALALM. "Code of Executive Board Decisions. Decision #102." http://salalm.org/about/code.html#code (accessed December 19, 2010).
72. Jane Garner, e-mail message to A.M. Cobos, August 22, 2007.
73. Herrera, 226–227.
74. Jane Garner, e-mail message to A.M. Cobos, September 16, 2007.
75. SALALM. "Code of Executive Board Decisions. Decision #23." http://salalm.org/about/code.html#code (accessed December 19, 2010).
76. SALALM. "Presidential Travel Fellowship." http://salalm.org/conference/ presidentialtravel.html (accessed December 19, 2010).
77. SALALM Secretariat. LALA-L posting. June 27, 2007.
78. *SALALM Newsletter*. June 2007, 107.
79. Gayle Williams, e-mail message to A.M. Cobos. June 25, 2007.
80. SALALM. "Code of Executive Board Decisions. Decision #99." http://salalm.org/about/code.html#code (accessed December 19, 2010).
81. SALALM. http://salalm.org/index.html (accessed December 19, 2010).
82. Sean Knowlton, e-mail message to A.M. Cobos, August 28, 2007.
83. SALALM. http://salalm.org/index.html (accessed December 19, 2010).
84. LARRP. Latin Americanist Research Resources Project. http://www.crl .edu/grn/larrp/index.asp (accessed December 19, 2010).
85. LAPTOC. Latin American Periodicals Tables of Contents. http://lanic .utexas.edu/larrp/laptoc.html (accessed December 19, 2010).
86. LAOAP. Latin American Open Archives Portal. http://lanic.utexas.edu/ project/laoap/ (accessed December 19, 2010).
87. LANIC. Latin American Information Network. http://lanic.utexas.edu/ (accessed December 19, 2010).
88. Kent Norsworthy, e-mail message to A.M. Cobos, September 13, 2007.
89. Jane Garner, e-mail message to A.M. Cobos, September 16, 2007.
90. America Reads Spanish. http://www.americareadsspanish.org (accessed December 19, 2010).

References

ALZAR. Academic Latina/o Zone of Activism and Research. http://salalm.org/alzar/index.html (accessed December 19, 2010).

America Reads Spanish. http://www.americareadsspanish.org (accessed December 19, 2010).

Block, David. E-mail message to Ana Maria Cobos. September 11, 2007.

Block, David, ed. "Introduction: Iberia, Latin America, and the Caribbean." In *Selection of Library Materials for Area Studies, Part I. Asia, Iberia, the Caribbean, and Latin America, Eastern Europe and the Soviet Union, and the South Pacific*, edited by Cecily Johns, 127–141. Chicago: American Library Association, 1990.

Center for Research Libraries. "LAMP." http://www.crl.edu/areastud ies/LAMP/ (accessed December 19, 2010).

Cline, Howard F. "The Latin American Studies Association: A Summary Survey with Appendix." *Latin American Research Review* 2, no. 1 (Autumn 1966): 57–79.

Deal, Carl. "The Latin American Microform Project." *Microform Review* 15, no. 1 (Winter 1986): 22–27.

Garner, Jane. E-mail message to Ana Maria Cobos. August 22, 2007.

Garner, Jane. E-mail messages to Ana Maria Cobos. September 16, 2007 (6:33 P.M., 8:36 P.M., 9:33 P.M.).

Garner, Jane, comp. *SALALM: Basic Documents of the Seminar on the Acquisition of Latin American Library Materials; Part III: Code of Executive Board Decisions.* http://salalm.org/about/code.html (accessed December 19, 2010).

Greenwood, David J. "Area Studies in the Twenty-First Century." In *SALALM and the Area Studies Community. Papers of the Thirty-Seventh Annual Meeting of the Seminar on the Acquisition of Latin American Library Materials, Nettie Lee Benson Latin American Collection, University of Texas at Austin. Austin, Texas, May 30-June 4, 1992,* edited by David Block, 3–10. Albuquerque: University of New Mexico, 1994.

Griego, Adán. Bibliography of Sexuality Studies in Latin America. http://www-sul.stanford.edu/depts/hasrg/latinam/balder.html (accessed December 19, 2010).

Griego, Adán. E-mail message to Ana Maria Cobos. September 13, 2007.

Grover, Mark L. "The Beginning of SALALM." In *Latin American Studies Research and Bibliography: Past, Present, and Future. Papers of the Fiftieth Annual Meeting of the Seminar on the Acquisition of Latin American Library Materials, University of Florida, Gainesville April 16–19, 2005,* edited by Pamela F. Howard-Reguindin, 16–42. New Orleans: SALALM, 2007.

Gutierrez, Ruby. E-mail message to Ana Maria Cobos. September 12, 2007.

HAPI Online. "History of HAPI as an Institution." http://hapi.ucla. edu/ web/free/aboutus.php (accessed September 14, 2007).

Hazen, Dan C. "*The Handbook of Latin American Studies* at (Volume) Fifty: Area Studies Bibliography in a Context of Change." *Revista interamericana de bibliografía=Interamerican Review of Bibliography* XLI (1991): 196–202.

Hazen, Dan C. "Seminar on the Acquisition of Latin American Library Materials." In *World Encyclopedia of Library and Information Science,* edited by Robert Wedgeworth, 753–754. Chicago: American Library Association, 1986.

Herrera, Luis. "SALALM and the Public Library." In *Latin American Studies into the Twenty-First Century: New Focus, New Formats, New Challenges. Papers of the Thirty-Six Annual Meeting of the Seminar on the Acquisition of Latin American Library Materials, University of California, San Diego and San Diego State University, San Diego, California, June 1–6, 1991,* edited by Deborah L. Jakubs, 224–227. Albuquerque: University of New Mexico, 1993.

Hodgman, Suzanne. "SALALM Membership, 1956–1990: A Brief Overview." In *Latin American Studies into the Twenty-First Century: New Focus, New Formats, New Challenges. Papers of the Thirty-Six Annual Meeting of the Seminar on the Acquisition of Latin American Library Materials, University of California, San Diego and San Diego State University, San Diego, California, June 1–6, 1991,* edited by Deborah L. Jakubs, 215–223. Albuquerque: University of New Mexico, 1993.

ISIS. Iberian Studies in SALALM. http://library.brown.edu/gateway/ISiS/index.php (accessed December 19, 2010).

Jackson, William V. "Twenty-Third Seminar on the Acquisition of Latin American Library Materials." In *Encyclopedia of Library and Information Science.* Vol. 33: 239–280. New York: Marcel Dekker, 1981.

Knowlton, Sean. E-mail message to Ana Maria Cobos. August 28, 2007.

LANIC. Latin American Network Information Center. http://lanic.utexas.edu/ (accessed December 19, 2010).

LAOAP. Latin American Open Archives Portal. http://lanic.utexas.edu/project/laoap/ (accessed December 19, 2010).

LAPTOC. Latin American Periodicals Tables of Contents. http://lanic.utexas.edu/larrp/laptoc.html (accessed December 19, 2010).

LARRP. Latin Americanist Research Resources Project. http://lanic.utexas.edu/larrp/ (accessed December 19, 2010).

Morse, Richard. "On Grooming Latin Americanists." In *New World Soundings.* Baltimore: Johns Hopkins University Press, 1989: 169–177.

Norsworthy, Kent. E-mail message to Ana Maria Cobos. September 13, 2007.

Read, Glen F., Jr. "SALALM: Thoughts on the Birth and Development of an Organization." In *Acquisitions from the Third World*, edited by D. A. Clarke, 177–191. London: Mansell, 1975.

SALALM. "Bylaws." http://www.salalm.org/about/constitution.html (accessed December 19, 2010).

SALALM. "Code of Executive Board Decisions." http://www.salalm.org/about/code.html (accessed December 19, 2010).

SALALM. "Constitution." http://www.salalm.org/about/constitution.html (accessed December 19, 2010).

SALALM. "Current Publications: Bibliography and Reference Series." http://www.salalm.org/publications/bibliography.html (accessed December 19, 2010).

SALALM. "Enlace Travel Awards." http://www.salalm.org/conference/enlace.html (accessed December 19, 2010).

SALALM. "Honorary Membership." http://www.salalm.org/honors/honorarymembership.html (accessed December 19, 2010).

SALALM. "José Toribio Medina Award." http://www.salalm.org/honors/toribiomedina.html (accessed December 19, 2010).

SALALM. LALA-L posting. June 27, 2007.

SALALM. "Past Enlace Fellows." http://salalm.org/conference/becarios.html (accessed December 19, 2010).

SALALM. "Presidential Travel Fellowship." http://salalm.org/conference/presidentialtravel.html (accessed December 19, 2010).

SALALM. "SALALM@50, Gainesville, Florida Executive Board Meeting, April 16, 2005, Minutes as Corrected." *SALALM Newsletter* 34, no. 6 (June 2007): 107.

SALALM. Secretariat. E-mail message to Ana Maria Cobos. August 27, 2007.

SALALM. Seminar on the Acquisition of Latin American Library Materials. http://www.salalm.org/ (accessed December 19, 2010).

Savary, Jennifer. "Library Cooperation in Latin America." In *Encyclopedia of Library and Information Science* Vol. 15: 214–245. New York: Marcel Dekker, 1981.

Stern, Peter. "The Growth of Latin American Studies and the American University Library." In *The Role of the American Academic Library in International Programs*, edited by Bruce D. Bonta and James G. Neal, 197–226. Greenwich, CT: JAI Press, 1992.

Williams, Gayle. E-mail message to Ana Maria Cobos. June 25, 2007.

Wisdom, Donald F. "The First Two Decades of SALALM: A Personal Account." In *SALALM and the Area Studies Community. Papers of the Thirty-Seventh Annual Meeting of the Seminar on the Acquisition of Latin American Library Materials, Nettie Lee Benson Latin American Collection, University of Texas at Austin. Austin, Texas, May 30-June 4, 1992*, edited by David Block, 118–152. Albuquerque: University of New Mexico, 1994.

ALA, IFLA, AND THEIR RELATIONSHIP WITH LATIN AMERICA

Loida Garcia-Febo

The American Library Association and the International Federation of Library Associations and Institutions (IFLA) are recognized worldwide professional associations with a strong presence in Latin America. They have a long history of collaboration to tackle issues affecting libraries and librarians from this region. Memberships to these organizations seem to be the life link of many Latino information professionals. This essay presents an overview of ALA and IFLA units and their work with Latin America, highlighting benefits of ALA and IFLA joint collaborations. This contributes to an examination of their collaboration record and the value of being a member of these organizations.

Associations at a Glance

Both ALA and IFLA follow the same goals of promoting and improving librarianship and library services and to advocate for the free flow of information. Of the two, ALA is the largest association with more than 66,000 members in over 80 countries, and at least 1 member in 12 Latin American countries. IFLA has more than 1,700 members in 155 countries, including most of Latin America. Although ALA has a more complex infrastructure and resources that allow it to employ specialized staff, IFLA as an international nongovernmental association (NGO) has close contact with international forums such as the World Intellectual Property Organization (WIPO) and the World Trade Organization (WTO). Also, "IFLA can call upon the expertise available in its world membership," said Peter Lohr, IFLA secretary general. This paves the way for IFLA to contribute an international perspective to complement ALA insights.

ALA

ALA maintains collaboration with international organizations, including library associations from Latin America via its International Relations Office (IRO) whose mission is to "increase ALA's presence in the global library community, to implement ALA policies concerning international librarianship, to promote greater understanding of international librarianship and international library issues within ALA, and to manage international library activities on behalf of the ALA." To this effect, the IRO partners with organizers of numerous activities around the globe, including conferences and book fairs such as the Guadalajara Book Fair. The office is the default link with international organizations such as IFLA.

The IRO works closely with ALA's International Relations Committee (IRC), which is charged with the association's international relations programs and projects. They recommend policies to ALA Council and encourage international professional exchanges and participation of U.S. librarians in efforts developed by international organizations. The committee suggests appointments and nominations for international organizations to the ALA Executive Board. The IRC hosts subcommittees covering different regions of the world with the purpose of promoting

ALA relations with these areas and the investigation of issues about them. The Americas Subcommittee includes 38 countries in North, Central, and South America, many of which have Spanish as its main language. Members of the Americas Subcommittee develop and maintain News and Contacts in the Americas, an online page with the most recent developments from countries in the region. Library associations from Latin America often send updates about their events to the Americas Subcommittee. These news items are added to the online page of the subcommittee on a regular basis. News and Contacts serves two purposes: it keeps librarians around the globe informed about initiatives in the Americas and, at the same time, provides an international forum for library associations from Latin America to share news with the world.

The International Relations Round Table (IRRT) functions as a link between the IRC and the association's members. The IRRT collaborates with ALA to encourage interest in international librarianship issues, coordination of international programs and activities, and hosting of international visiting librarians. The round table shares news about worldwide initiatives via its newsletter, *International Leads*. ALA's IRO, IRC, and IRRT synchronized work keeps its members informed of international decisions affecting libraries in the United States and around the globe.

IFLA

IFLA's activities in Latin America are lead by its regional office for Latin America; the Caribbean, the Latin America and the Caribbean Standing Committee (LAC); and the Action for Development through Libraries Programme Core Activity (ALP). These all play a key role in the developing of initiatives within countries in the region (Carvalho, 2004).

The regional office, based in São Paulo, Brazil, coordinates collaboration between LAC and other IFLA units and Core Activities. Since its creation in 1987, the regional office has worked with the ALP to develop innumerable projects in Latin America (Carvalho, 2004). Essential programs are established in cooperation with the ALP, which collaborates with developing countries from various regions of the world, including Latin America. The goal is to promote librarianship and library services such as information literacy and lifelong learning, create library associations, provide continued education and training, and promote the use of technologies. Working with IFLA regional offices and divisions, the ALP has developed initiatives such as fund-raising, scholarships, conferences, workshops, pilot projects, and publications.

Some of the activities coordinated by the ALP and the regional office include seminars about assessment of librarian's needs in Nicaragua and

Martinique, library services in rural and semi-urban areas in Peru, the UNESCO Public Library Manifesto in Brazil, IFLA/UNESCO manifestos for public and school libraries in Trinidad and Tobago, distance learning in Puerto Rico, and the creation of library associations in El Salvador. These projects have been supported by the LAC Section and its mission to promote access to information prioritizing literacy, reading, application of new technologies, and library services.

One of the highlights of the cooperation between the ALP and IFLA regional office is how indigenous libraries and librarians have taken a more active role in providing programs and services to the people in their library service areas (Aliaga, 2004). Bilingual information centers have opened in Bolivia, Colombia, Peru, and Venezuela. Cultural centers have been created in various cities in Peru. Reading projects were initiated in Colombia, Guatemala, and Mexico. A project to bring a bookmobile to Chile ethnic groups was successfully established, and a publishing house for writers of native languages continues to provide books in languages spoken by indigenous populations.

In 2007, the Committee on Free Access to Information and Freedom of Expression (FAIFE), an IFLA core activity, started presenting workshops in the region about the IFLA/UNESCO Internet Manifesto Guidelines. As stated on their website, FAIFE work is based on Article 19 of the United Nations Universal Declaration of Human Rights. "Its mission is to defend and promote the basic human rights," and the committee seeks "to promote free access to information and freedom of expression in all areas related to libraries and librarianship." Workshops coordinated in conjunction with the regional office to ensure access to information via the Internet have been presented in Brazil, Colombia, Costa Rica, Ecuador, Mexico, Puerto Rico, and Uruguay by FAIFE members.

The Library Services to Multicultural Populations Section of IFLA encourages the creation of international partnerships to promote library programs and services for all members of our society. Their *Guidelines for Library Services to Multicultural Populations* have been translated into Spanish and the other six IFLA languages. This includes sections discussing ethnic linguistic and cultural diversity, library services provided on languages preferred by populations served, cross-cultural materials and services, information and reference services, technical services, and staffing recommendations. Another publication, *Raison d'être for Multicultural Library Services*, explains 10 reasons to offer library services to such populations.

ALA and IFLA continue to strengthen links with Latin America via their work in the region. Their various committees and working groups constantly reach out to library associations to present workshops and establish programs to further access information for Latin Americans.

Initiatives in Latin America

The benefits of becoming a member of ALA or IFLA go beyond the obvious networking aspect. Both organizations provide an abundance of materials, programs, and avenues for members to enrich themselves as professionals and the services they provide. They include opportunities to partner with libraries from different regions of the world, quick access to translated documents, discounts for conferences, and a worldwide forum to develop ideas. Traditionally, however, ALA membership dues cost less than IFLA's. Although membership to IFLA is pursued by many information professionals, at times, associations have expressed their lack of funds to pay dues (Carvalho, 2004). Despite this limitation and that many countries have their own associations, librarians from Latin America continue to join ALA and IFLA. The real hook can be found on the projects, workshops, and initiatives developed in conjunction with libraries and professional associations in the region.

ALA's successful Sister Library Initiative is part of the IRRT. It builds on the idea of global communities to connect libraries sharing the same interests. Sister libraries help each other to develop projects, exchange printed materials, train staff on library and community issues, share expertise, and create cultural awareness. Types of partnerships go from informal to contract-signed agreements. As Sarah Ann Long, ALA president from 1999–2000 said when establishing this initiative, "becoming a Sister Library is an opportunity to build relationships with libraries in other cultures that can help us learn, understand and better serve our own community." Currently, libraries in the United States maintain sister library programs with academic and public libraries in Latin American countries such as Mexico, Ecuador, and Guatemala.

Every year, around 150 librarians participate in the ALA Free Pass Program, which provides financial assistance for ALA members to attend the Guadalajara Book Fair. This program, in conjunction with FIL and the Guadalajara Book Fair, includes registration, hotel, breakfasts, and a contribution toward airline fare. ALA maintains agreements with other library associations and organizations around the globe to meet the needs of U.S. librarians purchasing materials in languages other than English.

REFORMA hold a midwinter meeting and an annual meeting each year. These meetings attract librarians from the United States who serve Latinos and information professionals from Latin American countries who come to "learn, network, and keep abreast of trends within the profession," said Mario Ascencio, REFORMA president for 2007–2008. Michael Dowling, director of the IRO, confirmed that the ALA annual conference is attended by large numbers of librarians who speak Spanish, along with a smaller group of Portuguese speakers.

In light of this, ALA has translated a significant number of materials into Spanish. These include advocacy tools such as the Library Advocates Handbook. Various association documents are also available in Spanish, such as the Library Bill of Rights, ALA Code of Ethics, and Information Literacy Higher Competency Standards for Higher Education. Graphic materials in Spanish are available as well. Reduced rates for materials, conferences, and online workshops are available for members.

The year 1994 represented the beginning of a prolific relation between IFLA and Latin America. That year, La Habana hosted the first-ever IFLA Congress in a Latin American country. Around 940 delegates attended the historical event along with 400 librarians from Cuba. A total of 30 posters were presented by attendees from the region (Carvalho, 2004). In 2004, IFLA held another Congress in the region; this time, Buenos Aires welcomed thousands of delegates.

On that occasion, the IFLA journal dedicated an entire issue to Latin America and the Caribbean. It was the ultimate platform to share news from libraries and information centers within the region (Abad, 2004). ALA and IFLA united forces to create the Fellowship of the Americas to award funds to librarians from the region to attend the congress. This proved that it is of great benefit for the two associations to work together to achieve goals. In 2011, Puerto Rico will host the 77th IFLA General Conference and Assembly.

ALA and its Office of Intellectual Freedom (OIF) collaborated with IFLA in the creation of FAIFE in 1997. ALA brought to the table the OIF, its staff, and more than 40 years of experience to help shape FAIFE, which has become the international voice for libraries on intellectual freedom matters. In March of 2007, during a successful workshop about IFLA/UNESCO Internet Manifesto Guidelines in Costa Rica, librarians from Central and South America challenged IFLA to be present in their countries. Since then, FAIFE has worked with LAC and the regional office to develop workshops to promote access to information on the Internet. Seminars to train trainers have been instrumental in promoting the development of workshops concerning access to information by local librarians. This model allows FAIFE to reach out to a wider audience within the region.

Michael Dowling pointed out that cooperative efforts between ALA and IFLA have provided information to library communities from Latin America that has allowed them to engage in negotiations about discussions of U.S. efforts to create bilateral free trade agreements in Central America (CAFTA) and others in Latin America. The agreements will try to impose more restrictive U.S. copyright terms than the international standards require. Cooperative efforts in the area of advocacy have been vital for ALA and IFLA to increase awareness of the value of libraries in

Latin America. In 2001, these associations partnered to establish The Campaign for the World's Libraries, which was modeled after ALA's Campaign for America's Libraries, @ your library. Many countries have signed onto this world campaign including Latin American countries such as Argentina, El Salvador, Mexico, Nicaragua, Uruguay, and Venezuela. Brazil also joined this campaign in which the logo and materials have been translated into IFLA's official languages: English; Spanish; German; Chinese; French; Arabic; Russian; and other languages, including Armenian; Azeri; Bulgarian; Georgian; Icelandic; Italian; Japanese; Kazakh; Korean; Nepali; Portuguese; Romanian; Serbian; Turkish; and Vietnamese.

In general, IFLA enjoys an international platform that allows it to claim to represent the world's libraries, librarians, and library users. The more members IFLA has, the more credibility it has in international forums. It has become a given fact that IFLA as Shank (1982) called it is the chief and most prominent agency sponsoring an international meeting. IFLA congresses and meetings have become the most powerful networking events in librarianship. As Peter Lohr pointed out, there is definitely strength in numbers. IFLA gathers experts from all regions of the world "to exchange ideas, develop international cooperation, research and initiatives in all areas of library activity and information services." The association helps librarians to "protect their interests and to participate in finding solutions to global problems." One of the reasons why IFLA stands as the leading library association is because it wisely followed examples of "stronger and older national associations," as former IFLA president, Alex Byrne (2004), has mentioned, and in the process, "inspired new associations to promote the highest standards of professional services."

Having looked at ALA and IFLA work in Latin America and the Caribbean, and to the benefits of becoming a member of these two associations, it is now time to draft ways to continue developing projects in the region. It seems that the most pressing needs have to do with keeping up with library services and with technology. Scholarship opportunities for librarians of the region to attend conferences or to bring conferences to Latin American countries would serve as a link to connect them with new ideas, services, and programs. Increased partnership with strong technology companies will bring the Internet to rural areas—opening unsuspected information avenues to all, including indigenous populations.

For many decades, ALA and IFLA have promoted libraries and access to information in Latin America, proving that their quest goes beyond ideological or political reasons. They have also acted solo, and they have cooperated with each other's initiatives to establish robust programs. Each time they have proved that international joint work is the best basis on which to produce solid programs to benefit library services, librarianship, and foster free access to information.

References

Abad, Ramon. 2004. Why a special issue on Latin America and the Caribbean? *IFLA Journal 30*(2): 107.

Aliaga, Cesar Castro. 2004. Library services for Latin American indigenous populations. *IFLA Journal 30*(2): 134–140.

Byrne, Alex. 2004. IFLA and professional ethics. *Australian Library Journal 53*(1). Online. Available on the Internet at http://alianet.alia.org.au/publishing/alj/53.1/full.text/byrne.html; accessed October 18, 2007.

Ramos de Carvalho, Elizabet. 2004. Activities of the IFLA regional office for Latin America and the Caribbean. *IFLA Journal 30*(2): 166–174.

Shank, Russell. 1982. IFLA, ALA, & issues in international librarianship. *Library Journal 107*(13): 1299–1301.

Useful Links

- ALA Mission, about http://www.ala.org/ala/ourassociation/annualreport/aboutala/aboutala.htm
- ALA/ IRO http://www.ala.org/ala/iro/international.cfm
- ALA/IRC http://www.ala.org/ala/iro/internationalrelations.cfm
- ALA/IRC/Americas Subcommittee http://www.ala.org/ala/iro/americassubcommittee.cfm
- ALA/IRRT http://www.ala.org/ala/irrt/irrt.cfm
- ALA Sister Libraries http://www.ala.org/ala/ourassociation/othergroups/sisterlibraries/sisterlibraries.cfm
- @ your library, The Campaign for America's Libraries http://www.ala.org/ala/pio/campaign/campaignamericas.cfm
- The Campaign for the World's Libraries http://www.ifla.org/@yourlibrary/
- IFLA, about membership http://www.ifla.org/III/intro00.htm
- IFLA ALP http://www.ifla.org/VI/1/alp.htm
- IFLA Latin America and Caribbean Section http://www.ifla.org/VII/s27/index.htm
- IFLA Regional Offices http://www.ifla.org/III/ro/index.htm
- IFLA FAIFE http://www.ifla.org/faife/index.htm
- IFLA/UNESCO Internet Manifesto Guidelines
- http://www.ifla.org/faife/policy/iflastat/Internet-ManifestoGuidelines.pdf

REFORMA: A HISTORICAL OVERVIEW

Refugio Ramirez

My aim in profiling the history of the establishment of REFORMA is to shed light on the social impact that this organization has had on the profession and the Latino community. As a result of the civil rights movement era, REFORMA was founded by a group of bilingual librarians in July 1971 in Dallas, Texas, at the annual conference of the American Library Association (ALA).[1] The founding members sought "to pursue the ideals of reforming libraries' lack of outreach to Spanish-speaking people and create positive changes in the level of quality of library services to that community."[2] In essence, what is most revealing and compelling about this objective is that it highlights the fact that prior to REFORMA's existence, libraries (on a whole) were not significantly concerned about the Latino community in terms of providing equitable access and representation of library services and resources.

As an affiliate of the ALA, REFORMA "has grown into a truly national organization with twenty-five local and regional chapters across the nation. Its ranks have swelled from a small group of members in 1971 to over 1,000 members in 2008."[3] More specifically, each chapter functions "autonomously, working through their local library systems, state library associations, and local organizations to achieve local objectives."[4] Like many new organizations, REFORMA staggered at the beginning, due to a lack of funding and a small leadership core, yet it managed to grow considerably over the years with steadfast perseverance.[5] At its core, the REFORMA objectives include the development of Spanish language and Latino-oriented library collections; recruitment of bilingual, multicultural library personnel; promotion of public awareness of libraries and librarianship among Latinos; advocacy on behalf of the information needs of the Latino community; and a liaison to other professional organizations (About REFORMA, 2005). Considering the social climate that forged the emergence of REFORMA, I cannot help but stress just how radical and innovative this organization was in 1971 and how it continues to be so to this day.

Before discussing REFORMA's history and the kind of work it has done since its inception, it is important to understand my reasons for researching this topic and where I stand on this issue. Considering the fact that I was born in 1982 and probably did not step into a public library until the early 1990s, I cannot help but wonder how libraries must have been, prior to the existence of REFORMA. In light of this, I believe that well-resourced libraries have the potential to help serve as a positive mechanism to empower patrons from all walks of life. During my undergraduate career at the University of San Diego, for example, I recall walking into the Copley Library and learning about the small collection of Chicana/o literature. Considering the fact that the student population at my undergraduate campus is predominantly white, it was quite inspiring knowing there was literature on the shelf that I could identity with; in fact, it made me feel as if I was a part of the university.

With this, the founders of REFORMA had a clear understanding of just how detrimental it was for libraries to continue to neglect the Latino community, and as such, they sought to create an organization "aimed for societal change, so that libraries would move away from their tangential treatment of the Latino community to a new attitude of respect and enfranchisement."[6] More importantly, it is important to note that ethnic organizations such as REFORMA deserve tremendous recognition since they have played an important role in bridging the gap for groups of people who have historically been marginalized from such institutions. In light of this, with 1971 to 1995 as the time frame for the scope of this paper, I'll be examining REFORMA's early history as well as how it carried out its agenda during the harsh backlash made against the Latino community in the late 1980s and early 1990s with the English-only movement and the anti-affirmative action legislation. To do this, I will address the following questions:

- What led to the creation of REFORMA, and how was it established?
- How is REFORMA structured?
- What sociopolitical issues has REFORMA taken on over the years?
- How has REFORMA impacted the development of American librarianship?

Before I address these questions, it is critical that I briefly outline the events and changes that were taking place within the American Library Association as a result of the sociopolitical climate of the late 1960s. I will illustrate how these events and changes led to the formation of ethnic associations such as REFORMA.

Civil Rights Issue

There is very little literature before the 1970s regarding library services to the Latino community. In the article, "Latinos and Librarianship," Salvador Güereña and Edward Erazo illustrate that Gilda Baeza, the former president of REFORMA (1994–1995) and now university librarian at Western New Mexico University, discovered that the literature regarding the history of library services to Latinos was "virtually non-existent, despite the fact that a major component of that population . . . predates the arrival of the English speakers to the Southwestern United States'" (Güereña & Erazo, 2000, p. 139). It was not until the late 1960s that librarians such as Roberto P. Haro, Walton E. Kabler, William L. Ramirez, Arnulfo D. Trejo, and others began "writing and publishing about such services." It is for this reason that in discussing the contextual background, I decided to focus on the larger sociopolitical changes that were taking place in the ALA.

Dennis Thomison demonstrates in his book *A History of the American Library Association 1876–1972* that the association was not immune to the changes that were taking place in society in the late 1960s. However, it was the ALA's passive response to civil rights issue of the 1960s that set precedence for the formation of the ethnic library associations. According to the literature, the civil rights issue resurfaced at the 1962 midwinter meeting (Thomison, 1978, p. 216). At the time, the Intellectual Freedom Committee (IFC) conducted a survey that determined that black librarians were being barred from state chapters due to a conflict between "state laws and local ordinances which prevent fully integrated chapter meetings and a consequent lack of facilities for integrated meetings." In an effort to address this issue, Achie McNeal, IFC Chair, made recommendations in a statement to the ALA Council, and "although much debate ensued, including the canard that social change was not ALA's prime responsibility, a strong statement was adopted by ALA at the 1962 Annual Conference" (McCook, 2002). The statement was adopted and called "Statement on Individual Members, Chapter Status and Institutional Membership," and despite the fact that it declared that "membership in the association and its chapters had to be open to everyone regardless of race, religion, or personal belief" (McCook, 2002), the policy lacked "specifics about enforcement" (Thomison, 1978, p. 218).

Due to a lack of enforceability, many black librarians in the South, while having general ALA membership, were largely barred from attending state chapter functions (Thomison, 1978, p. 219). For example, Thomison further states that in 1964, after having been denied access "to attend a Georgia Library Association meeting at which an ALA staff member had been the principle speaker," Elonnie J. Josey introduced a resolution, which stated that "association should refrain from attending in official capacity the meetings of any sate associations unable to meet the requirements of chapter status in ALA." It is also worth mentioning that 1964 was also the year in which President Lyndon Johnson signed the Civil Rights Act, which "prohibits employment discrimination based on race, color, religion, sex and national origin" (Title VII). In hindsight, the adoption of EJ Josey's resolution was a great step in countering the Jim Crow legacy that plagued the structure of the ALA. Nevertheless, there was still a great deal to be done, and many librarians, particularly those of color, felt that the ALA still fell short in addressing their needs as information professionals and of library patrons of color.

Establishment of Units and Affiliations

Social Responsibilities Round Table (SRRT)

In the final years of the 1960s, there continued to be much debate about whether ALA should be neutral or proactive in dealing with the changes that were taking place in society. At the 1968 conference in Kansas City, a report was made, which strongly suggested that "the development and improvement of library services to the culturally disadvantaged and un-derprivileged be viewed as a major goal of the American Library Associa-tion as long as may be necessary" (Thomison, 1978, p. 224).

Thomison further states that the relevance of this report was momen-tous in that it appeared as if "The unrest, the outspoken dissent, and the violence that had characterized American society during much of the 1960s finally touched ALA." Thus, as Kathleen de la Peña McCook points out, "The 1968 Kansas City conference is viewed as pivotal in ALA's history as for it was there, on June 28, 1968 that the ALA Round Table on Social Re-sponsibilities of Libraries was established" (McCook, 2002). In an effort to address the social unrest, the SRRT would serve as "An outlet for expression of libraries' and librarians' concerns on these issues—race, violence, war and peace, inequality of justice and opportunity" (Thomison, 1978, p. 225).

At this point, it was quite evident that a sense of "symbolic change" was beginning to take place within the ALA. Yet, as Tami Echavarria and Andrew B Wertheimer point out in their article "Surveying the Role of Ethnic-American Library Associations," by the end of the 1960s, minority librarians who belong to the ALA still felt that "the association did not adequately represent them, did not provide opportunities to them to par-ticipate in decision-making, and responded to their needs too slowly and tentatively" (Echavarria & Wertheimer, 1997), and as a result, the 1970s marked the beginning of the formation of ethnic library associations.

Black Caucus of the American Library Association (BCALA)

The founding of the Black Caucus of the American Library Association (BCALA) is worth mentioning because its inception pre-dates REFORMA. I will not be discussing the formation of the BCALA because that is be-yond the scope of this paper. However, I do want to illustrate a point that E.J. Josey made regarding the demand for ethnic library associations. In the *Handbook of Black Librarianship* (1977), E.J. Josey wrote in the chapter titled "Black Caucus of the American Library Association":

Those black professionals in every discipline who were members of national professional organizations realized at the close of the 1960s that white racism was embedded in their professional organizations. . . . As a matter of survival, black and other minority groups saw themselves forced to seek involvement and control of a greater part of their professional lives. (Josey, 1977, p. 66)

This excerpt captures the essence of the veracity of what librarians of color felt at the time and, to some degree, still feel nowadays. In a telephone interview with John Ayala, former president of REFORMA, echoed Josey's sentiments by stating that the founding members felt the need to establish REFORMA, and that initially it was ignored by some of the leadership of ALA.[7] According to Ayala, much of the flak that they received had to do with why they were separating themselves. Yet, despite the criticism, the founding members felt that they needed their own organization because they did not want their concerns to get lost in the shuffle.[8]

Latino Community's Needs Unmet by ALA

Like each respective ethnic library association, the motivation that the founding members had in creating REFORMA had to do with issues of empowerment and achieving equity representation. In their article, Salvador Güereña and Edward Erazo eloquently state that this need for empowerment had to do with the fact that "For much of its history . . . [the] ALA was not known as a bastion of support for library services to Latinos. Even in the 1960s, many librarians like Lillian Lopez felt ill at ease in ALA because its nascent efforts at addressing the needs of Latinos lagged far behind those aimed at mainstream America" (Güereña & Erazo, 2000, p. 140). To help illustrate this point, Robert Haro conducted a survey between 1967 and 1969 in which

approximately six hundred Mexican Americans in East Los Angeles and Sacramento were interviewed and questioned in an effort to answer three questions about libraries and library service:

1. What are the library attitudes of Mexican Americans from various age groups?
2. What are the attitudes and practices of librarians serving these people?
3. What challenges and opportunities face librarians and libraries in providing more effective service to the Mexican American people? (Haro, 1970, pp. 736–737)

The findings revealed that there was a great disconnection between libraries and Mexican Americans. Of those interviewed, "Eight-nine percent ... would utilize their neighborhood libraries if Spanish were spoken and Spanish-language materials, especially those dealing with Mexican American and Hispanic themes, were available" (Haro, 1970, p. 738). What's more, in regard to the library attitudes of the youth, the survey also revealed that "On the whole, young Mexican-Americans wanted libraries to carry more activist literature about Mexican-American political movements, Brown power, and material on what makes Chicanos tick," while the "complaints by older Mexican-Americans ranged from a desire to see more Spanish-language materials available ... to a need for libraries to hire more Spanish-speaking clerks and librarians."

This survey, although it only focused on Mexican Americans, speaks volumes in the sense that it brought to light the fact that American librarianship severely lacked representation of Latina/o librarians and that many library collections were not representative of the communities they served. As the survey points out, nothing is more alarming than to learn that "while most disadvantaged Mexican-Americans generally perceive libraries indifferently and seldom frequent them, those that do, especially the young, harbor an uneasiness and a resentment toward them" (Haro, 1970, p. 738). As such, since the ALA was unwilling to address these problems in a reasonable fashion, the founding members took it upon themselves to create an organization that would serve to correct these issues.

History of REFORMA

I will now take this time to examine the history of REFORMA by drawing on the works from various prominent scholars such as Patrick Jose Dawson, who, for example, wrote a thorough analysis regarding REFORMA's role in reforming American librarianship. His chapter, "The History and Role of REFORMA," which was featured in *Latino Librarianship: A Handbook for Professionals* (1990) provides a comprehensive analysis regarding the history, structure, concerns and future of REFORMA.

As the literature points out, prior to REFORMA's inception, previous efforts had been made to provide library services to the Latino community (Dawson, 1990, p. 121). There was, for example, the Committee on Library Services to the Spanish Speaking; however, the Latino librarians in this committee "felt alienated from ALA and did not form a credible presence until many years later" (Güereña & Erazo, 2000, p. 141). There was also the Seminar for the Acquisition of Latin American Library Materials (SALALM), which was founded in 1956. As an international association of librarians, scholars, and book dealers, SALALM "provide[d] information on Latin American publications so that libraries and librarians can have ... a forum for information on the development of collections from and about Latin America" (Dawson, 1990, p. 121). Yet, since this association mainly focused on Latin America and on research libraries, Dawson further states many Latino librarians still felt a strong desire to create an association that would address the needs of the Spanish-speaking population within the United States, as well as be inclusive of public libraries.

Another prominent precursor to REFORMA was that "a Los Angeles-based group, led by a handful of librarians . . . had in 1968 already formed a group called the Committee to Recruit Mexican American Librarians whose hard work led to the founding of the Mexican-American Library Training Institute at California State University, Fullerton" (Güereña & Erazo, 2000, p. 155). Although this library school program was not accredited by the ALA, Güereña and Erazo point out it was the first of its kind that provided Latino librarians with specialized course work relating to the Latino community. Even though this program only ran from 1972 to 1975, it was soon followed by the Graduate Library Institute for Spanish-speaking Americans (GLISA) (1976–1980) at the University of Arizona; thus, these two programs combined graduated 104 Latina/o librarians (Güereña & Erazo, 2000, p. 155). Unfortunately, both programs ended due to budget cuts.

REFORMA was organized during the ALA annual conference in Dallas by a group of Latina/o librarians, which included Esperanza Acosta, Emma Morales Gonzalez, Alicia Iglesias, Modene Martin, Maria Mata, William Ramirez, and Arnulfo D. Trejo (Güereña & Erazo, 2000, p. 155). The idea for the organization came to Trejo after he and Elizabeth Martinez had showed *I Am Joaquin*, "a film based upon the poem of the same title by the Chicano poet Rodolfo 'Corky' Gonzalez" (Dawson, 1990, p. 122) at one of the programs of the convention. According to Dawson, the film was well received, and it was at that point in time that Trejo became "aware of the need for an organization which would serve as an outreach to the Latino population of the United States and as a forum for information and resource sharing."

At its inception, the organization was known as the National Association of Spanish-Speaking Librarians. Yet, as Zulema Navarro illustrates in her thesis "The History of REFORMA: Twelve years of Work on Behalf of Hispanics" (1984), the organization changed its name in 1972 after Dr. Trejo's visit to the University of California, Los Angeles. During this particular visit, Dr. Trejo came across the Californistas' old newspaper called *Reforma*, and as it turns out,

> Dr Trejo liked the name because 'reform' was what the organization intended to accomplish. The founding members wanted to make sure that new ideas would be introduced into librarianship, i.e. they wanted to 'reform' the existent situation. The name REFORMA is, therefore not an acronym . . . but is based on a concept. (Navarro, 1984).

Thus, it was then that the group became known as REFORMA, the National Association of Spanish-Speaking Librarians in the United States. What's more, other milestones worth mentioning are that 1972 also marked the year REFORMA adopted its constitution, while in 1973 the association published its first newsletter (Dawson, 1990, p. 123). As Dawson points out, the newsletter proved to be extremely effective in communicating news and events, as well as providing publicity for the organization.

Needless to say, as a new organization, REFORMA struggled tremendously because "There was not a large membership . . . and a viable financial base was lacking" (Dawson, 1990, p. 123). Much of REFORMA's financial problems had to do with the fact that it lacked the tax-exempt status and it was not until 1974, three years after its inception, that "REFORMA was officially incorporated as a nonprofit organization." Moreover, REFORMA experienced "organizational deficiency" since it lacked a national headquarters with support staff (Dawson, 1990, p. 124). As Güereña points out, "One of the major weaknesses of national REFORMA has been the continuing need to effect tighter lines of communication between the president, the executive board members, the general membership, and the local chapters" (Güereña, 1978). Therefore, in 1975, in an effort to help remedy this issue, REFORMA restructured itself by creating four regional chapters: Pacific-Southwest, Central, Northeast, and Southeast (Dawson, 1990, p. 124). In addition, 1975 also marked the year in which REFORMA became an official affiliate of ALA, which gave it more exposure, because "Membership increased to 129 through this period and into the next year" (Dawson, 1990, p. 124).

In an effort to increase recruitment, since REFORMA had a small membership base during the first couple of years, the board at the time, particularly the president, Arnulfo Trejo, felt it was important to implement an ALA-accredited program geared toward the "recruitment of Latinos into the library profession" (Dawson, 1990, p. 124). Therefore, Dawson notes that in 1975, after serving his presidency, Trejo created the Graduate Library Institute for Spanish-Speaking Americans, GLISA. Then, in 1978, REFORMA became more politically involved by pushing resolutions that opposed both California's Proposition 13, "where . . . many tax-funded services provided by the state and local governments had to be curtailed" and the "Supreme Court decision . . . in the case of the Regents of the University of California vs. Bakke," which required UC Davis to end its affirmative action practice of "reserving 16 percent of their places in medical school for minority candidates" (Dawson, 1990, p. 125). Dawson highlights that REFORMA made it a point to take a stance against these issues since they threatened library services and programs such as GLISA.

REFORMA's Structure

REFORMA underwent additional reorganization in 1978, which "allowed for . . . local chapters to develop their own by-laws and structure" (Dawson, 1990, p. 125). As such, the organization is governed by an executive board that includes the officers, committee chairs, and presidents of chapters, and each chapter functions "autonomously, working through their local library systems, state library associations and local organizations to achieve local objectives" (REFORMA and Castillo-Speed, 2001, p. xi). And as the years went by, REFORMA implemented the REFORMA National Scholarship in 1982 and continued to increase its visibility throughout the 1980s with ALA and honed in on serving the Spanish-speaking community. Another important issue that Dawson mentioned was that the first woman president, Susan Luévano, was elected in 1985. In addition, in the mid-1980s REFORMA formed "coalitions with other library and non-library groups with providing services to minorities" (Dawson, 1990, p. 127). In the sections that follow, I will demonstrate how these coalitions proved to be extremely effective for REFORMA.

Stance on Sociopolitical Issues

In 1985, the "English-only" movement fueled a wave of anti-Latino sentiment. Those behind this movement wanted "to amend the United States Constitution to make English the official language" (Dawson, 1990, p. 127). In response, REFORMA flexed its political clout by presenting a policy proposal opposing such legislation to the ALA Council via the Committee on Minority Concerns, which was adopted at the 1985 ALA Midwinter Meeting, and as such, REFORMA was elated that the ALA agreed to have its Washington office monitor and testify against such legislation (Dawson, 1990, p. 128).

In California, Proposition 63 threatened to make English the official language, and although the legislation was passed in 1986, it is worth noting that REFORMA put up a great fight. Commenting on the issue during a keynote address at the Joint Conference of the Arizona State Library Association in 1987, Salvador Güereña stated:

> I want to make it clear that the issue at hand is not to diminish our common language, which in fact is English, but rather, to oppose the discriminatory results of removing equal access to information, regardless of language orientation. For this reason, the California Library Association passed a resolution . . . underscoring its support for multilingual library materials and services. (Güereña, 1987)

On a similar note, while addressing REFORMA and the CSL Ad Hoc Committee on Minority Affairs in Long Beach, Gary Strong, who was the California State librarian at the time, said that public libraries have social responsibility in providing access to and disseminating information, and he urged all public libraries to "have clearly stated policies which address the inclusion of materials of all types and languages that meet the information and library needs of their users" (Strong, 1986). These efforts at language equity were further supported by a REFORMA position paper titled "Amending the Library Bill of Rights in Relation to Language." The document shows that an effort was made to have the word "language" inserted in Article I, following the word "background." Article I of the ALA's Bill of Rights states:

> Books and other library resources should be provided for the interest, information, and enlightenment of all people of the community the library serves. Materials should not be excluded because of the origin, background, or views of those contributing to their creation. (Library Bill of Rights)

According to this document, "The rationale for this explicit inclusion is to ensure that language equity . . . [is] considered as fundamental and basic 'origin, background, or views' of those who create the materials libraries acquire." Unfortunately, the proposal for this amendment was never ratified since the latest edition of the ALA's Bill of Rights does not include the word "language."

Impact on Development of American Librarianship

The ways in which REFORMA has impacted the development of American Librarianship are, without a doubt, infinite. For example, as Salvador Güereña points out, "it was not until after the Civil Rights Movement of the 1960s that the building of American ethnic research collections and archives became a conscious systematic goal anywhere" (Güereña & Erazo, 2000, p. 171), and there is no doubt that REFORMA, as an advocate for the collection development of Latino-related materials, played a role in this. In light of this, through its advocacy, "REFORMA has been successful in lobbying American publishers to produce Spanish language materials, including a recently released Spanish index" (Echavarria & Wertheimer, 1997). Moreover, with its annual scholarship drive and the REFORMA/UCLA Mentor Program, REFORMA has been instrumental in providing students with financial assistance and mentorship.

Another influential accomplishment worth noting is the impact that REFORMA had regarding the ALA's accreditation standards. REFORMA felt the ALA's standards for accreditation should require curriculum of master's programs to mindfully reflect "the needs of 'a rapidly changing multicultural, multiethnic, multilingual society including the needs of underserved groups" (Güereña & Erazo, 2000, p. 172). As it turns out, ALA's standards became inclusive in terms of multicultural, multiethnic, and multilingual nature of society because "REFORMA leaders took a leading role in aggressively advocating the inclusion of these provisos in the standards which were ultimately adopted by the ALA council" (Güereña & Erazo, 2000, p. 172).

Final Thoughts

There is no denying that REFORMA has accomplished a great deal during the past 40 years. Needless to say, as with most struggles, there is always more that could be done. Recruitment has long been, and continues to be, a top priority for REFORMA. Unfortunately, the fact of the matter is that "A shortage of Latino librarians still plagues the profession" (Echavarria & Wertheimer, 1997). In the article titled "Wanted: Latino Librarians," Isabel Espinal, humanities and anthropology librarian at the University of Massachusetts, notes that the number of Latina/o librarians is extremely low. The author states that the lack of Latina/o librarians negatively impacts the Latino community's perception of libraries. To illustrate her point, Espinal states:

> Imagine walking into a library time and time again and never seeing anyone who remotely looks like you. Imagine finding no one who speaks your language. Imagine knowing that there's a great collection of resources there that your tax dollars have paid for, but you don't know how it's organized or how to find what you need. Or imagine that you do speak a little English, but when you ask a question, the librarian appears not to understand what you're saying. This is the sad reality for many of the Spanish-dominant Latinos living in the United States. (Espinal, 2003)

According to Espinal, "For every 9,177 Latinos, there is only one Latino librarian, as opposed to one white, non-Latino librarian for every 1,830 white, non-Latinos" (Espinal, 2003). This disparity has to do with the alarming fact that

> From 1995 to 2001, MLS programs graduated 30,192 students, only ten percent of whom were students of color. Asian American MLS graduates are closet to achieving parity with their population.

Native Americans make up almost one percent of the population but less than four-tenths of one percent of MLS graduates. We need three times as many African American graduates and four times the number of Hispanic graduates to achieve parity with the U.S. population. (Adkins & Espinal, 2004)

The founders of REFORMA were well aware of this problem from the start, and it is an issue that the organization has continued to address. With that said, I would like to end by saying that REFORMA has become a well-recognized, vital player in its profession. Although starting off as a small group of devoted librarians, REFORMA has evolved into an influential national organization that has brought about a great deal of societal change.

Notes

1. Salvador Güereña, e-mail message to author, rough draft of finding aid titled "Guide to the REFORMA: The National Association to Promote Library and Information Services to Latinos and the Spanish Speaking Archives, 1972–2006," April 10, 2008.
2. Ibid.
3. Ibid.
4. Ibid.
5. Ibid.
6. Ibid.
7. John Ayala, personal telephone interview on May 20, 2008 at 1:00 P.M.
8. Ibid.

References

About REFORMA. 2005. Available at http://www.reforma.org/who.html; accessed on April 25, 2008.

Adkins, D., and Isabel Espinal. 2004. "The Diversity Mandate." *Library Journal* 129: 52–54.

Dawson, Patrick Jose. 1990. "The History and Role of REFORMA." In *Latino Librarianship: A Handbook for Professionals*, edited by Salvador Güereña, 121–134. Jefferson, NC: McFarland & Co.

Echavarria, Tami, and Andrew B. Wertheimer. 1997. "Surveying the Role of Ethnic-American Library Associations." *Library Trends* 46, no. 2: 373.

Espinal, Isabel. 2003. "Wanted: Latino Librarians." *Criticas* 3, no. 5: 19–24.

Güereña, Salvador. 1978. "REFORMA, The National Association of Spanish Speaking Librarians." MS, November 29, 1978. REFORMA Archives, collection number: CEMA 29; box 17; folder 2, California Ethnic and Multicultural Archives, Department of Special

Collections, Davidson Library, University of California, Santa Barbara (SRLF).

Güereña, Salvador. 1987. "English: The Official Language? Its Impacts Upon Equal Access to Information in California." MS, November 6, 1987. REFORMA Archives, collection number: CEMA 29; box 47; folder 1, California Ethnic and Multicultural Archives, Department of Special Collections, Davidson Library, University of California, Santa Barbara (SRLF).

Güereña, Salvador. 1991. Draft Position Paper: "Amending the Library Bill of Rights in Relation to Language." MS, 1991. REFORMA Archives, collection number: CEMA 29; box 47; folder 1, California Ethnic and Multicultural Archives, Department of Special Collections, Davidson Library, University of California, Santa Barbara (SRLF).

Güereña, Salvador, and Edward Erazo. 2000. "Latinos and Librarianship." *Library Trends* 49, no. 1: 138–181.

Haro, Robert P. 1970. "One Man's Survey: How Mexican-Americans View Libraries." *Wilson Library Bulletin* 44: 736–742.

Josey, E. J. 1977. "Black Caucus of the American Library Association." In *Handbook of Black Librarianship*, edited by E. J. Josey and Ann Allen Shockley, 66–77. Littleton, CO: Libraries Unlimited.

Library Bill of Rights. Available at http://www.ala.org/ala/oif/state mentspols/statementsif/librarybillrights.cfm; accessed on June 12, 2008.

McCook, Kathleen. 2002. "Rocks in the Whirlpool: Equity of Access and the American Library Association." Paper presented to the Executive Board at the annual conference of the American Library Association, New Orleans, LA, June 14, 2002.

Navarro, Zulema. 1984. Thesis titled "The History of REFORMA: Twelve Years of Work on Behalf of Hispanics." REFORMA Archives, collection number: CEMA 29; box 18; folder 2, California Ethnic and Multicultural Archives, Department of Special Collections, Davidson Library, University of California, Santa Barbara (SRLF).

REFORMA (Association), and Lillian Castillo-Speed. 2001. *The Power of Language = El Poder de la Palabra: Selected Papers From the Second REFORMA National Conference.* Englewood, CO: Libraries Unlimited.

Strong, Gary E. 1986. "English as the Official Language of California." MS, November 16, 1986. REFORMA Archives, collection number: CEMA 29; box 47; folder 1, California Ethnic and Multicultural Archives, Department of Special Collections, Davidson Library, University of California, Santa Barbara (SRLF).

Thomison, Dennis. 1978. *A History of the American Library Association 1876–1972.* Chicago: American Library Association.

Title VII of the Civil Rights Act of 1964. Available at http://www.eeoc.gov/laws/statutes/titlevii.cfm; accessed June 12, 2008.

Index

About the Editors and Contributors

JOHN L. AYALA was born August 28, 1943, and raised in Long Beach, California. He received his Bachelor's Degree in Modern History from California State University, Long Beach, in 1970; an MLIS in 1971 from Immaculate Heart College in Hollywood, California; and a second Masters in Public Administration from CSULB in 1982 (Magna Cum Laude). Mr. Ayala has been published in various professional journals and magazines and edited a chapter on Community College Library Service to Latinos in *Library Services to Latinos: An Anthology* (McFarland, 2000). He has received various professional awards and recognition, including the prestigious Librarian of the Year Award from REFORMA in 2001. Mr. Ayala retired from Fullerton Community College in 2006 as the Dean of the Library and Learning Resources and Study Abroad Administrator.

Dramatist and documentarian ERICA BENNETT is also Associate Professor, Library/Systems Librarian at Fullerton College. Ms. Bennett received a BA in Theatre Arts from California State University, Fullerton. She worked for over 10 years in dramatic television, film, and museum exhibit design for such companies as MGM, Warner Brothers, and BRC Imagination Arts before achieving a Masters of Library and Information Science (MLIS) in 2005 from UCLA with an emphasis in Archival Studies. Ms. Bennett is a member of the Orange County Playwrights Alliance, the Dramatists Guild of America, and the Society of California Archivists.

SERGIO CHAPARRO, PHD was born in Peru. He holds a BA in Literature and Linguistics and a BA in Library Science, both from the Pontificia Universidad Católica del Perú (PUC). After college he became a Linguistics teacher and an academic librarian and received a Fulbright Scholarship to pursue an MLS. He got his MLS and later his PhD at Rutgers, The State University of New Jersey. Dr. Chaparro has been a lecturer at Rutgers University in Communication and Library Science and an Assistant Professor at the Graduate School of Library and Information Science (GSLIS) at Simmons College. He is currently a lecturer at San Jose State Library School where he teaches long distance on Globalization and Diversity in the area of LIS. His areas of expertise are International Librarianship and Information Policy.

ANA MARÍA COBOS has been at Saddleback College since 1992. She previously worked at Stanford University and the UCLA Latin American Center. In 2002, Ms. Cobos and her colleague Analya Sater published *Latin American Studies: An Annotated Bibliography of Core Works*. This work received the Choice 2002 Outstanding Title. In 2005, Ms. Cobos received SALALM's Jose Toribio Medina Award. She has also contributed to previous titles by Sal Güereña.

Born in Villavicencio, Colombia, in 1961, TATIANA DE LA TIERRA's writings have been published since 1987. She is author of the books *Xía y las mil sirenas* (2009) and *For the Hard Ones: A Lesbian Phenomenology/Para las duras: Una fenomenología lesbiana* (2002). Ms. de la tierra's creative works have been published in anthologies such as *Lavanderia: A Mixed Load of Women, Wash and Words*; *Best Date Ever*; *Ultimate Lesbian Erotica*; *This Bridge We Call Home*; and *Without a Net: The Female Experience of Growing up Working Class*. Her poetry and prose have been published in periodicals including *Puerto del Sol*, *Curve*, *Mid-American Review*, *Journal of Lesbian Studies*, and *Aztlán*. Ms. de la tierra's library research and academic essays have been published in *Radical Cataloging*, *Encyclopedia Latina*, *Críticas*, *REFORMA Newsletter*, *Multicultural Review*, *LGBTQ America Today*, *Encyclopedia of American Ethnic Literature*, and *Lesbian and Gay Studies and the Teaching of English*. She was the cofounder and editor of the Latina lesbian publications published in the 1990s: *esto no tiene nombre*, *conmoción*, and *la telaraña*. And she has been on staff as a librarian at State University of New York at Buffalo and Inglewood Public Library in California.

MARÍA R. ESTORINO is a native of Miami, Florida. She is Deputy Chair and Chief Operations Manager of the Cuban Heritage Collection at the University of Miami Libraries, where she has served in various posts in special collections since 2001. Ms. Estorino received her MA in History from Northeastern University and her MS in Library Science from Simmons College. She also holds a Bachelor's in History from Loyola University New Orleans. Her interests focus on improving access to special collections materials, the documentation of underrepresented communities, Hispanic manuscript collections in U.S. repositories, and Latinos in the archival profession.

LOIDA GARCIA-FEBO was President of REFORMA for 2009–2010. She is the Assistant Coordinator of the New Americans Program and the Special Services units of Queens Library in New York. She was the former Manager of Queens Library's Special Services unit and the Spanish Language Collections and Cultural Arts for Queens Library's New Americans Program. Ms. Garcia-Febo was born, raised, and educated in Puerto Rico. She is a 2007 Library Journal Mover and Shaker, where she was recognized as a Freedom Fighter, and a 2007 Outstanding Woman for *Impremedia* and *El Diario/La Prensa*. Ms. Garcia-Febo is a member of ALA/IFC and IFRT Chair Elect, IFLA/FAIFE and works with IFLA/NPSIG, which she coestablished in 2004. As part of her work with IFLA, she has visited many countries around the globe including Brazil, Colombia, Costa Rica, Jamaica, Mexico, the Philippines, and Japan. She is also a member of the American Indian Library Association, Asian Pacific American Librarians Association, the Black Caucus of the American Library Association, Chinese American Library Association, and the Association of Caribbean University, Research and Institutional Libraries (ACURIL). Ms. Garcia-Febo has a video channel, Loida Time!; a blog, http://loidagarciafebo .wordpress.com/; and cowrote Multicultural Link for *Criticas Magazine*.

ORALIA GARZA DE CORTÉS is a leading voice for bilingual and multicultural children's literature and an ardent advocate of equity in library services for Latino children and families. A past president of REFORMA, Ms. de Cortés cofounded the Pura Belpré Award; cofounded the Children and Young Adult Services Committee of REFORMA and led REFORMA and the library community in implementing El día de los Niños/ El día de los libros, an annual national literacy event that celebrates children, books, languages, and cultures throughout the United States; and Noche de Cuentos, a Family Literacy Initiative of REFORMA. A native of Brownsville, Texas, Ms. de Cortés was the first Latina elected by the membership of ALSC in 1995 to serve on the Board of Directors of ALSC, the children's division of the American Library Association. She was also the first Latina children's librarian elected to serve on the 2000 Caldecott Committee. She has served on numerous children's book award committees, including the Pura Belpré Award; the Américas Children's Literature Award; the Tomás Rivera Mexican American Children's Book Award; the Hans Christian Andersen Award sponsored by the U.S. section of the International Board of Books for Young People (IBBY); and the Jane Addams Children's Book Award for Social Justice (2006–present).

An archivist, librarian, and writer, SALVADOR GÜEREÑA has directed, since 1988, the California Ethnic and Multicultural Archives (CEMA). CEMA is a part of the Department of Special Collections in the Davidson Library of the University of California, Santa Barbara (UCSB), and it is one of the leading repositories for the preservation of ethnic historical archives and manuscript collections in California. Mr. Güereña is a native of Santa Barbara, California. His BA is from Westmont College, and his MLS is from the University of Arizona. Prior to directing CEMA, he was in charge of the Chicano Studies library at UCSB Library and was Assistant Head of the Reference Department. Prior to his tenure at UCSB, Mr. Güereña directed the Santa Barbara Public Library's multicultural outreach program and managed one of its branch libraries. He is a past president of REFORMA. He has served on the governing council of the American Library Association and on the board of directors for the Society of California Archivists. Mr. Güereña has been a conference speaker and organizer on topics such as ethnic archives and manuscripts, library services to Latinos, library cultural diversity, community analysis, and digitizing for diversity. He has written numerous articles and compiled and coauthored several books in the field of library science, bibliography, and archives.

A librarian archivist, ALEXANDER HAUSCHILD has been working to advance information literacy using modern paradigms throughout his career. Building on his experience in education, photography, advertising, and publishing, his work seeks to unite brick-and-mortar library service with digital access. He developed Chicano digital art collections for the California Ethnic and Multicultural Archives (CEMA) and the California Digital Library (CDL), once among the largest online Chicano art collections in the world. Currently at work with the Architecture and Design Collection at the University Art Museum of the UC Santa Barbara, Mr. Hauschild continues to expand upon methods of integrating legacy archival finding aids, modern asset management forms, and techniques with an eye toward specific user needs.

LUIS HERRERA is the City Librarian for the City and County of San Francisco. Prior to assuming his current position, he served for 10 years as the Director of the Pasadena Public Library. Previously, he served in public library management in San Diego and Long Beach, California, and his hometown of El Paso, Texas. Mr. Herrera is also a former middle school librarian. He holds a BS from the University of Texas at El Paso and an MLS from the University of Arizona. He also earned a Master of Public Administration degree from California State University, Long Beach where he received the Future Urban Administrator Award. His leadership includes service as President of the Public Library Association, the California Library Association, and REFORMA. Mr. Herrera serves on the California Council for the Humanities and the Latino Community Foundation. He is also the author of numerous articles on library strategic planning and the role of libraries in forging community partnerships. His vision is to promote libraries as innovative and dynamic organizations that help build strong and vibrant communities.

SUSAN C. LUÉVANO is a graduate of the University of Oregon, School of Library Science. She has worked in academic libraries in California and Texas for over 30 years. Since 1995, Ms. Luévano has been the Anthropology, Ethnic and Women's Studies Librarian at California State University, Long Beach. Her areas of research and publication include library services to immigrant and undocumented populations, diversity issues in higher education, faculty-centered information literacy, and mentoring. She is also a past national president of REFORMA and is currently a board member of the Trejo Foster Foundation for Hispanic Library Education. A scholar activist, Ms. Luévano takes her inspiration for serving others from her parents and the struggles and triumphs of the Latino community.

SARA MARTÍNEZ coordinates the Hispanic Resource Center for Tulsa City-County Library. She is responsible for collection development of Spanish language materials and works closely with the Latino and Spanish-speaking community in Tulsa. She received her MLIS from the University of Oklahoma and has a BA in Comparative Literature from the University of California, Berkeley. Ms. Martínez did postgraduate work at the Universidad Nacional Autónoma de México in Latin American Studies with an emphasis on Literature.

PHILIP S. McCLEOD currently serves as Emory University's Librarian for Spanish, Portuguese, Latin American, and Caribbean Studies. He holds an MA and PhD in Latin American Studies from Tulane University. McCleod previously worked as the Curator of Manuscripts for Tulane University's Latin American Library; a Latin American Project Archivist and Assistant to the Latin American Curator at the Yale University Libraries; and the Research Librarian for Spanish, Portuguese and Latin American Studies for the University of California, Irvine.

ALMA C. ORTEGA is a tenured librarian at the University of San Diego in San Diego, California. At Copley Library, she is a Librarian and Bibliographer for History (World and United States), Theology and Religious Studies, Spanish Language and Literatures, Latin American Studies, Medieval and Renaissance Studies, Ethnic Studies, Mission and Ministry, and the Trans-Border Institute. She also teaches course integrated sessions, works with archival collections and conducts research on collection management, archives' place in libraries, recruitment to the profession, Library/Web 2.0 including multiuser virtual environments, such as Second Life, as well as conduct research on Romance philology. Ms. Ortega earned a BA in Peace and Conflict Studies and another one in Spanish (Iberian languages and literatures) from the University of California at Berkeley.

She earned her masters' degrees in Library and Information Studies, and in Latin American Studies at the University of California, Los Angeles.

MARISOL RAMOS has worked both in libraries and archives since 2000. She obtained her MLIS degree with an archival concentration from the University of California, Los Angeles. Ms. Ramos obtained a BA in Anthropology from the University of Puerto Rico and an MA in Latin American and Caribbean Studies at SUNY-Albany. She worked as the first archivist at the Chicano Studies Research Center at UCLA; as a Marine Science Librarian at the Cabrillo Marine Aquarium, Los Angeles; and currently she is the Subject/Liaison Librarian for Latin American and Caribbean Studies, Puerto Rican and Latinos Studies and Spanish, in addition to working as the curator for the Latin American and Caribbean Collections at the Thomas J. Dodd Research Center at the University of Connecticut, Storrs. Her research interests include recruitment and mentoring of underrepresented students into library and archives, the use of Web 2.0 tools for instruction and networking in libraries and archives, archives and libraries relationships in academic settings, and diversity issues in archives.

REFUGIO RAMIREZ was born in Visalia, California, in 1982. He received his BA in Ethnic Studies and Sociology from the University of San Diego in 2005 and his MLIS in 2009 from the University of California, Los Angeles, where he was awarded a Graduate Opportunity Fellowship, Marie Saito Fellowship, and a Spectrum Scholarship. After graduate school, Refugio will begin working as the Law Library Resident at the Georgetown University Law Center.

YOLANDA RETTER VARGAS had many nicknames. One was Yolanda the Terrible because nothing held her back from speaking up against racism, sexism, classism, and homophobia. Another was "gadfly on the body politic," but my favorite was Knight for Higher. Yolanda would help when help was needed, whether it was to rescue a kitty who had been thrown onto the freeway shoulder or someone whose car had broken down. She was the person you would want to be with in case of emergency or disaster. Yolanda encouraged all she knew to pursue higher education and even though she had her PhD (in addition to two masters degrees, a woodworking certificate, and an airplane mechanics license), she did not want people to call her Dr. Retter. She was passionate about improving the lives of lesbians, women, and people of color. Yolanda had *chispa*. Yolanda left her body in 2007 without time to complete various projects but hopefully not without impacting the lives of many people.

ROMELIA SALINAS earned a doctoral degree from the Graduate School of Education and Information Studies at the University of California, Los Angeles. Her dissertation work examined the barriers that Latino undergraduates encounter in the access of digital information to meet their academic needs. Her areas of research include the social implication of new technologies, information services to the Latino community, and information equity. Ms. Salinas is currently the Head of Access Services at California State University, Los Angeles and is an Adjunct Lecturer at the UCLA Library School. She has published articles on the lack of relevant web content about Latinas, how to partner with nonprofit organizations to bring information technology into low-income communities, as well as on the history of library services to the Latino community. In prior positions she has been involved in initiatives to develop information and computer literacy in underserved communities and in the production of digital content for the Latino community. She served as President of the Los Angeles Chapter of REFORMA for multiple years and was a founding member of the REFORMA Information Technology Committee and the REFORMA Web Team.

TIFFINI A. TRAVIS received her Masters in Library and Information Science from the University of California at Los Angeles. She has been a member of the library faculty at CSU Long Beach since 1999. For the last four years, she has been the Director of Information Literacy and Outreach Services. In this role, she provides outreach to on- and off-campus groups and facilitates student success and retention by arranging collaborative research and writing workshops at the library. In her time with the CSU, system she has been awarded four Information Competence Grants and been a strong advocate for information literacy efforts at her campus. Her varied research interests include social media, the evolution of instructional technologies, and measuring the library's role in student success. Recently she was named as one of the newest additions to ACRL's nationally recognized Immersion Faculty.

EILEEN WAKIJI is the California State University, Long Beach Nursing and Allied Health Librarian. She received her MSLS from the University of Southern California. In addition to working at CSULB University Library since 1991, Ms. Wakiji has worked in public, hospital, medical society, and academic health sciences libraries. Since 2001 she has been involved in developing ethnic studies faculty-centered information literacy training, assessments for information fluency, curriculum mapping, and has lectured and written on these topics. Ms. Wakiji presented at the First Joint Conference of Librarians of Color on an information literacy project with the CSULB Black Studies Department. The tutorial she created with her colleagues, Susan Luévano and Tiffini Travis, for this information literacy project has been highly reviewed. It was highlighted as an ACRL Peer-Reviewed Instructional Materials Online site. Currently, Ms. Wakiji is writing about team mentoring and outreach in academic libraries.

Edwards Brothers, Inc.
Thorofare, NJ USA
November 28, 2011